Children First

Children First

Working with Young Children in Inclusive Group Care Settings in Canada

Joanne Baxter
Mount Royal College

Malcolm V. Read
Medicine Hat College

HARCOURT BRACE
CANADA

Harcourt Brace & Company, Canada
Toronto Montreal Fort Worth New York Orlando
Philadelphia San Diego London Sydney Tokyo

Copyright © 1999
Harcourt Brace & Company Canada, Ltd.
All rights reserved

No part of this publication may be reproduced or transmitted in any form or by any means, electronic or mechanical, including photocopy, recording, or any information storage and retrieval system, without permission in writing from the publisher.

Requests for permission to make copies of any part of the work should be mailed to: Permissions, College Division, Harcourt Brace & Company, Canada, 55 Horner Avenue, Toronto, Ontario M8Z 4X6.

Every reasonable effort has been made to acquire permission for copyright material used in this text, and to acknowledge all such indebtedness accurately. Any errors and omissions called to the publisher's attention will be corrected in future printings.

Canadian Cataloguing in Publication Data

Baxter, Joanne M. (Joanne Marlena), 1955-
    Children first: Working with Young Children in Inclusive Group Care Settings in Canada

Includes bibliographical references and index.
ISBN 0-7747-3583-X

1. Inclusive education. 2. Handicapped children — Education (Early childhood). I. Read, Malcolm V. (Malcolm Victor), 1945- . II. Title.

LC1200.B39 1998   371.9'0472   C98-930982-7

Acquisitions Editor: Joanna Cotton
Senior Developmental Editor: Laura Paterson Forbes
Production Editor: Stacey Roderick
Copy Editor: John Eerkes
Senior Production Coordinator: Sue-Ann Becker
Cover Design: Avril Orloff
Typesetting and Assembly: Danni Stor
Technical Art: Danni Stor
Cover Art: *Jellybean Painting* (1996) by Jénayr Radajkovic
Interior Art: Cathie Archbould, Chapters 2, 10; Carissa Baxter, Chapter 4; Chelsea Baxter, Chapter 9;
       Joel Carston, Chapter 7; Steven Carston, Chapter 3; Paul Till, Chapters 1, 5, 6, 8
Printing and Binding: Tri-Graphic Printing

This book was printed in Canada.

1 2 3 4 5   03 02 01 00 99

PREFACE

In our experiences as teachers and in practice, we have typically seen two types of professionals interacting with children with special needs. Professionals with an education or early childhood education orientation typically work in the context of child development and are prepared to work with children in group settings. They often feel inadequate or unsure about meeting the unique or special needs of individual children. Professionals from a rehabilitation or special education background often have the skills to assess individuals and intervene on an individual basis, but they find it difficult to work with children who have special needs in a group of their normally developing peers.

Students from a rehabilitation orientation may be asked to complete practicums with children who have special needs in day-care settings. They often go through a period of intense frustration, feeling that they don't know what to do — "All they do is play all day." Although these students have learned specific assessment and intervention techniques, they lack knowledge about the relationship between the development of young children and play. There is no easy way to learn about development and play and about how to integrate the various approaches. On the other hand, students from an early childhood background may feel inept and afraid of working with children who have special needs. The apparent incongruence between traditional approaches to working with children who have special needs and the philosophical basis and structure of typical early childhood care and education settings is not recent. Safford and Rosen (1981) observed that

> Mainstreaming programs brings into focus a confrontation of beliefs and values and a disparity in method. The problem is one of integrating the specialised methods required in a manner congruent with the situational context of the regular classroom. (p. 43)

As you read this book, you will find points that you agree with and others that you disagree with. In some areas, your similar experiences will cause you to share the same perspective, while other experiences may cause you to disagree with or fail to understand our perspective. We, as authors, while sharing many ideas and opinions, also see some things in different ways because of our different experiences.

We urge you not to toss this book aside when you encounter an idea you do not share. Attempt to understand the perspective that we present — it is the result of our experience. You may be working with parents, professionals, and colleagues who have different perspectives and do not share your background or experiences in your day-to-day interactions. By recognizing and giving voice to those other perspectives, you may grow and be better able to deal with the myriad people who you will interact with throughout your professional career.

About this Book

This book is written for early childhood professionals working with children who have special and diverse needs in a integrated group-care setting. It is not intended for professionals whose focus is special education. Many excellent, more comprehensive resources are available to special needs workers or special educators, such as Deiner (1993); Allen, Paasche, Cornell, and Engel (1994); and Winzer (1997). These comprehensive books review the theories, approaches, and strategies in much more detail.

This book will help professionals who regularly interact with children who have special needs. Although these professionals may not have particular responsibilities for diagnosis and treatment, they live and work with children who have diverse and special needs for many hours each day. They often act in loco parentis and attempt to provide appropriate, worthwhile, and inclusive experiences for children.

You, as caregivers, likely know more about caring for children with special needs than you realize. If you know about child development and have had experience with children, you know a great deal about children with special needs because they are children first and development is the focal point of reference (Chandler, 1994).

Canadian children have a wide range of special needs in group-care settings, especially at the preschool age. This occurs for a variety of reasons.

1. A family may want their child to be in inclusive settings so that the child has an opportunity to interact with his or her peers in as many settings as possible.
2. Parents may be encouraged by the positive effects of modelling.
3. Parents may believe that their child has the right to be in environments like those of other children.
4. A young child may not have yet been diagnosed as having special needs, or those needs may not yet have been recognized. This is common among children under the age of two because special needs are often not recognized unless they are severe or until the child begins to miss major milestones such as walking and talking. Other special needs are typically not diagnosed until school age, such as learning disabilities or attention deficit disorders. These types of problems become noticeable in school, when children are expected to sit for long periods and learn in a group setting.

Because of the nature and purpose of group-care settings for preschool children, these difficulties are typically not relevant or noticeable. For example, a child may be considered "active" in a day-care centre that focuses on play and motor activities for much of the day. However, in a school setting, where attention to the teacher and to the task is central, that same child may be considered a problem. Also, resources may not be available to meet the child's special needs. For example, as a result of cutbacks, many outreach services required by young children with special needs, such as speech therapy, physiotherapy, and occupational therapy, may be reduced. Often children with special needs are in group-care settings with minimal or no supports. For example, one half-hour a week of physiotherapy still leaves early childhood professionals with many hours to meet the individual and unique needs of a child. Thus, it is not unusual to have children with a wide range of skills and abilities in child-care settings that have a limited range of supports available.

This book is intended to address the needs of the early childhood professional who works with children with diverse needs in his or her playroom and who may be unable to access supports and resources to meet each child's diverse needs. It attempts to combine the knowledge, skills, and attitudes traditionally taught to early childhood professionals with the knowledge, skills, and attitudes traditionally taught to the special-needs worker or special educator. This goal is accomplished by presenting children from different perspectives and by examining curriculum holistically, as it exists in the real world, not in isolated skill-specific content areas. By doing this, children with special needs will construct knowledge of their world alongside their peers. Professionals involved with these children will see them as children, not merely objects of particular teaching strategies, and they will be better able to develop the approaches best suited to the children's continued growth and development.

An important aspect of the work of early childhood professionals who care for children with diverse and special needs is that they work in collaboration with others. The theme of teamwork is repeated throughout this book. Given the complexity of various delays and disabilities and their effects on development, it is clear that no individual will have all the knowledge and skills necessary to optimize every child's development. Success in inclusive programming in early childhood settings depends on the extent to which early childhood professionals and members of other disciplines (speech pathology, physiotherapy, and psychology) work together. In a team approach, knowledge and methods are shared. Each member of the team does not work in a specialized or clinical manner with the child. In this way, preparation and planning for the inclusion of all children, whatever their needs, may be successfully accomplished.

THE APPROACH OF THIS BOOK

This book is presented from the perspective of traditional handicapping conditions. The decision to organize the book in this way was one of the more difficult choices we made. Early childhood professionals are more familiar with talking about children in terms of developmental domains — physical, cognitive, social, and emotional. They are less familiar with descriptions of children's diagnostic categories or labels. It is difficult to discuss an area of development such as social behaviour without also looking at the interaction of the child's physical, emotional, cognitive, and language development. However, in the case of a child with special needs, the condition of the child may affect all areas of development. This approach can also lead to problems. If we consider the child through the use of a diagnostic category such as hearing impairment and deafness, we must be careful not to lose sight of the child as a child first, who has environmental, biological, and developmental needs in common with his or her "normally" hearing peers.

Our decision to organize the book from the perspective of diagnostic categories was eventually made for several reasons.

1. Early childhood professionals typically work in collaboration with a variety of other professionals. In many fields, the use of labels and handicapping conditions is still prevalent. For example, psychologists continue to utilize handicapping conditions in their diagnosis of children, and it is still relatively common for access to programs and funding for children with special needs to be based on a diagnostic label. Thus, as much as some groups dislike labels and recognize that labels may cause as many problems as they solve, they serve a purpose and continue to be widely used by many professionals. Therefore, it is important that early childhood professionals become familiar with these labels as a means of facilitating the communication that must occur between professionals. Early childhood professionals should know the labels, understand their implications, and ask relevant questions to obtain the desired information. In turn, the early childhood professional will be better able to assist parents in understanding the language of professionals so that they can function as a member of the team.

2. If used appropriately, labels can be helpful and efficient. They may help early childhood professionals to understand some of the child's needs from the medical professional's perspective. They can assist an early childhood professional in better understanding the child's particular needs. It is important to realize the difference between using the categorizations in a meaningful, purposeful way and "labelling." Labelling can lead to stigmatizing or devaluing, discrimination, and generalization (Frost, 1992). We can all recall the emotional effects of being labelled in some way. Early childhood professionals must remember that all children are different: they have unique characteristics, personalities, temperaments, and home environments. When professionals mention conditions or labels in the proper context, they may provide some understanding in a quick and efficient way. When labels are used improperly, prejudgements, misunderstanding, and prejudices potentially can result.

3. Typically, a review of handicapping conditions concentrates on a condition and its characteristics. For instance, a review of visual impairments includes all of the possible concerns related to vision, usually from a medical perspective, and the resulting difficulties or characteristics typically manifested in the individual. From there, diagnosis and treatment plans can be formulated on the basis of this knowledge and an understanding of the handicapping condition itself. In this book, we will attempt to present information regarding handicapping conditions in a holistic manner. For example, a visual impairment has obvious effects on a child's ability to see, but there are also effects, related to the child's developing motor skills, communication abilities, social abilities, cognitive understanding, self-care, and self-esteem. All of these areas will be considered and discussed in the overview of handicapping conditions so that readers may come to understand the child better.

SCENARIO

An elementary school teacher related his experience with Jennie, a 7-year-old girl who is blind. He was teaching Jennie how to operate a brailler. The girl was hesitant and resistant during the first few attempts, and the teacher was unsure about why this was occurring. Jennie seemed to be ready to learn this particular skill. After several attempts, the teacher again attempted to demonstrate and explained that the sheet went in the top of the brailler.

Jennie burst into laughter and said, "How do I get a big sheet into a little machine like that?" After questioning Jennie, the teacher realized that Jennie was thinking about a sheet that her mother put on her bed at home. She could not comprehend how this size of sheet could possibly fit into a little machine. This misunderstanding was the cause of her hesitation.

Jennie's behaviour in this scenario might have resulted in her being labelled as resistant and having a behavioural problem. However, a consideration of the whole child and the interplay between the areas of development leads to a better understanding of Jennie's reaction and subsequent behaviour.

Thus, this text begins with a discussion of traditional handicapping conditions but also provides a different perspective by considering the whole child. Accordingly, it considers the interplay and interaction between developmental domains. This approach provides the opportunity to consider the child first and the handicapping condition second, rather than focusing primarily on the disability. It should enhance the reader's understanding of the whole child and subsequently your practice.

Terminology

The terminology used in this book is based on the authors' perspectives. The terms "children with special needs" and "children at risk" include:

- children who have diagnosed conditions that interfere with their learning and development;
- children who have developmental delays but no apparent biological impairments; and
- children who are at risk of developmental delays because of environmental and/or biological factors.

Although diagnostic categories or labels are used in this book, the children referred to have some needs that are shared by all children and other needs that are not shared by other children. To successfully include these children in early childhood care and education settings requires early childhood professionals "who are competent in meeting the needs of all young children and who will work cooperatively to meet the particular needs of children with disabilities" (Wolery, Strain, and Bailey, 1992).

References to early childhood professionals or caregivers include day-care staff, day-care directors, nursery school or preschool teachers, and family day-home providers. Caregivers are referred to as she and he interchangeably. The use of the term "parents" recognizes that both mothers and fathers play an important role in the lives of their children and that typically both wish to be involved in the growth and development of their child.

The care settings are referred to as early childhood care and education settings or group care. These are settings where children are left in the care of adults who are not their parents for some part of the day. This book focuses on professionals who work in an environment dedicated to care and development rather than on a school setting, where predetermined educational goals dominate. The emphasis is on an integrated curriculum approach, which is usually found in child-care settings.

OUTLINE OF THIS BOOK

Chapter 1 provides an overview of the historical and social context of early childhood care and education settings and children with special needs. It ends with an explanation of the key issues or themes of this book, including those relevant to inclusive settings, such as play, friendships, environment, and cultural diversity.

The remaining chapters are divided by diagnostic categories. Each begins with an overview of the condition, including a discussion of classification, causes, and associated characteristics. The overview provides basic information in a simple manner and includes information and resources for early childhood professionals. Next, the implications of the disability are discussed. This is done in relation to the child by considering the potential implications of the disability on all areas of development. The implications for others, both adults and children, will then be discussed. They may include implications for the child in the group context, the physical setting, and emotional and social issues such as rejection.

Each chapter ends by considering the role of the early childhood professional. After a discussion of attitudes, general strategies for including the child are considered. In addition, ideas are presented to ensure that all aspects of development are planned in the group-care setting. The options and ideas presented in each chapter may be useful for children with other special needs. The intent is to present a range of ideas and alternatives that early childhood professionals may draw upon in their practice to meet the particular needs of the children in their care.

It is hoped that this book will be used in conjunction with other resource materials, which are useful in providing supplementary and thorough information about the various handicapping conditions. This book contextualizes that information for the child within the group setting and moves beyond to consider approaches and strategies that are based on a developmental framework in inclusive settings.

Acknowledegments

Writing this book proved to be a most interesting journey. It began with two instructors on two different paths, independently teaching the same course about children with special needs to early childhood education students in different colleges in different cities. Both of us struggled with the available materials because the majority of books were so comprehensive and detailed that it was almost impossible to teach it all in one course. Further, we felt that early childhood graduates did not require this level of information in the roles that they would eventually assume with children with special needs included in regular child-centred programs. When we began to teach together and dialogue about students' needs in a course about children with special needs in inclusive settings, we were amazed at how similar our past experiences and perspectives were. The journey to capture these similarities in written word began there. It has been a journey of shared thoughts, writings, and discussions, along with the construction of new ideas and approaches along the way. This journey has ended with the completion of this manuscript, and another journey in a new direction can now begin.

Our thanks to several people who reviewed the book during its development and provided suggestions for improvement: Cindy Brandon, Centennial College; Mary Ellen Meunier, Camosun College; Wendy Mitchell, St. Lawrence College, and Lynda Rice.

I wish to acknowledge and thank my husband Dave, who has always encouraged me to follow new dreams and then lovingly supported me through the journey. Thanks also to my daughters Chelsea and Carissa for allowing me the time to complete this project. My gratitude also goes to the Mount Royal College Early Childhood Education and Development graduating class of 1998 who field-tested the manuscript and the many students along the way who offered their unique perspectives on caring for children with special needs in inclusive settings.
— Joanne

I, too, am indebted to many people. In particular to Brenda, whose advice, support, and faith in me were, as always, invaluable. My thanks also to the Early Childhood Development diploma class of 1998 at Medicine Hat College who provided insights and suggestions that are incorporated into the book.
— Malcolm

Contents

CHAPTER 1	AN INTRODUCTION TO WORKING WITH YOUNG CHILDREN WITH SPECIAL NEEDS	1
	Introduction	1
	Historical Traditions	2
	Child Care	2
	Nursery Schools	2
	Kindergarten	3
	Project Head Start	3
	Parental Involvement	3
	Early Intervention	4
	Approaches	5
	Behavioural Approaches	5
	Integration	6
	Inclusion	6
	Interactionist Approaches	7
	Constructivist Approach	7
	Summary	8
	Key Issues	8
	Play	8
	Environments	11
	Friendships and Peer Relationships	13
	Attitudes of Non-Disabled Children	16
	Diversity Issues	17
	Planning Approach	19
	Summary	23
	Activities	24
	Discussion Questions	24
CHAPTER 2	CHILDREN WITH DEVELOPMENTAL DELAYS	27
	Introduction	27
	Classification	28
	Specific Conditions	29
	Down Syndrome	29
	Causes	29
	Diagnosis and Assessment	30
	Implications for the Child's Development	30
	Role of the Early Childhood Professional	35
	Attitudes	36

	Strategies	37
	Planning in a Developmental Context	38
	Play	38
	Social	39
	Emotional	39
	Cognitive	40
	Sensory	41
	Physical	41
	Language and Communication	42
	Summary	43
	Activities	43
	Discussion Questions	44
CHAPTER 3	**CHILDREN WITH PHYSICAL IMPAIRMENTS**	45
	Introduction	45
	Classification	45
	Causes	46
	Specific Conditions	46
	Cerebral Palsy	46
	Muscular Dystrophy	47
	Spina Bifida	48
	Absent Limbs	49
	Head and Spinal Cord Injury	49
	Correctable Orthopedic Impairment	49
	Implications	50
	Implications for the Child's Development	50
	Implications for Others	53
	Role of the Early Childhood Professional	55
	Strategies	56
	Planning in a Developmental Context	58
	Motor	58
	Play	59
	Social	59
	Emotional	60
	Language	60
	Sensory and Cognitive	60
	Summary	61
	Activities	61
	Discussion Questions	62
CHAPTER 4	**CHILDREN WITH VISUAL IMPAIRMENTS**	63
	Introduction	63
	Classification	64

Contents • xv

Causes	65
Diagnosis and Assessment	65
Implications	67
Implications for the Child's Development	67
Implications for Others	69
Role of the Early Childhood Professional	70
Attitude	70
Strategies	70
Planning in a Developmental Context	72
Emotional	72
Sensory	72
Play	73
Physical	73
Cognitive	74
Social	75
Summary	75
Activities	75
Discussion Questions	76

CHAPTER 5   CHILDREN WITH HEARING IMPAIRMENTS   77

Introduction	77
Causes	78
Conductive Hearing Loss	78
Sensorineural Hearing Loss	79
Diagnosis and Assessment	79
Implications for the Child's Development	80
Role of the Early Childhood Professional	83
Attitudes	83
Strategies	85
Planning in a Developmental Context	86
Play	86
Social	87
Emotional	88
Cognitive	88
Sensory	89
Summary	89
Activities	90
Discussion Questions	90

CHAPTER 6   CHILDREN WITH COMMUNICATION DIFFICULTIES   91

Introduction	91
Causes	93
Sensory Deprivation	93

Experiential Disadvantage	94
Emotional and Social Difficulties	94
Central Nervous System Impairment	95
Diagnosis and Assessment	95
Implications	96
Implications for the Child's Development	96
Implications for Others	97
Role of the Early Childhood Professional	97
Attitude	98
Strategies	99
Planning in a Developmental Context	101
Play	101
Social	102
Emotional	103
Cognitive	103
Summary	104
Activities	104
Discussion Questions	104

CHAPTER 7   BEHAVIOURAL AND EMOTIONAL CHALLENGES   105

Introduction	105
Temperament	106
Causes and Etiology	110
Diagnosis and Assessment	111
Classification	112
Specific Conditions	113
Pervasive Developmental Disorders	113
Fragile X Syndrome	114
Attention Deficit Disorder and Attention Deficit Hyperactive Disorder	114
Fetal Alcohol Syndrome (FAS)	115
Implications	116
Implications for the Child's Development	116
Implications for Others	117
Role of the Early Childhood Professional	118
Attitudes	119
Strategies	119
Planning in a Developmental Context	122
Emotional	122
Play	122
Social	123
Language	123
Cognitive	123

	Sensory	124
	Physical	124
	Summary	125
	Activities	125
	Discussion Questions	126
CHAPTER 8	**CHILDREN AT RISK**	127
	Introduction	127
	Children with Health Needs	128
	Allergies	128
	Asthma	129
	Cystic Fibrosis	129
	Diabetes	129
	Epilepsy	132
	Hemophilia	133
	Heart Problems	133
	Implications	133
	Implications for the Child's Development	133
	Implications for Others	134
	Role of the Early Childhood Professional	135
	Children at Developmental Risk	137
	Implications	138
	Implications for the Child's Development	138
	Implications for Others	139
	Role of the Early Childhood Professional	139
	Children in Stress	140
	Implications for the Child's Development	141
	Role of the Early Childhood Professional	141
	Summary	142
	Activities	144
	Discussion Questions	145
CHAPTER 9	**PARENTAL INVOLVEMENT**	147
	Introduction	147
	Parents of Children with Special Needs	148
	Understanding the Experience	148
	Shock	149
	Denial	149
	Anger and Guilt	149
	Depression	149
	Detachment	149
	Reorganization	150
	Adaptation	150

	Other Influences on the Family	151
	Ecological Approach	152
	Role of the Early Childhood Professional	152
	Advocacy	152
	Showing Respect for the Child and Family	155
	Providing Emotional Support	156
	Knowledge, Attitudes, and Skills	157
	Summary	160
	Activities	160
	Discussion Questions	160
Chapter 10	**Collaboration for Success**	161
	Introduction	161
	Collaboration	164
	Role of the Early Childhood Professional	165
	Knowledge	167
	Skills	169
	Attitudes	170
	Summary	171
	Activities	171
	Discussion Questions	172
	References	173
	Index	178

CHAPTER 1

An Introduction to Working with Young Children with Special Needs

Introduction

Working with children with diverse needs in an early childhood care and education setting can be challenging, rewarding, and frustrating, often all at the same moment. Early childhood professionals are typically responsible for meeting the needs of all children under their care, including children with special and diverse needs. The challenge, then, is to meet the child's unique needs while ensuring that the needs of all other children in the group are met at the same time.

This chapter is the beginning of our quest to examine this challenge. It begins with a historical review of early childhood care and education programs and of the care of children with identified special and diverse needs. This review will establish the context for the services offered and approaches used today and will explain the diverse approaches being used. Following the review, the fundamental issues and ideas pertaining to meeting the diverse and special needs of children in inclusive settings will be discussed.

After reading this chapter, you should have a better understanding of:

- the historical and theoretical traditions inherent in the practices dealing with children with diverse needs today;
- key issues relating to the inclusion of young children
  - play
  - setting up environments
  - social competence and friendships
  - attitudes of children in the playroom
  - cultural diversity
- programming approaches suitable for children with diverse needs.

Historical Traditions

This section highlights the major influences on the care of young children, particularly the care of young children with special needs. This is a review of the major milestones and influences that have shaped today's services. In addition, this overview will explain the diverse range of attitudes and approaches existing in practice with young children today.

CHILD CARE

From the early history of Canada, there were child-care settings available for young children. Day nurseries were part of a broad social reform aimed at improving the lives of young children (Prochner, 1994). They were protective, custodial services provided by wealthy, benevolent women and typically did not include educational goals. This need for day-care services was created by the disruption of normal family life caused by industrialization and urbanization (Shimoni, 1990). Child neglect due to the parents' death, divorce, separation, and, most often, the need to work outside the home was common. Day nurseries and day care were available to mothers who needed to enter the work force, and when older siblings, required to attend school, were unavailable to care for younger children.

In time, the prevailing view became that women should be home with their children and that mothers were best capable of providing the moral roots that young children required (Spodek, 1985). There was concern that day care might undermine women's responsibilities for child rearing, and accordingly, only families that required day care were admitted. These settings became the domain of social workers, and day care was established as a temporary service, required only until the family could resume "normalcy" — until the mother could return home to care for her children (Shimoni, 1990).

At the same time, social policies and financial assistance were enabling mothers to stay at home with their children. As a result of these changes in services and day care, poverty alone was considered insufficient for admittance into day care, and families had to be considered dysfunctional in order to qualify. Social workers and a case-work approach were then used to provide protective, custodial services. This social service perspective remains influential in day care today and is exemplified by the fact that day care continues to be administered under the Department of Social Services in many provinces.

NURSERY SCHOOLS

The nursery school movement was associated primarily with universities and colleges. This resulted when many key people involved with the establishment of kindergarten programs moved into university positions and established child-development laboratories (Bloch, 1992). These nursery school programs served two functions: they were a means of developing more extensive information on child development, the subject of a new and developing science; and they provided a means of making the theoretical psychology of child development more practical. This was done at the same time that young women were trained, predominantly in home economics programs, to care for young children (Bloch, 1992).

Nursery school programs have subsequently maintained their child development orientation and have remained an alternative for young children. Despite the lack of public funding or affiliation with public education, they have survived. This is likely a result of a variety of factors: their teaching approach, which is based on the observation of young children; the use of developmental theory as their foundation; their promotion of emotional and social growth; and their emphasis on parental involvement.

KINDERGARTEN

Simultaneously, the kindergarten movement was being established. From its earliest days, it had an educational focus and was part of the educational system. Kindergarten became more relevant and important in the 1950s and 1960s, when it was recognized that the first five years of life were critical to intellectual development (Bloom, 1964), and Russian technological advances led North Americans, particularly Americans, to question the educational options available to children under the age of five.

PROJECT HEAD START

Developments in the field of psychology, scrutiny of the educational system, and the American civil rights movement's highlighting of the plight of children living in poverty led to the establishment of Project Head Start in the United States in 1965 (Shimoni, 1990). Federal funding and programs were established to deal with the educational concerns of children living in poverty. Project Head Start's goals included physical health, emotional and social development, conceptual and verbal skills, and the promotion of a sense of dignity and self-worth for disadvantaged children and their families (Shimoni, 1990).

Community and parent involvement were key components of all Head Start programs. The project's educational practices were based on behavioural principles and developmental theory. Head Start programs have been evaluated regularly, with mixed results. Research tended to suggest minimal positive effects on children's cognitive and socioemotional abilities, but more positive results for families in terms of education, health care, and social services (McKey et al., 1985). Although Project Head Start was an American initiative, the resulting research findings have been used as a model for programs across North America.

As Project Head Start became established and developed to meet the changing needs of children, its programs expanded to include children with special needs. Expansion of the programs to include children with a higher level of special needs seemed to be a logical direction for growth.

PARENTAL INVOLVEMENT

The other relevant historical or cultural factor influencing the education of children with special needs was the focus on parental involvement. This was a focal point of Project Head Start, and many benefits to the child and to the family were documented as part of the Project Head Start programs. The programs emphasized the involvement of parents as teachers who affect the child's growth and development outside of program hours and beyond the child's involvement, well into the school years.

This positive outcome of the Head Start programs was adopted by many programs dealing with children with special needs. It was recognized that parents could learn to act as therapists and teachers and so could positively influence developmental activities at home. Parents were asked to carry out range of motion programs, behavioural programs, self-help programs, and language programs at home. In fact, some programs required parents to sign a contract stating that they would consistently carry out all the prescribed programs at home prior to being admitted to the program.

EARLY INTERVENTION

The 1960s were also the time that early intervention programs were being introduced. Early intervention programs were initially directed at younger children with special needs, that is, those under the age of two years. Research suggested that long-term disabilities could be prevented or lessened by starting therapy and programming early. For example, an early start of range of motion and physiotherapy programs for young children with cerebral palsy could not only lessen the effects of cerebral palsy but also serve to prevent major complications from occurring, such as a severe tightening of muscles, which might require surgery. Parents were considered instrumental in early intervention programs both because of the lack of public funding and programs, and because of the parents' predominance in the child's daily life at this age. Programs were developed that had as their major goal teaching parents to teach and educate their child. Experts were brought in to assess the child's needs and develop treatment plans. Parents were then taught to carry out written programs created by professionals in all areas of development.

These parents were expected to carry out all forms of programs and therapy for their child at home because it was believed that all these programs would benefit the child. They typically carried out these treatment plans willingly. Parents routinely devoted large amounts of time to meet the individual programming requirements of the child with special needs. In busy families that included other siblings, this was often difficult to manage, despite the parents' best efforts and intentions. Many parents began to question their roles. They were expected to be teachers, therapists, and programmers, but frustrations arose: "When do I get to be the mom? When do I get to cuddle, comfort, and enjoy my baby? When do I get to decide what is best or what is too much?"

Since there was almost an exclusive emphasis on teaching, the difficult task of parenting was sometimes left unaddressed. This approach led to the polarization of parents and professionals. Parents came to feel that they did not know what their child needed and that they must depend on professionals to provide the answers. Professionals, "the experts," were then supposed to tell the parents what to do and how to do it. Parents often felt isolated, helpless, left out of the decision-making process, and dependent on the all-knowing professionals to determine what their child needed. As a result, the early intervention movement lost momentum. Professionals continue to struggle with issues of parental involvement today (Shimoni and Baxter, 1996).

SCENARIO

A young professional woman, Nola, adopted a very young infant and later discovered that the baby was severely delayed in motor and cognitive development. For the first few years, Nola worked tirelessly with a range of professionals and services to ensure that her daughter received the best possible care and education. When her daughter was 6 years old, several factors in their family life changed, and Nola realized that she required additional support and couldn't do it alone.

As she became immersed in her search for assistance, she commented that professionals expected her to be the expert — to know and do everything for her daughter. Nola reflected that this was quite a reversal: the professionals she had dealt with earlier had always made her feel incompetent, and she had relied on their knowledge and advice because they were the experts.

This scenario illustrates a shift in how parents and professionals work together. In six short years, Nola had moved from involvement with professionals who told her what to do, to involvement with professionals who expected her to know it all.

Approaches

In addition to various movements in the education and care of preschool children, there were approaches to teaching and learning that also influenced services for children with special needs.

Behavioural Approaches

Another factor contributing to the education of young children with diverse needs was the acceptance and widespread use of the behavioural approach as a viable teaching tool. Behavioural psychology developed in the 1960s as a result of the work of Alfred Watson and B.F. Skinner, which was based on the premise that behaviours could be shaped and that factors in the environment were important for learning. For example, behaviours could be increased or decreased by adding or removing a reinforcing event or "punisher" following the occurrence of a particular behaviour.

Behavioural psychology grew rapidly, and many techniques and methods were developed that could increase or decrease behaviours and learning. These theories were put into practice in developing teaching strategies for children and for individuals with special needs. Through the 1960s and 1970s, it was shown repeatedly that children and adults with special needs could learn by using behavioural strategies and techniques. The strategies and techniques were used in a variety of settings, including schools and residential schools, with both children and adults. Over and over, skill development occurred in areas where it had not previously occurred, such as personal skills, language development, and intellectual skills. Programs were expanded to include children of all ages and all levels in all settings.

Behavioural approaches were developed in the belief that anything could be taught, given the right behavioural method — teachers just had to be willing to try another way (Gold, 1980). The philosophical underpinnings of rehabilitation were challenged as people with disabilities proved that they could develop the skills and abilities needed to live independently and productively in society. Program structures evolved to become more community based and came to recognize the positive benefits for children with special needs of being with their normally developing peers.

Integration

The movement toward the integration and inclusion of children with special needs began in the 1970s and 1980s. It was based on the availability of a teaching technology and upon the work of Wolf Wolfensberger (1972), who advocated a more "normal" or typical lifestyle for individuals with disabilities. Changes in the attitudes and beliefs of society toward children and adults with special needs was required to ensure that normalization could occur. Accordingly, in the early years, much of the focus and research on integration centred on this philosophical debate. Research focussed on the intellectual and social benefits of integration for the child with special needs.

The debate around integration focussed on several key points. It was demonstrated that children with special needs learn more appropriate behaviours from socially appropriate role models, that is, normally developing children (Chandler, 1994). The social and emotional benefits of this approach were consistently noted in the research. In addition, integrated settings led to more realistic expectations for children with special needs. Integration contributed to a more challenging environment and enhanced skill development. Lastly, evidence suggests that integration can affect the attitudinal development of all children (Chandler, 1994). These research findings contributed to more integration and to the establishment of legislation in certain jurisdictions ensuring this right for the child with special needs.

Since the 1970s, integrating children with special needs in child-care programs has become more common. In Canada, integration occurs on a voluntary basis. In the United States, federal policy and legislation provides free and appropriate education for all children 3 to 21 years of age and prohibits children with a disability from being excluded. Neither federal nor provincial integration policy and legislation exist in Canada, but most provinces support integration through funding, education, and resources (Hope Irwin, 1997).

Inclusion

The preceding section discussed the integration of children with special needs. However, the recent change in emphasis from integration to inclusion represents an evolution and carries with it an essential shift in conceptualization that has important implications for practice. Integration refers to the process by which social and physical opportunities are created for children with disabilities to participate with others in regular or typical settings (Taylor, Biklen, Lehr, & Searle, 1987). The reality of integration, however, is that one group is considered the "mainstream" and the other is not. The result is that "one group must 'push-in' to the settings and activities occupied by the other" (Salisbury, 1991). Thus, although integration is generally considered more desirable than segregation, the "push-in" approach appears hierarchical and unequal.

The notion of inclusion implies a different value to thinking about and planning the care, education, and development of all young children. "The underlying supposition in inclusive programs is that all children will be based in the *rooms* they would attend if they did not have a disability. Teachers, students, parents, and administrators (in fact, all stakeholders) define the *program* and *room* culture as including children with diverse backgrounds, abilities and contributions" (Salisbury, 1991, p 148) (emphasis added).

Inclusion programs accommodate the diverse needs of all children as much as possible within the general curriculum and in the provision of appropriate experiences and activities. Collaboration in planning, teamwork, and transformational leadership provide a framework for success. Driven by the vision that early childhood settings are places where all children develop and learn well, inclusive settings become creative and successful environments both for the adults (early childhood professionals and parents) and for the children they serve.

Interactionist Approaches

Throughout the twentieth century and in parallel with the development of preschool programs, early childhood care and education programs evolved approaches to working with children that emphasize the importance of interactions among children and with materials. These interactionist approaches, inspired largely by the work of Jean Piaget, are based on the belief that children construct their knowledge and understanding of themselves and their world. This belief led to the creation of early childhood programs with a strong orientation toward play as an important vehicle for children's development and learning. This approach to curriculum, which may be described as child-centred, emergent, or generative, appears to conflict with the behavioural approaches traditionally provided for children with special needs.

Constructivist Approach

An approach that appears promising in working with children with special needs is the constructivist approach, which allows children to create their own knowledge through interactive experiences with their social and physical world (Winzer, 1997). A central feature of the interactionist–constructivist approach is that of "providing experiences which make it possible for children to try out, shift backward as well as forward, to create where necessary the opportunities for the kind of interaction that is essential for the assimilation of experience, the achievement of new integrations, and the resolution of conflict in both cognitive and emotional realms" (Shapiro and Biber, 1972, p. 37).

By contrast, traditional behavioural approaches to curriculum for young children with special needs, emphasize that "many, if not all, handicapped children are in particular need of a high degree of structure in their learning environments.... Often they do not have a repertoire of basic skills that both motivate and enable them to explore, experiment and thus learn almost spontaneously from play." (Allen, 1991, p. 15).

The apparent incongruence between these theoretical positions — behaviourism and constructivism — may cause difficulty for early childhood professionals. Often medical and educational rehabilitation personnel who provide early intervention and special education programs for young children work from behaviourist orientations focussing on particular skill training that use adult-directed teaching models. Early childhood professionals, however, whose training has focussed on the theories of Piaget (1962) and the teaching models of Bank Street (Shapiro and Biber, 1972), Devries (1984), Kamii (1985), and Pacific Oaks (Jones and Prescott, 1989) practise constructivist approaches and emphasize the importance of the medium of play.

Summary

This brief review of influences highlights the multitude of influences in the education and care of young children, particularly the education and care of those with special needs. Thus, many types of programs based on many philosophies and approaches exist today. Most programs are based on developmental curriculum and use behavioural strategies for teaching. However, other models exist, causing difficulties for parents who must often search for the model and program that fit their values, beliefs, and needs.

Early childhood professionals working with children with special needs in group care settings also experience difficulties because the various methods often do not work with the developmental approach. Child caregivers are typically left with few resources and little funding to meet individual needs in a diverse group of children. It must be recognized that different historical and sociological factors have shaped attitudes toward children with special needs and influenced the various approaches and strategies.

Key Issues

Early childhood professionals must identify and interpret the variety of theoretical and philosophical positions and the resulting approaches used by the programs and professionals with whom they are involved. Following is a review of the fundamental or key issues relevant to the provision of inclusive services for children with diverse and special needs. These key issues will be revisited throughout the book in discussions of the practical approaches and strategies to be considered in working with young children with special needs.

PLAY

All over the world children play. Whatever their age and situation, children engage in playing peekaboo, rope jumping, pretending to be heroes, and much more. The fact that play is so universal and persistent suggests that it has an important role in development. The key to understanding the link between play and development is that play changes as children develop. As children mature, their play reflects changes that point to maturation. Their social interactions, expressions of feelings, and evolving understanding of possibilities in play all signal these changes. It is through play that children enact and practise their increased understanding of the world.

Erikson described play as a child's way "to deal with experience by creating model situations and to master reality by experiment and planning" (1950, p. 220). Play also reflects a child's ability to concentrate, to be inventive, to organize and pay attention to detail, and to participate with others. Whether children engage in play as a preparation for life, to practise new skills or roles, or for pure pleasure and enjoyment, play is inexorably linked to development.

Although play is difficult to define, several characteristics provide useful reference points. Play is:

- free of imposed rules and tasks;
- intrinsically motivated;
- voluntary and often spontaneous;
- something that requires the active involvement of the player;
- non-literal; that is, it requires the player to enter a world of make-believe and to bridge imaginary and real worlds by assuming an "as if" mode.

Play includes a wide variety of types or levels. Children interact with toys or other objects in different ways, as well as with other children in play in different ways. Classic work by Parten (1932) and Smilansky (1968) resulted in a proliferation of information about play and the development of play abilities for all children.

A brief comparison of Piaget's theory of cognitive development with play activities of children illuminates the relationship between play and development. For instance, playing peekaboo for pleasure and with persistence and inventiveness is characteristic of children in the first year of life. However, a child cannot engage in this play until she or he has understood that people still exist when not in sight. Piaget described this phenomenon as "object permanence," an accomplishment critical to the child's learning during the sensorimotor stage of development. At about the same age, children are learning to pretend — to understand that objects may be used as a symbolic representation of other objects or people.

SCENARIO

Recently my wife, Brenda, was playing with our 16-month-old nephew, Talus. He was bringing her an object, simply giving it to her, and then going to get another. As he gave her a plastic cup she stopped him and said, "M'mmm, juice. Thank you for the juice," and put the cup to her lips, pretending to drink. "Nice juice," she said.

Talus watched this episode intently. He took the cup from Brenda, looked inside it, tipped it upside down, then looked toward his mother. Brenda said, "More juice?" Talus looked at her, held on to the cup, and put it to his lips, pretending to drink. He gave the cup to Brenda. "Nice juice," she repeated, pretending to drink again. "Talus have a drink?" He smiled, took the cup, and walked over to his mother. Holding the cup toward her, he said, "Juice?"

Talus appears to be at the beginning of make-believe play, imitating an adult's actions in an attempt to make sense of an experience. Over the next few months, he will probably engage in more representational play, taking on different roles and playing imaginatively. In a few years Talus, as a five-year-old, may be inventing play with others in which they construct complex roles or take on superhuman characteristics. The play may be planned, may require intense preparation, and may be sustained over several days. Piaget proposed that in this period of pre-operational thinking, children use play as a bridge between inner experience and the world "out there," between private understanding and socially validated knowledge.

Engagement in play is as critical for a child with a disability as for other children. Play involves the functions of thinking, feeling, controlling, creating, experimenting, and practising, and it brings enjoyment and pleasure. Because play is pleasurable, children will continue to practise and build on the skills they already have. Unfortunately, programs sometimes focus so much on helping children to overcome or compensate for the area of concern that little provision is made for play. In extreme situations, play is used as a form of reward when the child has accomplished a particular task.

SCENARIO

Three-year-old Tae attended a speech pathology session twice a week. The pathologist identified speech sounds that Tae needed to practise and developed a program for him to practise them. At each session, the pathologist put him through a series of specific rehearsals. Only after Tae had completed these exercises to her satisfaction was he allowed to select toys or books and play.

Was Tae provided with the opportunity to "play," given the definitions and descriptions of play that were discussed earlier? Could play have been used in this situation to promote the development of communication skills?

Children acquire play skills at different times in their lives and in conjunction with their development. Young children may play alone but be learning to play next to others and to share toys. One 3-year-old child may have very good turn-taking skills and be able to play with others co-operatively, while another 5-year-old may still be struggling to master the social skills that would enable her to accept the ideas of others. Early childhood professionals, through their knowledge of play and development, identify the skills that children need to learn to become "master" players and assist children in acquiring those skills. Through the knowledge and experience gained by working with diverse children in a group setting, these professionals assist children to use and acquire skills so that they benefit from play with peers.

Early childhood professionals can promote play opportunities in many ways:
- being aware of the various levels and types of play, so that their expectations for play are appropriate to the child's level of overall development.

- being aware of their role as caregivers in play experiences. Their role should not be unidimensional (i.e, leading, initiating) but rather vary based on the child's needs, interests, and abilities. Accordingly, they may initiate, follow the child's lead, extend, build skills, or observe.
- ensuring blocks of time for uninterrupted play in which children can explore, experiment, and practise. An additional benefit of large blocks of time is the reduction of transition times, which typically are disruptive for children.
- ensuring that a range of materials is accessible to children so that they can make choices and enhance their abilities in all areas. Children with special needs need to have not only toys suited to their level of development (to promote refinement of skills and repetition) but also toys that will challenge their development. Toys that promote a range of skills, such as those that promote sharing as well as toys for solitary play, are desirable.
- attempting, as much as possible, to use toys that are part of the typical environment and to introduce adapted toys only where needed.
- ensuring that play spaces are adequate in terms of size and location. For example, children may need large spaces to spread materials out, or they may need to be away from high-traffic areas to eliminate disruptions.

These are only a few ideas regarding play. More specific ideas can be found in subsequent chapters.

ENVIRONMENTS

Including all children in the preschool program has implications for arranging their environment while in care. The early childhood professional must pay particular attention to the environment in which children eat, sleep, play, listen, talk, pretend, and express their joys, fears, and frustrations. This includes more than the amount of physical space; it affects the arrangement of space, materials, and equipment, and the ways in which they are displayed and made accessible. Special consideration should be given to children with special needs. For example, accessibility is a key issue for children with visual or orthopaedic impairments.

Environment also includes the tone and atmosphere of the setting. Although these are difficult concepts to describe they are key to the success of inclusive programs. Early childhood professionals must ask themselves how they can create an atmosphere of inclusion, in which all children, regardless of ability, belong. The environment should not be one in which children with a disability are invited to participate only in particular events and thereby treated as marginal participants. This aspect of inclusion involves the attitudes of both adults and children.

Decisions about the care environment are influenced by many things, including the ages of the children, their interests, the focus of their play, and the image of child care brought by each of the early childhood professionals. The last factor may be the most critical. For instance, professionals who view themselves primarily as teachers may attempt to create an environment for learning experiences to occur, perhaps to create a classroom setting, with accompanying expectations and learning centres. By contrast, professionals who see themselves as parents, or as acting in loco parentis, may attempt to make the environment as homelike as possible by selecting furniture, colours, and room arrangements to promote comfort.

SCENARIO

Victoria enrolled her 3-year-old son, Liam, in a nursery school program. He had just accomplished toileting. In the first three weeks of nursery school, he had two "accidents." After the second, the teacher loudly announced to his mother that Liam was not toilet trained. Victoria was embarrassed. She explained to Liam that this was bad and that if it continued, he would not be able to go to nursery school anymore. After considering the situation, it occurred to her that Liam had just learned to use the toilet independently and that since he was in a new situation (the bathroom was down the hall) and the teacher was unfamiliar to him, it probably wasn't all his fault.

The next day, Victoria told the teacher that she and Liam had talked about it and that Liam was going to try really hard. Victoria asked if there was any way that she could support him, since he had just mastered this skill. The teacher replied, "Sure. The next time he wets his pants, I'll call you so that you can come and change him," and walked away. Liam's mother felt that this environment was likely not conducive to meeting Liam's three-year-old needs.

In this scenario, how does the caregiver view herself and her role? Is there a way that the environment and the caregiver could better meet Liam's needs?

The environments that early childhood professionals create are critically important to the well-being and development of each child (Winter, Bell, and Dempsey, 1994). Ensuring a physical space that is safe, and that invites and welcomes each child to engage in interactions and experiences that are appropriate, meaningful, and worthwhile is the responsibility of each early childhood professional. Adaptations to the physical environment should be made only to accommodate a child with a disability when it is developmentally appropriate to do so or when it is done for safety (Chandler, 1994).

The environmental task of early childhood professionals is to create environments in which both they and the children in their care may live together for several hours each day in an atmosphere that is engaging and provides a sense of belonging. In that respect, caregivers should consider the following issues.

- Children with special needs require private spaces as well as spaces to play with others in both small and large groups, opportunities to create complex play events using various materials, and a variety of hard and soft areas.
- Physical health and safety may be a priority for some children with special needs.

- Space may need to be rearranged to ensure that children move and act as independently as possible.
- Caregivers may need to ensure that toys, materials, and equipment are accessible to all children. This may necessitate, for example, ensuring that toys are available at floor level for children who crawl or use scooter boards.
- The use of space may need to be considered in light of behavioural expectations. For example, it is not uncommon for child-sized tables to be used for lunch, at which the expectations include eating, being quiet, being patient, sitting, and learning table manners. The same tables may be used later in the day for table-top activities such as playing with play dough, during which the expectations are not to eat, to interact, and to have fun without reference to noise level, table manners, or even sitting. For some children, environmental cues are useful in guiding behaviour and may warrant consideration by caregivers.

These are only a few considerations regarding the physical environment. More can be found in the chapters to follow.

FRIENDSHIPS AND PEER RELATIONSHIPS

Social competence, rather than cognitive development, has become a focus for children with special needs (Carr, 1997). However, exposure to same-age peers and appropriate activities alone will not enhance interactions with peers or foster social development. Special strategies to promote play and increase interactions will always be necessary (Cook, Tessier, and Klein, 1996).

When children are denied access to or rejected from play, not only are there social and emotional effects, but these children are also denied opportunities for learning (Matthews, 1996). The importance of the social aspects of learning was emphasized by the writings of Vygotsky (1976), and it has been demonstrated repeatedly that peer relationships are critical to inclusion (Guralnick, 1990; Matthews, 1996). Children gain many social abilities in their interactions with peers (Buzzelli and File, 1989).

Not only are friendships important to inclusion, but peer relationships are critical to healthy development (Lawson, 1997). The early years seem to be the ideal time to assist children in developing peer relationships (Kemple and Hartle, 1997). However, there is evidence that in inclusive settings typically developing children interact with typically developing peers more frequently than with children with special needs. Thus, it is critical to make specific efforts to teach children with special needs social abilities that will enhance their interaction with peers and promote participation with the group (Buzzelli and File, 1989).

A healthy, positive parent–child attachment is considered the foundation for social development. There is a common belief that children with special needs and their parents experience difficulties in this kind of attachment. It is believed that the presence of a disability may lower the child's responsiveness, which may in turn lead adults to be less responsive (Dunlap, 1997a). Interruptions in attachment occur for children with facial deformities, malnourished babies, and children with brain damage (Trawicki-Smith, 1997). However, others contend that this assumption has not been supported by research (Trawicki-Smith, 1997). Most parents and children with special needs attach in ways similar to those of normally developing children and their parents, despite stresses and complications. The mental health and healthy functioning of adults appear to be more relevant to attachment than any special needs the child may have. Bearing this in mind, it is important for caregivers to be aware of attachment and to foster it with parents and other significant people as much as possible.

Research into friendship patterns demonstrates that, within groups, some children are accepted, others are neglected, and some are rejected, and that these groups are treated differently by their peers (Matthews, 1996). Accepted or popular children are attentive to other children, respond to others in positive ways, and are sought out for friendship. They are more likely to demonstrate friendship-making abilities (such as greeting peers or inviting peers to participate), to display appropriate behaviours within the group, and to engage in positive interactions with their peers. Children who are rejected by their peers, on the other hand, engage in more aggressive behaviour, are more disagreeable, and try to exert control over their peers. They may attempt to use imposing strategies like demanding or becoming the centre of attention in order to be noticed or included.

This research describing socially competent children can provide a good starting point for developing and enhancing the social skills of children with special needs. It is particularly important that early childhood professionals be aware of friendship and relationship issues and attempt to provide children with every opportunity to develop the social abilities necessary to interact with their peers and make friends.

The development of peer relationships among children does not simply happen because children are in close and regular contact in the playroom or playground. Negative interactions are likely to occur in such situations. Developing children's social competence requires the attention of caregivers who understand the abilities and social needs of young children and who know how and when to provide appropriate support and guidance (Kemple and Hartle, 1997). Although it is important to assist children with special needs in acquiring social competencies and skills, it is just as important to assist non-disabled children in understanding, accepting, and interacting with children with special needs. Early childhood professionals can support the development of social competence in many ways.

- Typically, programs oriented toward children with special needs become so focussed on skill development and enhancement that they neglect the importance of play in the development of young children. Caregivers should ensure that children have sufficient time for free play. This play is less likely to be interrupted, and children will feel less need to compete for toys or time, so more opportunities to learn and practise social skills are available.
- It is important to create an environment in which all children feel safe and comfortable to play and interact with other children. This may necessitate the caregiver spending time with each child, being sensitive and responsive, ensuring that children have a voice, and being a good, positive role model.
- All children need to experience success. This may require caregivers to do more planning and to be aware of small successes. In addition, peers can help recognize abilities.

By doing this, children come to recognize that learning is a process in which all children, including those with special needs, are engaged, even though they may be at different stages (Chandler, 1994).
- Caregivers should consider the impact and arrangement of the physical environment on peer interactions. Settings, toys, and materials can encourage or discourage positive peer interactions.
- The attitudes of significant adults contribute to an environment conducive to learning and acceptance. Young children will imitate the behaviours, words, and actions of these significant adults. Modelling the behaviours that caregivers would most like children to develop promotes inclusion and enhances opportunities for learning through peers.
- Guidance and support for children resolving conflicts can be provided by giving them the tools they need. Stating "You need to use your words" is helpful if children know what words to use and if they understand the other child's perspective. Helping a child to develop an awareness of the other child's perspective, feelings, and developing vocabulary will be effective both immediately and in his or her continuing development of social abilities. Early childhood professionals can be helpful in developing not only the skills necessary for conflict resolution but also those required for initiating and maintaining interactions and expressing needs and feelings.
- Young children develop their language skills at an incredible rate. Thus, although they may know the right word, they may not understand what they are saying, especially in the realm of feelings. For example, young children often say "I hate you," or "I'm bored," without understanding the implications of these words. Early childhood professionals need not only to help children build their vocabulary but also to help them develop the emotional and social dimensions of defining and understanding those feelings and feeling words.
- Children with special needs need to feel that they are free to express their feelings and thoughts. Caregivers should create an atmosphere in which the child can be heard and then use the opportunity for learning. If caregivers respond to children's hurting remarks and questions openly and with clear, accurate information, they will let children know that it is acceptable to discuss differences. The discussion can be used as an opportunity to learn about, understand, and appreciate differences (Youcha and Wood, 1995).
- At one time or another, most children will tease and be teased. Those who are short or tall, fat or skinny, have red hair, wear glasses, or are different in any way will be subjected to hurtful comments from other children. All children need to learn that making such remarks hurts others. They also need to learn to cope with teasing. Rather than minimizing the child's concerns, the caregiver should let the child talk about the teasing and how it felt. Other children also need to hear how the child with special needs feels so they realize that children with special needs have the same feelings.
- Although children with special needs may occasionally require direct guidance or teaching strategies, they may also benefit from more natural interventions, or interventions that would naturally be used for any child (Kemple and Hartle, 1997; Odom and Brown, 1993). Thus, different strategies and approaches should be used for various

children. For example, the use of peers and peer interactions is one strategy. Often, skills modelled by a peer are more effective than those modelled by an adult. In addition, normally developing children may also develop more positive attitudes by peer modelling (Trepanier-Street and Romatowski, 1996).
- Early childhood professionals may find resources aimed directly at social competence development useful as a starting point or for generating new approaches or strategies. For example, "The Friendship Circle" (CCIF) and Anne Carr's "Making Friends," a video about social integration, are very popular.

Peer interactions and social development are key features in any early childhood care and education setting. Caregivers need to be aware of this for all children in their care, but especially for children who have particular needs in this area. A variety of strategies should be used to guide and support children in an environment in which caregivers are ever-present as positive social role models.

As a role model for the children in your care, you must be careful to communicate positive values. If you fail to respond to a question or choose to ignore a comment, the child may believe that the question is not a topic open for discussion or that the comment is correct. Instead, when inappropriate comments are made or awkward questions are raised, you can seize the opportunity to communicate positive values by providing children with a simple explanation in words that the child will understand, perhaps an explanation related to the child's experience.

It is important to acknowledge the feeling behind the child's question — the fear, uncertainty, or apprehension. Pay attention to the child's facial expression and tone of voice. The comment should be addressed openly. Sometimes an opener such as "Some children wonder... Some children think... Some children feel..." may be helpful. Acknowledging and labelling these reactions may help the child to understand. By communicating positive values, such as the fact that children with special needs are more alike than different, and by openly discussing questions and concerns, you as a caregiver can help foster positive attitudes and inclusion.

ATTITUDES OF NON-DISABLED CHILDREN

Inclusion has typically focussed on the needs of children with special needs. Studies of inclusion have repeatedly acknowledged its benefits for children with diverse and special needs, especially in regard to cognitive and social development (Trepanier-Street and Romatowski, 1996). The impact of inclusion on normally developing children has not been studied to the same extent.

Research suggests that young non-disabled children perceive children with special needs in terms of their limitations and have a narrow view of their ability to make contributions (Cruz, 1987). However, by spending time with special-needs children, non-disabled children can develop empathy and acceptance, but only through planned intervention by early childhood professionals (Trepanier-Street and Romatowski, 1996). Positive attitudes toward children with special needs will not occur by accident; early childhood professionals must plan for this to occur, for both children with special needs and normally developing children (Buzzelli and File, 1989). This intervention may include direct contact such as guidance in play situations and use of curricular materials such as books, videos, and modelling by adults.

A further consideration is that parents of non-disabled children often feel that their children may be affected by the presence of special-needs children in the playroom. They may believe that their normally developing child will receive less attention from caregivers and that he or she will develop inappropriate behaviours by interacting with children with special needs.

SCENARIO

Sergei was a 3-year-old boy attending an inclusive day-care centre. In his playroom there were two children with Down Syndrome, one child with emotional concerns, and one child with language delays. Sergei's parents were aware of all of the children in the room and their needs. Several weeks after Sergei arrived at the centre, his mother demanded that he be moved to a room that had no children with special needs. She explained that when Sergei started, he knew the word for milk and was capable of saying "Milk, please" and "I want milk." Now he grunted "Mi-mi" and expected his milk to be given to him.

Sergei's mother was adamant that not only had he learned this in the day-care centre, but that the caregivers were accepting this as acceptable behaviour from him. The caregivers tried to explain that all children will imitate and that the caregivers had different expectations for the various children in their care. The parents, however, contended that the development of their child was being compromised by the presence of children with special needs and removed their child from the day-care centre.

Sergei's mother obviously had some strong feelings about the inclusion of children with special needs in a child-care setting. What could you have said to alleviate her fears? How might the children have been approached in this situation?

Early childhood professionals must be aware of these potential concerns and be prepared to deal with them. All parents want to be assured that their child's needs are being met in the group setting and that the needs of one child are not being ignored in favour of the special needs of another. Parents may need concrete examples of the attention being given to their child or may need to spend time observing the children interacting to be reassured that this occurs.

DIVERSITY ISSUES

Early childhood professionals are increasingly working with young children from linguistically and culturally diverse backgrounds. These children and/or their parents may not speak English, may have had very different life experiences, and may have expectations about child development or parenting approaches that are very different from those of the caregivers. They may also have very diverse ideas about children with special needs. Thus, the early childhood professional may feel frustration both in meeting the needs of the child within the group and in working with the child's family.

The children that early childhood professionals work with embody diversity in size, age, abilities, race, religion, cultural background, and family structure (Youcha & Wood, 1995). Caregivers need to recognize and acknowledge all aspects of diversity and the contribution of these aspects to the uniqueness of each child (Dotsch, 1997). Sometimes this is difficult to do.

SCENARIO

One of the authors of this book was quite excited to find a textbook that considered development from a multicultural perspective. The text presented development in the context of a variety of cultural influences and was sensitive to the ways in which race, culture, and religion may affect development. The point that all children are different was made repeatedly throughout the book.

However, in discussing children with special needs, the word "difference" was abandoned in favour of terms such as "abnormal," "having deficits," or "deficiencies." Although the text was sensitive to cultural aspects of diversity, it was not sensitive to another area of potential difference.

Early childhood professionals need to be mindful not to fall into the same trap. One of the first steps they should take is to examine their own attitudes and beliefs. This may not be easy, since no one wants to consider himself or herself as, for example, a racist. But it is important to be aware of one's beliefs and attitudes, because they will emerge in words and actions.

SCENARIO

A newly immigrated Asian family had their three children in day care. The three children were 8 months, 3 years, and 5 years of age. The parents told the caregivers at the outset that each child was to learn "to mind." Disobedience and not listening were not to be tolerated. The parents gave the caregivers permission to punish the child physically if this occurred. The caregivers discussed this situation at a regular staff meeting. They were shocked at the parents' attitudes and expectations. The staff felt that although the parents' expectations did not meet with the caregivers' developmental expectations, they could compromise on these but that they could not compromise on the punishment. They further decided that they would closely watch the children for signs of abuse.

One of the caregivers from the family's Asian culture sat quietly through this discussion but then felt that she had to speak. She explained that the situation resulted from different perspectives and different values. Whereas North Americans value and promote autonomy and independence in young children, some Asian cultures value and promote dependency and respect. This, not bad parenting or abuse, is what was underlying the parents' request.

Different values and beliefs underlie the care of children with special needs. The first step is for you as a caregiver to examine and become aware of your attitudes and perspectives. Upon reflection, it may not be necessary to change them but to recognize their impact on your behaviour.

SCENARIO

In a class on children with special needs, the discussion centred on attitudes. One student told the following story. In high school, she was involved in a peer tutoring program. A class of adolescents with special needs was integrated in the school, and she tutored them as well. One day she was physically assaulted by one of the students with special needs. Even though it was explained to her why he did this and she was able to better understand his behaviour, her fear of some people with special needs remains.

Upon reflection, she concluded that this discussion made her realize what her attitudes toward people with developmental disabilities actually were. She realized that she needed to understand this in the context of the situation in which it occurred and not generalize it to others. Although she might not change her attitude toward some people with developmental delays, it might change her approach to others.

Early childhood professionals need to find resources, either parents or other individuals, who can provide information regarding others' values, beliefs, and approaches. Find a person with whom you feel comfortable in asking the questions in order to check potential areas of difference or diversity before they arise as issues or concerns. Try to create a language-rich environment, consisting primarily of English but also including the child's native language.

Playrooms should be evaluated from the perspective of diverse cultures. Are all groups represented and treated in valuing ways? Can the same can be said of children with special needs? Early childhood professionals need to be aware of diversity needs in the widest possible context. It cannot be assumed that this will occur automatically. Thinking about diversity includes tolerating, accepting, and respecting as well as embracing and celebrating differences (Chud and Fuhlman, 1995).

PLANNING APPROACH

The predominant use of the behavioural approach for children with special needs has had lasting effects. One result has been the legacy of the deficit model. Behavioural strategies are founded on the premise that the professional should identify and assess the areas of deficit for each child. This is typically done by using developmental assessments that help to determine which skills the child has mastered and which skills the child will need to learn next. Programming strategies and approaches are then developed on the basis of deficits. By concentrating on what the child lacks or needs to learn in order to catch up or stay on track developmentally, this approach leads people to focus on the development of specific skills. Somewhere along the way, the "child" gets lost. Parents are often most sensitive to this approach and have the most difficulty in dealing with it. They often want to talk about "my child," rather than with the bits and pieces that each professional is concerned about.

SCENARIO

I was asked to provide some information to a mother who had a 4-year-old son in an integrated day-care setting. Keigo was experiencing some difficulties in toilet training. The special-needs worker and the mother had tried a number of techniques, schedules, and programs. When the mother called for some advice on a new program, I asked her some questions about the child and the setting. She replied that Keigo played well with his peers. He loved to play and sometimes just got so involved that he forgot to go to the bathroom. I suggested that he was a "normal" boy who normally forgot.

There was a long pause, after which his mother asked if I was saying that her son was normal. "Yes," I replied, "he is." She said, "That's the first time anyone, any professional, has ever said that." Our conversation after that was very different in tone and content. She no longer looked for a program but instead considered what she had done with her older children in the same situation. I later realized that it hadn't taken very long for this mother to become trained to look at her child in terms of deficits and that this perspective affected her whole view of her son.

This scenario shows how attitudes and beliefs about children can affect the practices of early childhood professionals. The deficit model permeates the perspective of professionals who work with the child. It focusses on correcting deficits, rather than considering the whole child, including personality, temperament, family, and their individual strengths and other positive attributes.

Likewise, professionals combining behavioural strategies with developmental curriculum approaches encounter difficulties. In preschool settings, the developmental approach predominates. Developmentally appropriate practices (Bredekamp, 1987) have become the foundation of programming for young children across North America. Many assessment tools exist that assist professionals in determining the developmental level or age of children with special needs. For example, there are broad-based screening devices such as the Denver Developmental

Screening Device and in-depth assessments such as the Brigance, Koontz, and Vulpe scales. All of these devices present children with a standard set of tasks based on normal developmental sequences. Then professionals determine which developmental skills the child has and which skills the child will need to learn. A program or treatment plan based on the next developmental skill to be learned is developed, using behavioural techniques such as task analysis, chaining, and reinforcement to teach the skill. Teaching then focusses on the learning of specific skills and subsequent maintenance (ensuring that the skill continues to be used after the program is done) and generalization (expanding the skill to related activities). The skill-based model looks like this:

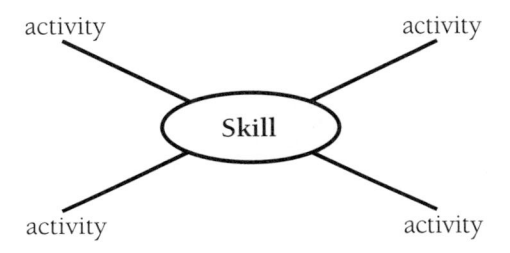

```
    activity              activity
         \                /
          \              /
           ( Skill )
          /              \
         /                \
    activity              activity
```

If the developmental skill to be learned is eye–hand co-ordination, the initial program outlines how to teach eye–hand co-ordination, perhaps by developing a task analysis (breaking the skill down to its component parts) and then by teaching one step at a time, using reinforcement to increase the probability of learning. The initial teaching may occur by giving a child either a functional, meaningful task, such as eating, or a non-functional task, such as picking up different-shaped objects. After the child has learned the skill, other activities are added so that the child can practise, maintain, and generalize the skill. For example:

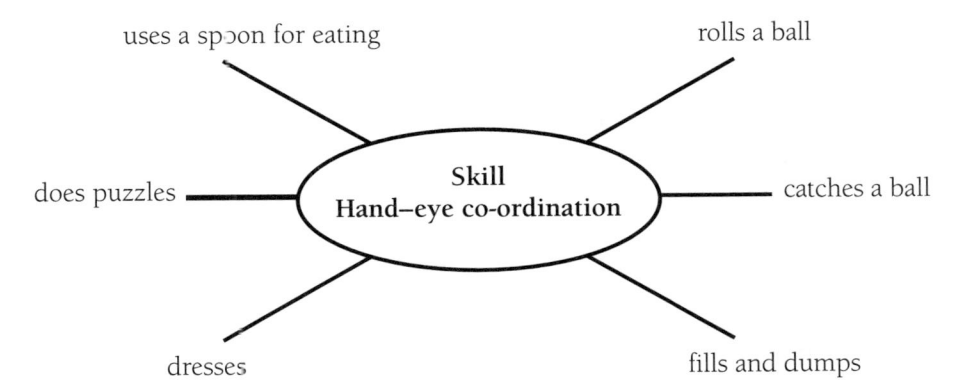

```
       uses a spoon for eating          rolls a ball
              \                          /
               \                        /
                                          
 does puzzles ─────  Skill              ──── catches a ball
                    Hand–eye co-ordination
               /                        \
              /                          \
           dresses                    fills and dumps
```

This behavioural approach continues either by adding more activities that involve this skill, to ensure maintenance and generalization, or by adding new skills as determined by the developmental assessment. Although this approach has predominated, it has shortcomings. One concern is that it focusses on isolated skills and does little to integrate skills in different areas.

SCENARIO

A rehabilitation practicum student working with Sandra, a 4-year-old developmentally delayed child in a segregated setting, related this story. The daily schedule was set out: circle time, language, fine motor, cognitive, and gross motor activities in half-hour blocks. During the language session, the student was teaching Sandra two phrases: "Can I" and "May I." The session involved a series of questions, and Sandra's correct responses were reinforced.

An hour later, in the cognitive session, the class was given choices of activities that promoted cognitive development. Here, it was appropriate and meaningful for Sandra to use the two-word phrases, "Can I" and "May I." However, there was no such expectation, and Sandra was no longer reinforced or even noticed when she used these phrases. So, when she used them appropriately, nothing happened. The student was perplexed about what she was trying to teach from one half-hour slot to the next. She assumed that Sandra must be just as confused, because she wasn't able to tell time and did not understand why her earlier correct responses were no longer relevant.

This scenario shows how the skill-based approach often leads to isolated teaching events, typically based on need rather than on a consideration of the whole child and all of his or her abilities. This focus on skills and specific skill areas inadvertently reinforces and maintains the deficit model. It continues to force parents and professionals alike to focus on areas of deficit and need rather than on the whole child.

Skill-based teaching models tend to be teacher-directed. The teacher must determine what the child needs to learn, and arranges the program, setting, and materials so that the child learns. Those who work with young children understand how difficult it can be to direct children's learning in such a way, especially when it requires taking children away from something that they have chosen (such as playing) to engage in a skill development activity.

Skill training tends to focus on the major developmental domains of cognitive, language, personal, and motor skills. There is very little emphasis on integrating these skills or teaching skills outside the traditional domains, such as emotional, social, or play skills. How to incorporate skill development into play is still a major concern. Professionals, who typically have medical training (for example, speech therapy, physiotherapy, or occupational therapy), have little background education in play and the development of play skills. Early childhood professionals, on the other hand, have learned extensively about the development of play and teaching in the context of play or ongoing routines, but they do not have skills in assessment and programming or in integrating the two approaches.

A third approach, called an integrated curriculum approach (Stone, 1996), can function as a balance to skill-based teaching. It is an experience-based approach, which requires a different perspective and different set of abilities from the professional. Professionals must know development and must understand activities well enough to know when to intervene, by taking the child's lead. For example, learning to ride a tricycle may be the means to learn the gross motor skill of peddling, and perhaps balance, but this activity involves many other skills and has the potential to develop many other skills. All of these skills need not be developed at the same time. For example:

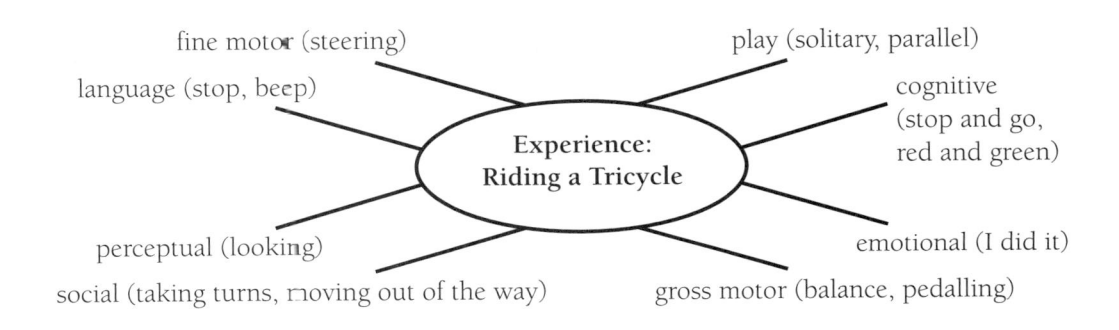

```
         fine motor (steering)                      play (solitary, parallel)
  language (stop, beep)                                    cognitive
                                                           (stop and go,
                          Experience:                      red and green)
                         Riding a Tricycle

      perceptual (looking)                          emotional (I did it)
  social (taking turns, moving out of the way)   gross motor (balance, pedalling)
```

In using this approach, the caregiver must be familiar with the specific developmental tasks that the child needs to learn and how these come together in order for the child to engage in the experience. The caregiver must also be sensitive to the child's interests. When the child chooses to ride the tricycle, the caregiver must determine either what to teach or what the child wishes to get out of this experience. She may focus on one ability considered important for the child's development, such as learning to pedal or maintaining balance or steering, or she may pick up on the child's interest in the words that accompany riding (toot toot, stop, watch out) and focus on language or cognitive abilities, such as turning. She may focus on one ability or develop several related skills simultaneously — pedalling, eye–hand co-ordination, hand–foot co-ordination, and language and cognitive skills.

This approach allows the caregiver to develop the child's skills by considering the child's development, needs, and interests in a natural way, using play as the medium. It is a holistic, integrated approach to the child and to the curriculum, incorporating teachable moments (Shimoni, Baxter, and Kugelmass, 1992) in play and routine-care activities. It also involves planning participation experiences that provide the child with the opportunity to learn and practise abilities in all areas of his or her development. Early childhood professionals may find this strategy useful in a play-based setting to ensure that development is fostered and children are challenged.

Summary

This chapter has reviewed some of the key factors associated with the practices used with children with special needs in child-care settings. There appears to be much confusion about approaches and methods; integration and inclusion remain topics for debate and discussion. Early childhood professionals must determine the most appropriate strategies. It is important to move beyond the philosophical debate of inclusion and offer early childhood professionals a new perspective so that they can provide an environment conducive to development for all children in their care. This book is not intended to be a recipe book of programs. It is intended to challenge and stimulate attitudes, beliefs, and resulting approaches to children with special needs. A "shopping bag" of ideas will be presented, from which caregivers can choose the approaches and strategies that best meet the needs, interests, and abilities of the children in their care.

ACTIVITIES

1. Observe the activities in a playroom. Make notes regarding:
   - the inclusion of children with special needs;
   - the inclusion of children from diverse cultures;
   - how children with special needs are represented and valued;
   - how children from diverse cultures are represented and valued;
   - friendship patterns.

   Consider these issues in the room both generally and specifically in relation to children with diverse and special needs.

2. Make observations regarding the playroom environment. Does it meet the diverse needs of children with various special needs? What needs are met? How can the physical setting be changed to accommodate all children with special needs?

3. At a parent–caregiver meeting, discuss the topic of meeting diverse needs to determine what parents expect and how their needs can be met.

4. Do some research in a library to find books pertaining to children with diverse and special needs. Are there any books that you would recommend to parents? Which books would you use for children in your playroom? Which would you use for your own professional use?

5. Review the books in your playroom. How many of them include images of children with special or diverse needs? What messages do the books convey about children with special needs?

DISCUSSION QUESTIONS

1. Discuss the diverse needs of the children in your playroom that result from different cultural, linguistic, or religious factors. Find ways to gather more information if necessary.

2. Discuss play as it relates to children with diverse and special needs. In what ways will it be the same, and how will it be different? How will you meet these needs within your playroom?

3. Discuss the needs of the normally developing children in your playroom. Are all of their needs met? Have you considered ways to develop positive attitudes and to promote positive interactions between non-disabled children and children with special needs? What other strategies could be considered?

4. Children with special needs often show variation across developmental areas. If children in the centre are grouped by age, where will an older child with developmental delays be placed? For example, a 4-year-old child with developmental delays may function in the 2-year range in most areas of development. Discuss the choice you might make and the rationale behind that choice.

5. Staff in centres should examine facets of program policies to ensure that inclusion can occur. For example:
   - Are all areas accessible (e.g., parks, playgrounds)?
   - Can the centre accommodate special diets or feeding requests?
   - What procedures are needed for fire drills?
   - What provisions may need to be made for field trips?
   - Are policies in place for dispensing medication?

   These are but a few considerations. Make a list of considerations relevant to your centre and of its current policies. Research the policies and procedures of other centres to gain a wider perspective.

6. The use of one-to-one assistants has been common in schools, nursery schools, and child-care centres. Discuss the benefits and drawbacks of this model. Consider its impact from the perspective of the child with special needs, the children in the centre, the staff, and the program.

7. Some jurisdictions are moving away from the use of one-to-one assistants and are using "enhanced ratios" with children who have diverse needs. Discuss the benefits and drawbacks of this approach. Consider its impact from the perspective of the child with special needs, the children in the area, the staff, and the program.

8. Consider the diverse needs of caregivers working and interacting with children with special needs. Are there cultural beliefs that may restrict interactions with some caregivers? How could these be managed in an inclusive group-care setting?

CHAPTER 2

Children with Developmental Delays

Introduction

Developmental delays is a widely used generic term referring to a variety of disabilities. The key common factor is a delay in the development of intellectual, language, or motor skills. Children with developmental delays tend to fail to achieve age-appropriate developmental milestones, which are based on the typical sequence of development (Batshaw and Shapiro, 1997). The terms used to identify this group have included mentally retarded and mentally handicapped.

Changes in terminology have been accompanied by changing descriptions of who these people are and how society has valued or devalued them. For example, early classification systems used categories such as imbecile, idiot, and moron. Later the term mentally retarded became common, but it too became part of the vernacular and as a result became inappropriate. People who were considered mentally retarded were generally devalued and put into institutions "to keep society safe." More recently, partly due to the principle of normalization (Wolfensberger, 1972) and to civil rights movements, many people with developmental delays have been moved back into community settings as much as possible and are considered functioning members of society. But myths and prejudices about developmental delays remain.

The most widely used current definition of mental retardation states that "mental retardation refers to significantly sub average general intellectual functioning resulting in, or associated with, impairments in adaptive behavior, and manifested during the developmental period" (American Psychiatric Association, 1994). The definition includes three main points.

1. Intellectual functioning is affected to some degree.
2. Adaptive behaviour is impaired. This point concerns people's ability to adapt to the environmental demands of their age or cultural group in any two of the following areas: com-

munication, self-care, home living, social, interpersonal, use of community resources, self-direction, functional academics, work, leisure, health, and safety (Batshaw and Shapiro, 1997).
3. The above two indicators must be noticed before the person is 18 years of age.

The definition of mental retardation does not include any mention of etiology or cause. After reading this chapter, you should have a better understanding of:
- developmental delays;
- the extent to which the development of children with developmental delays may affect their participation in a group-care setting;
- the role of the early childhood professional in including children with developmental delays in the playroom.

CLASSIFICATION

Children with developmental delays do not develop in typical ways. Generally, they do not acquire skills, particularly cognitive or thinking skills, as quickly as other children. These cognitive delays may affect development in other areas. As is the case with other disabilities, developmental disabilities are typically organized into levels based on the level of services required for the child to function in inclusive environments.

Children with a mild degree of developmental delay typically attend preschool and school settings that require occasional assistance. They are usually not noticed during the preschool years because they fit into a group setting readily. Caregivers may notice that these children are slower to develop speech skills or to walk, but these delays may be part of normal development. It is not usually until the child reaches school age that developmental problems are noticed and identified.

Moderate developmental delays become apparent early in the child's cognitive, speech, and motor development. The child will likely require assistance in self-care areas and have difficulties in social relationships. Children with moderate developmental delays are increasingly being included in day-care and school settings. Since their delays are more noticeable, their successful inclusion in the playroom requires planning and intervention.

Children with a severe developmental delay are delayed in all areas of development and require intensive support. Increasingly, they are being served in regular day-care and school settings. They require assistance in all areas of development and may require supplementary services to meet their unique needs. For example, children with severe delays often receive support from physiotherapists, communication therapists, and occupational therapists.

Developmental delays are typically not classified according to particular conditions, since often there are no discernible causes and the characteristics are so varied. There are several syndromes or conditions in which developmental delays coexist with other disabilities, such as autism, cerebral palsy, and fragile X syndrome. These syndromes are discussed in later chapters of this book. The one condition typically associated with developmental delays, Down Syndrome, is discussed here.

Specific Conditions

DOWN SYNDROME

Down Syndrome is a genetic disorder whose most common effects include:

- a small, round head and a flattened face;
- folds of skin at the inner corners of the eye;
- a low bridge of the nose;
- low-set ears;
- a tongue with low muscle tone, so that it tends to protrude from the mouth;
- short fingers and toes;
- a simian crease (a single crease across the palm, rather than the usual two creases);
- developmental delays that range from mild to severe.

Children with Down Syndrome may also experience complications such as congenital heart disease, chronic respiratory impairments, and sensory impairments. They are typically hypotonic, that is, they have low muscle tone, which may lead to implications for gross motor-skill development. In addition, children with Down Syndrome tend to be short in stature and have a low metabolism, which results in a tendency to be overweight (Roizen, 1997).

A wide range of abilities and characteristics is associated with children with Down Syndrome. Some affected children have great difficulty in acquiring and using speech, whereas other children are quite verbal. Typically, cognitive, language, and motor development are areas of particular concern for children with Down Syndrome. These children tend to be quite sociable and fit well into group settings. However, as with all children with special needs, the attitudes of other children and adults may be problematic.

CAUSES

The causes of developmental delays can be identified in only a very small number of those affected (Winzer, 1990). They may include factors such as:

- infections, including rubella, herpes simplex, and toxoplasmosis;
- intoxicants, such as drugs and alcohol;
- trauma, such as anoxia or hemorrhaging in the brain;
- metabolic disorders, including phenylketonuria;
- chromosomal abnormalities, such as Down Syndrome, Cri-du-chat, fragile X syndrome, Tay-Sachs disease;
- gestational concerns, such as prematurity or low birth weight;
- environmental influences, such as sensory deprivation;
- unknown influences leading to hydrocephaly or myelomeningocele.

Needless to say, the range and diversity of disorders affects the range and diversity of developmental difficulties.

Diagnosis and Assessment

Developmental disabilities typically are diagnosed by using both formal and informal measures, including tests, measures, inventories, scales, and observations. However, many of these tools are inadequate in assessing or predicting the later intellectual development of young children (Winzer, 1990). Generally, the more severe the disability, the earlier it is recognized (Allen et al., 1994; Batshaw and Shapiro, 1997). The more severe impairments are usually identified in infancy, whereas milder forms may not be noticed until kindergarten or school age. In addition, the earlier the problem is identified, the more severe its consequences will likely be (Batshaw and Shapiro, 1997).

Delays in early developmental milestones such as sitting, crawling, walking, and talking are often the first indication that there may be difficulties of any kind. So it is not unusual that children are not diagnosed or labelled until they are school-aged, when there are expectations and skills that the child is unable to master. It is also not unusual that early childhood professionals are the first to observe or recognize a developmental delay, because they spend time with the child and other children at the same developmental stage. Since early childhood professionals know and understand development, they may be among the first to recognize unmastered milestones or different developmental patterns.

Developmental delay is a slowing down but not a stopping of development, specifically in intellectual and adaptive behaviours. The ability of children with developmental delays to learn and to put this learning to use may be limited, but it is not non-existent. Children who are developmentally delayed appear to go through the same developmental stages as normally developing children and in the same order, but they do so at a slower rate (Dunlap, 1997b; Saracho and Spodek, 1987). Thus, these children typically reach developmental milestones, but later and perhaps with the aid of developmental assistance or intervention.

The amount of intervention required and the length of the developmental delay are determined by the severity of the delay. For example, children with mild delays will often reach milestones closer to the normal range and will require less intervention. Children who are more severely challenged often are more delayed in reaching milestones and require more intervention, such as assistance and therapy to develop speech and motor skills.

Thus, it is common for normal developmental sequences to be combined with a behavioural teaching approach for children who are developmentally delayed. However, no literature exists that prescribes normal developmental patterns for children with any type of disability.

Implications for the Child's Development

Since so many areas of children's development and ability can be affected to varying degrees, children will learn very differently, even when they have been diagnosed similarly. The typical classifications address the severity of developmental delays but not the interaction of various levels of ability that a child may possess. For example, a child may be severely delayed in language development but mildly delayed in physical development.

Usually, children with developmental delays are delayed in cognitive or intellectual development. Since cognitive development does not occur in isolation, effects may be noticeable in other areas of development, to varying degrees. Also, the child's particular disability may manifest itself in many different ways. So, for example, one child may lag in language development while being close to the norm for physical development, while the next child experiences the opposite phenomenon.

SCENARIO

In an integrated day-care centre, two 4-year-old Down Syndrome children were in the same playroom. Both little boys had characteristic protruding tongues and were generally quite flaccid in muscle tone. But there the similarities ended. The first little boy, Jared, was quiet and withdrawn and engaged in solitary, functional play quite often. He had a large vocabulary and could make his needs known. He was uncomfortable in large-muscle activities and tended to be passive when outdoors, and he needed much prompting and support in the gym.

The other boy, Travis, was active and busy all the time. He loved to be outside and never stopped moving in the classroom and the gym. Travis was a risk-taker and thrived on physical activity. His high level of activity often left him playing in solitary activities, but he would readily join other children if they were engaged in active play. His language was quite delayed, and the staff were attempting to teach him sign language as an initial form of communication.

This scenario illustrates how children may be very different, even though their diagnoses may be similar.

Significant difficulties often occur in learning and memory. Children with these developmental delays typically are slow learners. They have difficulty in gaining insight into reasoning, in concept development, in transferring and generalizing skills, and in the acquisition of language and speech skills (Saracho and Spodek, 1987).

Children with developmental delays often have difficulty in gaining social skills. This may occur for several reasons. Social behaviours abound in every situation, yet they are usually not articulated. Deciding what kind of clothes to wear and how to behave in a group is determined by the individual in relation to a particular situation. Although adults generally become skilled in determining what is appropriate in a specific situation, they sometimes misjudge the situation and end up feeling very uncomfortable. For example, they may wear blue jeans to a formal event or drink a bit too much at a party and say inappropriate things about their boss. Children need guidance about their behaviour in social situations, for example, being quiet in church and polite to others. Over time and with repeated practice, more and more of these social behaviours are learned, and through practice children become better able to judge and predict new and unfamiliar situations.

Children with developmental delays typically have delays in language. This may range from speech that is difficult to understand, small vocabularies, and speech limited to simple sentences to a complete absence of speech, as a result of which children are taught alternative forms of communication to have their needs met.

The self-esteem of the child with developmental delays may be affected over time. It begins when people do not explain to the child what is expected, believing that the child will not understand. When the child is provided with the rationale on several occasions and continues to behave or misbehave in the same manner, then the adult's belief that the child does not understand is reinforced, and explanations are less likely to occur. Over time, the child with developmental delays may experience failures more often than normally developing children and come to see himself or herself as a failure. This leads to a self-defeating cycle in which the child becomes passive and waits for direction rather than risk failure or punishment once again.

The cycle of failure affects not only the children's motivation, initiative, and sense of achievement, but also other aspects of development. For example, as they become passive and dependent, they act less on their environment and may not experience normal opportunities of cause and effect. Accordingly, cognitive development may be compromised because they do not develop an awareness that they can affect the environment in some way. They see others as affecting their world, but they do not see that they have this ability. This is often compounded by so many things being done for them — meals are served on a schedule unrelated to their internal needs (not when they feel hunger), and toileting times are not scheduled according to their needs. It is easy to see how these children come to feel powerless and controlled by others.

Some literature suggests that the play skills of children with developmental delays are quantitatively and qualitatively different from those of non-disabled children (Covel, 1997). Their play appears to be less organized and less complex, and these children engage in less group play. Given the importance of play in development, it is surmised that this could affect other areas of development.

Children with developmental delays may not have obvious delays or problems associated with gross or fine motor development or sensory skills. However, caregivers need to be aware of the potential implications of cognitive delays.

SCENARIO

Yoshi was 4 years old. He had Down Syndrome and his speech was delayed, but he had very typical physical abilities and was very active. His parents enrolled him in a local creative-movement class on Saturday mornings. Yoshi initially required some assistance in understanding guidelines and needed some physical support to try activities out, but once he caught on, he engaged in a range of movement experiences. One morning, a wood-and-rope climber was opened for the children to use. It spanned half the gym and rose right to the ceiling, about six metres high. All the children enthusiastically began to climb the structure while the leaders spotted children at the bottom. Each child took a turn, climbing up and down at different spots.

Yoshi, however, continued straight up to the very top and did not move. The leaders were unsure about what to do — Yoshi had good motor skills and had free-climbed to the top easily, but now he was in an unsecured and unsafe spot. The leaders tried to talk to him, but he did not respond. Three leaders scaled the structure to offer physical support, but any attempts to get close to Yoshi resulted in crying and screaming.

Eventually, while one leader distracted Yoshi, another leader got close enough to grab him and carry him down to the bottom. Once he was down, Yoshi appeared to be unharmed, but the three leaders were shaken. They had not realized the implications of Yoshi's cognitive development and the impact on other areas of his functioning.

Caregivers must consider all the needs, abilities, and interests of each child. Focussing on one area may create problems in other areas.

Delays in development can also affect the responses of other children and adults. For example, if the child is slow to respond, adults and children alike may assume that the child did not understand and will not follow through. Then, others end up doing things for the child because the child does not complete the task. This may lead to the child becoming dependent, lacking initiative, or not developing a sense of cause and effect. For example, the child may not self-initiate when playing with other children. This may lead the other children to assume that the child does not want to play or interact with them, or it may result in the child with special needs being taken advantage of by other children who know that the child may not react or seek adult help. Thus, it is important that both adults and children learn to be patient with the child who is developmentally delayed and give the child sufficient opportunity to respond.

Normally developing children are provided with reasons for and alternatives to their behaviour. Accordingly, normally developing children will learn about their environment and about their behaviour in that environment; that is, they will be told what is appropriate and what is not. If it is assumed that children with developmental delays do not understand, they may simply be told "No" to stop the behaviour and not be provided with any positive means to deal with it. As a result, they are not provided with information about their world or with a means of behaving on the next similar occasion. It is likely then that they will not have learned from this inappropriate behaviour and may repeat the behaviour the next time the occasion arises.

Other people's perspectives may influence how particular behaviours are interpreted, as is illustrated in the following scenario.

SCENARIO

Mikhail was an 8-year-old developmentally delayed boy who lived at home with his parents. One of Mikhail's interests was cleaning the bathroom sinks. He would spend hours wiping out the sinks so that they sparkled and not a drop of water could be seen in them. Mikhail would even get up late at night to work on his hobby. He was usually quite accommodating; he would let others use the bathroom when needed and then clean up after them. Mikhail moved to a group home when he was nine. Initially he continued with his hobby there. It soon became a problem because Mikhail used so many towels, since there were more sinks at his disposal.

The staff attempted to accommodate this by replacing the cloth towels with paper towels. Mikhail readily adapted. Soon, however, cost again became a factor because Mikhail was using so many paper towels. The staff began to discourage this behaviour and to punish Mikhail for engaging in it. Mikhail again readily adapted by cleaning the sink with paper towels and then eating the towels, thus leaving no paper trail of his activities.

This scenario illuminates several points. First, Mikhail's behaviour was considered a hobby when it did not interfere with others. The hobby turned into a behaviour problem when it no longer served a useful purpose (the group home had cleaning staff) and when it became an expense. Thus, the interpretation of the behaviour changes with the circumstances. Second, this scenario may be understood as a description of a behavioural problem or as a story about the adaptability of an individual. Mikhail quite easily and readily adapted to the changes in his environment without any direction from others.

Other children, too, may not understand why a certain child acts in a particular way — for instance, why the child does not ask for toys but just grabs; why the child is still in diapers; or why the child needs to be fed at lunch time. These unanswered questions may lead other children in the group to avoid the child with special needs, especially if the child behaves inappropriately. For example, if one child is always taking toys or hitting, other children will not want to play with him or her. This not only has implications for the group in the present; but will affect the child's development of social skills in the long term.

It is important for all children to be made aware of and understand other children's needs and behaviours. This requires a very simple explanation from the adult in the area. When the adult does not respond or provide information, children often create their own explanations, which may be worse.

SCENARIO

A friend related this story regarding her 3-year-old daughter, Maggie. Maggie was shopping in the local mall with her mother. They were in a restaurant at lunch when a young man at the next table got very loud and then had a seizure. He fell to the floor and knocked his table and chair over in the process. He continued to be loud, and people crowded around. Maggie's mother was not sure what to do and left as quickly as possible, thinking that clearing the area would be the most appropriate thing to do. Also, she wasn't sure what to say to Maggie. Because they left in such a hurry, nothing was said, although it was not forgotten.

Maggie wasn't sure what to ask but she thought about that man and had nightmares about him flying across the room to get her. After several midnight crying sessions and attempted explanations, Maggie's mother remembered the incident, and the similarity between the nightmare and the incident became evident. In the morning, she talked to Maggie about it. Maggie confessed that she wasn't sure what the incident in the restaurant was all about. She had assumed that the man was a monster of some sort who had tried to get her in the restaurant and then later in her dreams.

This is not an unusual scenario. Adults who are unsure about how to explain something unpleasant to young children say nothing, believing that the child will forget about it. Chances are that the child will not forget but will make up an interpretation that may or may not be accurate. Thus, it is important to give children some type of explanation, even if it means saying, "I don't know, but let's find out." Children, when given the opportunity, will ask questions. It is up to the adults to provide the answers.

Role of the Early Childhood Professional

The varying needs of the child determine the role of the caregiver. This chapter has discussed, for example, the need to be patient, to create situations for learning language and social skills, and to provide explanations both to the child with special needs and to other children in the group. But the role of the early childhood professional extends beyond these practices.

To begin, it is important for the caregiver to understand the special needs of the child. This requires the caregiver to talk to the parents and to get relevant information from them. Parents are often the best source of information, since they not only have the technical and medical information, but they have coped with the child in a very practical way, so they understand handling and care needs as well. The parents likely know the child's temperament and personality best. Early childhood professionals may also want to get further information from publications (see the "References" list at the back of this book) and other professionals. Typically, associations representing people with various disabilities have excellent reference materials and resource people for presentations. For example, the local epilepsy association may be able to provide excellent in-services for day-care personnel. Consult local resources and associations for more information.

ATTITUDES

Once early childhood professionals understand the disability, it is important for them to review their attitudes regarding the disability. For example, do you feel sorry for the child with a disability? Do you feel that this child cannot learn or that he or she will be a menace in the playroom? These views of the child will influence your behaviour as a caregiver.

SCENARIO

A young student was doing her first early childhood education practicum in an integrated playroom of 4-year-old children. She had never worked with children with special needs previously. At first she avoided the two children with special needs, but toward the middle of the practicum she began to spend more time with them. This became a problem, however, since she began to do everything for one child. She greeted him in the morning, removed his coat, put on his shoes, helped him in the bathroom, fed him, and intervened in the child's play.

The supervisor noted her actions and spoke to her about them. The student responded that initially she was scared of the children with special needs and did not know what to do, but then she felt sorry for them and tried to help, especially when the other children would "pick" on them. Through the discussion, she came to realize how her attitudes and feelings affected her behaviour and that her actions were not necessarily benefiting the children with special needs.

This scenario points to the importance of caregivers examining their attitudes from time to time. Attitudes will affect practice, so it is critical for early childhood professionals to be aware of their values and beliefs.

Early childhood professionals must always remember that children observe and model them all the time. Children will pick up the attitudes of caregivers from both their words and their actions. If the child with special needs is felt to be a menace or bother, that attitude will be evident in how the caregiver interacts with the child. All the children in the room will notice, even though the caregiver may never have uttered a word suggesting this. On the other hand, if the caregiver models caring, acceptance, and understanding, children of all ages will observe and learn this.

STRATEGIES

Early childhood professionals must consider and plan their environment and schedules according to the needs of all children. Creating an environment that meets children's developmental needs can go a long way. For example, it is important to ensure that a variety of materials is available to meet a diverse range of abilities and skill areas. Changing toys regularly to provide challenges is beneficial for all children, including those with special needs. Ensuring that children's basic needs for security are met by establishing some routines and predictability will be useful for all children.

Children with special needs need to have their social and emotional needs met just as all other children do; thus, planning that includes the needs of all members of the group should include the special or unique needs of individual children. Caregivers typically plan this way, but may feel inadequate in meeting the different needs of the child with special needs.

Professionals who emphasize differences and request special accommodations increase the likelihood that the child's differences will be attended to rather than their similarities — that they are children who want security, love, and care. Early childhood professionals are often left to manage and balance the two. It is not the planning that may create difficulties for caregivers but the constant balancing of demands in meeting each child's particular needs as well as the demands of parents and professionals. If early childhood professionals can keep this perspective, planning and maintaining environments will be easier.

It would be easy to say that the child, first and foremost, needs to be treated like a child and to be a part of the group, but likely the child will need support for this to occur. In planning, then, it is critical for the caregiver to remember all aspects of development and consider the whole child. It is common for the early childhood professional to receive information from therapists who deal with one aspect of development; from the doctor, who deals with another aspect; from the psychologist, who deals with a third aspect; and the parents, who may deal with yet another aspect. The early childhood professional is typically the person who pulls all the bits of information together to provide a whole program for the child. Sometimes time and resources are restraining factors. If so, the caregiver must prioritize and balance the needs of the child and the needs of the group with the resources available. As part of this planning, early childhood professionals need to consider all areas, including areas that other professionals may not have considered. The following scenario concerns not only the child with special needs but ways of promoting interactions for all children within the group.

SCENARIO

Jamil was a 4-year-old boy with Down Syndrome attending day care. He had good language skills but was having difficulty interacting with the other children in the group. Cynthia, a rehabilitation services practicum student, volunteered to develop a program for Jamil to form some friendships. The program Cynthia developed focussed on Jamil initiating interactions with other children.

Cynthia initially worked with Jamil to establish the routine for getting ready to go outside. Once outside, the children could ask for play equipment, such as balls. This became the second step of the program — Jamil learned to dress quickly and then get a ball. Balls were chosen because Jamil liked to play with balls, he was good at playing with them, and balls were usually popular. A third step was to ask another child to play with him. Cynthia taught Jamil some key phrases, which he easily learned. The first day, Jamil dressed, got the ball, and asked a child to play. The child said "No," as did the second and the third.

Jamil was confused, and so was Cynthia. The program had looked good, and Jamil had easily learned all of the required steps. They tried again the next day and the same thing happened. Cynthia convinced Jamil to try one more day, with the same result. She then felt that the solution would be to put some of the other children on a complementary program, but no one agreed with that solution.

The bottom line is that a program can be written that looks comprehensive and manageable, but not all factors can always be controlled. Jamil's behaviour can be programmed, but friendship with others cannot. The needs of all the children in the playroom must be considered.

Early childhood professionals can use some basic strategies in their playroom that will benefit children with developmental delays. They can arrange activities and experiences so that children have ample opportunity to practise skills. They should be careful not to move on to the next step as soon as the child has mastered the skill, but to allow time for overlearning. Because learning can be difficult, it is useful to teach in short intervals and make learning as meaningful as possible. Picking up Cheerios may be a more meaningful way to learn to use a pincer grasp than picking up paper clips or screws. When activities are functional, they will likely be more easily generalized. Routine times during the day should be used for teaching specific skills. Fine motor skills can be taught and practised when children are eating, doing up zippers, tying shoes, or brushing their hair and teeth. Using these teachable moments ensures that learning is meaningful, that many opportunities for practice are available, and that generalization occurs. In addition, children will learn to become more independent and capable.

PLANNING IN A DEVELOPMENTAL CONTEXT

The previous scenario illustrates that planning must consider all the people in the playroom rather than targeting just one area of the development of one child. The experience webs discussed in Chapter 1 may be useful in conceptualizing how planning may occur. It is also important for early childhood professionals to consider each area of development, as follows:

Play

Play is often neglected as an area requiring attention. Children with developmental delays generally have fewer opportunities to play, fewer materials to play with, and fewer play areas designed for their play (Frost, 1992). Adults either think that all children know how to play naturally and therefore do not need to be taught, or they think that children with special needs have other, more important skills to learn. These attitudes result in play becoming an unimportant and forgotten area of curriculum. Thus, play in segregated settings is typically relegated to free play times during caregivers' coffee breaks and after children's nap times.

Two beliefs prevail about play: children with developmental delays do not play, and play is merely a good way to pass the time. In fact, children with developmental delays often fail to play because the environment is not stimulating, it does not take into account their abilities and needs, and the group-care setting provides few or no play opportunities (Frost, 1992). Consequently, children with developmental delays may not have the opportunity to develop play skills, or they get stuck engaging in the same type of play over and over.

There has been limited writing on play and children with developmental delays, and many people still believe that these children may not have the ability to develop play skills, that they have difficulties that make play impossible, or that they are more likely to be injured during play (Frost, 1992). Planning, however, will ensure that the child with special needs has learned ways to play and is provided with opportunities to develop new ways to play. For example, even if the child plays well alone, teaching the child to play next to and then with others is recommended not only to maintain interest but also to further social skills.

Social

Children with developmental delays may not have a repertoire of ways to initiate and maintain contact with others. There may also be few ways for the other children to interact and solve problems that may arise in the course of interactions. As a result, children with developmental delays may be isolated or may disrupt other children during their play in an attempt to get involved. Early childhood professionals should observe the children and support attempts to initiate and maintain interactions. Using ongoing interactions as a teaching time may also be more beneficial than practising skills at other times during the day.

Children with developmental delays also learn by watching both adults and other children. Pairing them with socially competent children in the group could promote learning, but the learning may take some time, even when both children are willing participants.

Caregivers need to be mindful of how other children in the playroom are involved with the special-needs child. If one child is a special helper, constantly paired with the child with special needs, that child may not recognize his or her role as a friend, but only as a helper. Although the child with special needs should be encouraged to have a variety of social contacts during the day, other children should be free to make choices about social contacts as well.

Emotional

Children with developmental delays often require much adult support and attention in completing tasks. Throughout the day, it is essential to consider ways to enhance the child's self-esteem and to provide opportunities for the child to make choices and demonstrate responsibility. Children with special needs, like all children, have security, identity, and belonging needs that should be addressed to ensure the child's continued social and emotional development. For example, children with developmental delays may be teased or ostracized by their peers and suffer the same resulting feelings. Although these issues are often considered when thinking about development for children, they are often neglected or forgotten with special-needs children. Caregivers need to attend to these situations. As a first step, welcome and accept all children into your playroom. They will observe and learn from the example of adults — if you ignore or neglect, if you reject, if you devalue in words or in actions, children will observe and will learn from you.

Observe children in the playroom to determine the times or events during which they may be able to act independently or make choices. The choices need not be major; for example, the choice between eating a sandwich or having a drink first is not major, but it provides a forum for developing the ability to make choices. Practice in effecting change and demonstrating independence skills can also happen in the same way. Observing the child and thinking about creating opportunities, however small, may be the first step for the child developing such abilities.

SCENARIO

Chu was an 18-month-old Down Syndrome boy starting day care for the first time. His parents had been advised by their doctor and therapist team that Chu needed to be with other children in a setting where his special needs could be met. Chu cried incessantly for the first two weeks in the centre. After an initial period of adjustment, the caregivers called in the psychologist to observe and make recommendations. After observing, the psychologist and playroom caregivers met.

The psychologist began by stating that he felt that the behaviour had extended beyond normal time limits, that this was a display of inappropriate behaviour to gain attention, and that the situation should be treated accordingly. The staff felt that Chu was still adjusting and needed some extra displays of affection, and that in time he would realize that they could be trusted. One caregiver who seemed to have some rapport with Chu volunteered to take on this task for the next week. Chu's behaviour changed significantly within that week.

This scenario illustrates the importance of considering the child's emotional needs as part of the whole child. What would your reaction be in this situation?

Cognitive

Although cognitive development is typically considered a significant area of learning for children with developmental delays, sometimes the way that tasks are presented stifles development. For example, children are often presented with the same tasks over and over, until they "reach criterion," or demonstrate proficiency. Sometimes learning is so structured that children are provided with only a small range of materials and equipment. This limiting of materials and insistence upon mastery may lead the child to feel unchallenged and, in turn, stifle learning. Children often move from one activity to another, returning to more challenging tasks over and over again, gradually piecing together information.

Allowing learning to occur in a more natural, child-driven manner may promote learning and intensify the child's interest in the environment. Try to include a variety of tasks and experiences that build on sensory, motor, and preoperational skills, not only in skill-building exercises but throughout the day. For example, children may develop the notion of cause and effect if they are allowed to behave in such a way that their actions have some effect on their environment. This may begin with simple, day-to-day activities so that children develop a variety of skills and begin to see themselves as competent, worthy individuals. Tasks such as helping to set the table by matching to sample, independently pulling on tube socks, or helping to tidy up at the end of the day not only encourage the development of specific skills but also further the development of critical cognitive skills in functional and meaningful ways. In working with young and severely disabled children, careful observation of the child's abilities and the environment may be required. You may be able to use these tasks as a way of letting other children realize that the child with special needs has certain abilities, for it is often common for other children to see this child as basically incompetent.

Sensory

Children with developmental delays may have difficulties in other areas of development, particularly with sensory skills. This is more likely for children with severe delays or with problems resulting from brain damage. Often these problems remain untreated either because the child is unable to verbalize difficulties or because it is difficult to determine the source of the difficulty. For example, does the child fail to respond to the doorbell because of the developmental delay or because he or she did not hear it, and how would the cause be determined? Is it due to attitudes, for example, feeling that hearing aids or glasses won't help the developmental delay, so why bother? Whatever the situation, observe the sensory abilities of all children, including children with developmental delays, to ensure that sensory abilities are not forgotten in the day's routine. Providing opportunities for the child to use sensory abilities and to associate the stimulus with something in the environment is critical for the development of sensory skills. Children also need opportunities to develop body awareness. You can provide some by naming body parts in many different ways — in play, while dressing, and in songs.

Physical

Children may appear hesitant when attempting to make sense of their environment, and adults may be very protective of them. Ensure that children with developmental delays have a range of supervised experiences and are permitted to attempt new activities, perhaps initially with adult support. Protecting children by holding them back may interfere with their development of a full range of physical skills.

The development of fine motor skills may be similarly affected when children are not given ample opportunity to attempt tasks on their own. They need sufficient time to dress themselves and feed themselves on their own with some assistance if required. Consider introducing them to adaptive aids or items that may be more easily managed by them. For example, Velcro or slip-on shoes are much easier to put on than laced shoes; special cutlery may allow children to feed themselves; clothing such as tube socks and elasticized waist bands may promote independence and broaden opportunities to develop other fine-motor and self-help skills. Again, examine your attitudes; some people think these aids provide the "easy way" out and bypass real teaching, but the bottom line is the developmental needs of the child.

Promoting fine-motor skills in the context of self-help and personal care skills serves a dual purpose. Not only are children's specific skills enhanced, but children may begin to see themselves as capable and independent, thereby further developing their emotional skills. With this in mind, provide a variety of pencils, brushes, and crayons. Use a variety of objects for children to grasp and hold, so that a variety of grasp patterns are practised. Larger items may be easier to hold. Add grips or built-up handles. Pair fine-motor with large-motor activities, such as holding onto an object while walking, or pushing a cart so that the co-ordination of abilities is enhanced.

Language and Communication

One of the challenges facing caregivers is providing a reason for the child to communicate. Often, when the child has a high level of need, it is necessary and easier to do things for the child. Hence, if mealtimes are regular the child may never have the opportunity to ask for something to eat, and if toileting is routine the child may not ask to go to the toilet. This is not to imply that routines should be abolished, but you may want to attempt to create situations in which the child must communicate a desire or need. The other side of this issue is that you should be available to listen to and respond to the child; communication skills will not be used for long if attempts to communicate go unheard or unanswered. Teaching the child functional and meaningful words and phrases that many people will understand may enhance the child's communication skills.

Consider what may be functional, meaningful, and useful vocabulary in a variety of settings where people may not be as aware or tolerant. Teach children words they will use — words that focus on the child, body parts, family, clothing, personal care, and the child's environment, both at home and at day care. At the same time, encourage children to talk and communicate whenever possible. It is often easier and faster for adults to anticipate and provide for children's needs, but learning opportunities are diminished in the process.

The ideas presented are not meant to be mutually exclusive, so you may find ideas in other chapters of this book that may be helpful when planning for your particular child with special needs. You will likely not have just one child with special needs or several children with the same concerns; you will more likely be planning for the diverse needs of a diverse range of children. If so, consider all the strategies presented, and choose those that provide the most benefit for a particular child yet suit the other children with special needs. For example, children with developmental delays require a high degree of auditory and visual stimulation, while children with behavioural or emotional concerns may require little stimulation. Your task is to balance these two sets of diverse needs within the playroom setting.

Summary

The child who is developmentally delayed has particular learning and developmental needs. Children labelled in this way tend to be very different, since they vary in terms of severity, degree, and skill areas affected. Just as there is no one profile of children with developmental delays, there is no one strategy or set of techniques that will be most appropriate with them. Early childhood professionals need to understand the delay, understand their own perspective regarding the disability, and plan their playrooms accordingly, taking into account the needs of all the children. Understanding the unique needs of each child while remembering that this is a child with developmental needs similar to those of other children will be helpful in providing the best program possible.

ACTIVITIES

1. Interview adults from various cultural and religious backgrounds. Ask them about their beliefs regarding children who are developmentally delayed.

2. In the mass media, what are the popular images of children and adults with developmental delays? What myths are associated with these individuals? How will these portrayals and myths affect the child's acceptance into the community?

3. Observe children in a playroom. What adaptations would you make to ensure that the needs of the child with developmental delays are met?

4. How would you talk to other children in your playroom about children with developmental delays and their needs? How would you promote inclusion and friendships?

5. Given the attitudes and myths prevalent in society, how would you explain the child with severe developmental delays to other parents?

6. Discuss temperamental traits in relation to children with developmental delays. Which behaviours may be considered temperamental traits, and which may be considered behavioural problems? What is the difference between the two kinds of behaviour?

7. Check your local library or bookstore for books related to children with developmental delays. Which books would you recommend for parents, for use within your playroom, and for your professional use?

8. Look at the books in your playroom. How many of these books contain images of children with developmental delays? Are these positive images? What messages would they send to the children?

DISCUSSION QUESTIONS

1. Discuss the range and diversity of children with developmental delays. What are the major delays? How would a child with these delays fit into your playroom? What adaptations would need to be made?

2. Discuss how the images of and terminology describing individuals with developmental delays have changed over time. It is not long ago that society had a very different view. How has this changed? How have earlier images hurt children with developmental delays?

3. What characteristics and behaviour would you look for to determine if a child has developmental delays? How would you relay this information to his or her parents?

4. Which resources in your community may be useful for children with developmental delays and their families?

Children with Physical Impairments

CHAPTER 3

Introduction

Children with physical or orthopedic impairments are a diverse group. They may have minor difficulties that interfere marginally with their mobility or severe motor problems that cause concerns for inclusion in group-care settings. Unlike mobile children, who move continuously during the day, children with physical disabilities are at a distinct disadvantage because moving themselves to other locations or rearranging their own learning settings presents major obstacles. This disadvantage may lead to concerns for development across all domains.

After reading this chapter, you should have a better understanding of:

- the varieties of physical or orthopedic impairments, including cerebral palsy, muscular dystrophy, spina bifida, head and spinal cord injuries;
- the implications of these impairments on the child's development;
- the role of early childhood professionals in working with physical impairments including their attitudes; strategies, and planning in a developmental context.

CLASSIFICATION

Physical disabilities are often termed orthopedic impairments (Allen et al., 1994). The term includes a wide range of conditions but generally refers to any problem that interferes with normal functioning of the bones, muscles, or joints. Children with physical disabilities are grouped according to three factors: the severity of the disability, the clinical type of the disability, and the parts of the body that are affected.

In relation to severity, children with a mild degree of physical impairment typically can walk, perhaps by using aids, and can communicate clearly enough to make their needs known.

45

They can do most of the things that those without impairments can do, but perhaps require a bit more time. Children with a moderate level of impairment require more assistance in all areas and often require adaptive aids for mobility. Children with a severe degree of impairment require a wheelchair or need others to move them and have delays in all areas of development.

The terminology used for physical disabilities that are categorized by the part of the body affected includes:

- hemiplegia: one side of the body is affected;
- quadriplegia: all four limbs are affected;
- paraplegia: only the legs are affected;
- diplegia: the legs are more affected than the arms.

Causes

Although most causes for physical challenges are unknown, several are known. Injury to the brain or lack of oxygen to the brain at any time during development may cause brain damage and lead to physical impairments. Diseases that affect the brain, such as meningitis or encephalitis, also cause impairments, as do accidents and injury.

Specific Conditions

Cerebral Palsy

Cerebral palsy (CP) refers to an "impairment of the coordination of muscle action with an inability to maintain normal postures and balance and perform normal movements" (Bobath and Bobath, 1984, p. 29). CP results in a broad category of conditions that affect muscle tone, movement, reflexes, and posture (Howard et al., 1997). It is caused by injury to the brain, usually around 26 – 32 weeks of gestation, but it may occur at any point in development. This injury affects the connections related to muscle tone and muscle control (Pellegrino, 1997). CP is non-progressive but permanent. All affected children will have difficulty with movement and posture. Many impairments associated with central nervous system damage, such as developmental delays, visual delays, hearing delays and seizures, may also be present (Pellegrino, 1997).

To better understand the dynamics of cerebral palsy, it is helpful to understand muscles and muscle tone. Muscle tone refers to the amount of tension in the muscles. When we move, the amount of tension increases. Damage to the brain may result in abnormal muscle patterns, which lead to unco-ordinated movements. Normal muscle tone refers to the condition of muscles at rest. Children who are hypertonic have too much tension in their muscle, so they are stiff and move with jerky movements. Children who are hypotonic have low muscle tone, so they tend to be "floppy." Children with high, low, or inconsistent muscle tone have difficulty with all movements but particularly with small motor movements because of the precision involved in these movements.

Cerebral palsy is typically classified into a number of categories. Athetoid or spastic CP involves muscles that are very tight and difficult to move, making voluntary movements difficult. It may affect all four limbs, the trunk, and the muscles of the tongue and mouth, thereby affecting feeding and speech.

Another variety is dyskinetic, in which muscle tone goes from one extreme to the other. The child may alternate from hypotonic to hypertonic. Children with dyskinetic CP tend to also have difficulty in developing voluntary muscle control because their primitive reflexes do not fade. In addition, they may make involuntary movements that are either rapid and jerky or writhing movements.

Ataxia refers to a lack of motor co-ordination. Poor balance and involuntary muscle responses make purposeful activity difficult, but more muscle control is possible with ataxia. For example, the child may have difficulties in controlling hand or arm movements while reaching or in the timing of reaching and grasping.

There are other categories of cerebral palsy in which the different types may be mixed together in a range of variations.

Eating typically is a concern for children with more severe degrees of CP (Howard et al., 1997). Children may experience poor chewing and swallowing muscle actions, which result in long, difficult feeding sessions. Over the years, the child's nutrition and energy levels may be affected by diet and feeding difficulties.

Cerebral palsy is a lifelong condition. The goal of treatment is to maximize the child's functioning while minimizing the disability and potential complications (Pelligrino, 1997). Some problems may be prevented by orthotic devices such as braces and splints to maintain a range of motion while controlling involuntary movements. Positioning of the child is also important, both to prevent difficulties later and to prevent abnormal movement patterns that interfere with the child's movements. Positioning may include the use of static devices such as seating systems, standing frames, or wedges. Children with CP will likely use aids such as scooters, tricycles, or wheelchairs to increase their mobility. The ways in which caregivers handle and position children can make a vast difference in the children's muscle control and involuntary movements. Finnie (1981) is a classic reference for positioning and handling.

MUSCULAR DYSTROPHY

Muscular dystrophy (MD) is a term describing a group of progressive, chronic impairments that affect the muscles. MD is hereditary, and typically the symptoms begin when the child is a toddler. Warning signs include a waddling gait, frequent falling, trouble getting up, difficulty climbing stairs, and walking on one's toes. Since many of these signs characterize toddlers' movements generally, MD may be difficult to diagnose early on. Generally, children with MD will learn to walk before the muscles begin to deteriorate. The condition progresses from affecting the muscles closest to the body (such as the neck, hips, or shoulders) to affecting the extremities (hands and fingers), resulting in gradual muscle weakness and decline.

Muscular dystrophy progresses at its own rate. It may progress quickly in one child and very slowly in another. Once it has started, however, its progress is predictable. It is painless, and the affected person's intellectual functioning is not impaired. Children with MD typically have normal feeling in their limbs, even though they may not be able to move them. Depending on the child's age at the onset and the condition's progress, children with MD may present diverse concerns in your group.

Spina Bifida

Spina bifida refers to a split of the vertebrae, the bony structure that covers and protects the spine. This split may be undetected and cause no concern, or it may include a protruding sac that contains part of the spinal cord. When the spinal cord does not close completely, the child is born with a malformed spine. Surgery immediately after birth is done to remove the protruding sac, if necessary, in order to protect the exposed structures and prevent infection (Liptak, 1997).

It is believed that spina bifida occurs within 26 days after fertilization, when the neural tube has folded over to become the spinal cord, the beginnings of the central nervous system. During this folding, if a portion of the neural tube does not close, the spinal cord may be malformed (Liptak, 1997). The incidence of spina bifida appears to be declining because of increased knowledge (for example, about the role of folic acid) and prenatal screening. In addition, the treatment of spina bifida has benefited from advances in medical and surgical care. The severity of the condition depends upon the location of the opening. If the opening is high, bowel and bladder control may be affected and the severity increases.

The most common type of spina bifida is spina bifida occulta, in which there is a defect in the vertebrae covering the spinal cord. This type typically goes unnoticed and causes no concerns related to growth and development.

The type that causes more difficulties is myelomeningocele, in which a cyst-like sac containing nerve roots and a part of the spinal cord protrudes through the spinal cord. Children with this condition often experience several related problems. The first is paralysis and a sensory loss of the limbs below the point of the spinal cord defect. Second, children may also have no sensation associated with bladder or bowel activity, so they may not have bowel or bladder control.

Children with spina bifida who have bladder and bowel dysfunction may be more prone to infection. They can begin to learn to use the toilet at around 3 or 4 years of age. This may involve routine, timed toileting and learning good hygiene practices. Achieving both bladder and bowel continence is a realistic goal and important to the development of self-esteem (Liptak, 1997).

In some children, the circulation of fluid in the brain may be blocked, which puts pressure on brain tissue and may cause brain damage. This condition is referred to as hydrocephalus. The child may require a shunt to drain fluid away from the brain in order to prevent brain injury. It is important to know if the child has been shunted and whether any special precautions are associated with it. Signs of a blocked or infected shunt include lethargy, headache, vomiting, and irritability as the pressure builds. Early detection of potential problems related to the shunt is critical.

Children with spina bifida often have decreased feeling and movement in their legs. Special precautions must be taken to prevent injury to their legs because their bones are not strong and fracture easily. Keeping children's feet warm and protected while moving is important. Due to the lack of sensation and poor circulation, these children are more at risk of skin breakdown (Howard et al., 1997).

Children can learn to move independently by using their upper body to crawl on their tummies, they may learn to four-point crawl, or they may use scooter boards. They may be able to stand with the support of a standing frame and may learn to walk with braces. The likelihood of ambulation will depend on the site of the spinal opening and other factors. For example, if children have developmental delays resulting from hydrocephalus, they may need to use a wheelchair occasionally or for longer periods of time. An associated risk is that children with spina bifida may become overweight because of their decreased activity level. It may be necessary to pay special attention to their physical activity and diet.

ABSENT LIMBS

Children may be born with deformed or absent limbs. This usually is the result of an injury or insult early in fetal development. They may also have limbs amputated as a result of disease or accident. Typically, children are fitted with prosthetic devices, but the age of fitting is controversial. Some believe that the younger the child, the easier and more natural the adaptation to the prosthetic device will be. Others feel that it is better to wait until the child is older and can care for and control the device better. Early childhood professionals should be aware of how to fit and care for the prosthetic device.

HEAD AND SPINAL CORD INJURY

Head and spinal cord injury is an increasingly frequent cause of physical impairments. As many as one in 25 children will seek medical attention for a head injury (Michaud, Duhaime, and Lazare, 1997). Injuries are commonly caused by falls, automobile accidents, and bicycle accidents. The effects of head and spinal cord injury vary significantly, from minor difficulties to major motor, sensory, intellectual, memory, and emotional difficulties. These problems may be temporary or permanent.

Spinal cord injuries do not usually involve any damage to the brain, but children with spinal cord injury will not receive neural messages from areas below the injury. They may experience a loss of sensation in these limbs as well. Caregivers should be aware of this to prevent further problems.

The type of head injury often depends on the nature and severity of the force that caused it. The injury may be caused by an exterior impact when the head is struck or strikes something, or it may be caused by interior forces when the brain is exposed to movement inside the skull that results in tears to nerve fibres and blood vessels when, for example, young children are shaken (Michaud et al., 1997). Outcomes range from full recovery to little recovery, which requires lengthy rehabilitation. Brain injury may affect motor abilities, feeding, vision, hearing, speech, and cognition and causes changes in personality and behaviour. Most head injuries are preventable by using seat belts in cars, helmets on bicycles and motorcycles, and safety precautions in playgrounds.

CORRECTABLE ORTHOPEDIC IMPAIRMENT

A variety of orthopedic problems can be treated in the preschool years. If they are treated early, the prognosis is favourable. If left untreated, some degree of physical impairment for the child will result. These conditions often necessitate surgery, casts, braces, and physiotherapy.

Children may have inwardly rotated feet or bowlegs, which are noticeable when the child begins to walk. These conditions usually correct themselves with normal growth, but they may require braces, casts, or sometimes surgery to correct the problem. Club feet are typically treated with casts, splints, and physiotherapy. Congenital hip problems occur when the femur does not fit properly into the socket joint of the hip. These problems may require a brace, traction, casting, or surgery.

Orthopedic conditions can be treated and usually cause few problems for the child's future physical development. However, at the time of treatment the restriction of movement can be frustrating and the treatment can be painful. These concerns may cause affected children to see themselves as different from others or other children to treat children with an orthopedic device as different. Children may require additional support and understanding through this time period. Usually the problems and treatments are short-lived, and the difficulties experienced afterward are minimal.

Implications

IMPLICATIONS FOR THE CHILD'S DEVELOPMENT

The characteristics of each child and each impairment vary significantly in terms of what part(s) of the body are affected and how severely they are affected. Children with physical disabilities may have associated conditions that affect development, such as associated neurological concerns, developmental delays, or sensory impairments, depending on what part of the brain was damaged. In addition, children with physical challenges may experience health and medical concerns requiring surgery, catheterization, hospitalization, medications, and feeding tubes. They may be more prone to illness and infection because they are immobile or sitting or reclining for long periods of time. As a caregiver, you should familiarize yourself with these potential complications and ways in which they may be prevented or managed.

Most children with physical disabilities use prosthetic devices or adaptive aids to assist their mobility. Some aids are very simple to fit and maintain, while others are more complex and may require instruction or training in order to use them properly. In addition, children may require assistance in transferring, that is, moving from the floor to their wheelchair or from their wheelchair to the toilet. Transfers should be done by two people, one to support the child's head and trunk while the other moves the lower half of the body and the legs. Before the transfer be sure to tell the child that you are moving him or her, and enlist the child's assistance as much as possible. This may entail shifting the child's weight or keeping his or her arms or knees bent.

Children with physical disabilities may use adaptive devices such as braces, crutches, standing frames, walkers, scooters, strollers, or wheelchairs. Most of this equipment is made exclusively for and fitted to the child. As a caregiver, you may need to learn how to fit or remove these devices. For example, you may need to know how to fit braces on the child or how to put a child into a customized stroller or wheelchair. Parents and physiotherapists may be able to offer you assistance or training, if required. Again, be sure to tell the child what you are doing and to elicit whatever assistance is possible. Always secure wheelchairs and strollers with brakes and secure the child with a seat belt.

Allow children sufficient time to pick themselves up after a fall. The movements associated with this activity will not only benefit the child's motor development, but can be just as important to his or her emotional development and a sense of independence. It can give the child the sense that "I can do it myself. I can be like the other children."

SCENARIO

Rebia was a 5-year-old who wore braces on both legs for a minor orthopedic impairment. She was a determined and fiercely independent little girl who adamantly opposed any assistance when she fell. One day she confided in her caregiver, "It's okay to fall. Sometimes it takes me longer to get back up, but I can do it. When you run over and help me, all the kids stare, and that makes me feel handicapped."

This scenario comes directly from the experiences of a young child. It offers a thoughtful perspective to caregivers. How will you know when to intervene? How much time should you give the child to try on her own?

Allowing able-bodied children the opportunity to explore and experiment with adaptive aids may help all children to become more comfortable with others' disabilities because it may lessen any fears or anxieties that they may have (Chandler, 1994). This opportunity should be provided with parental approval and under supervision, because some equipment is expensive and fitted specifically for the child. But it is an excellent opportunity for peers to develop a better understanding of adaptive aids and of the child with physical disabilities.

Some people believe that awareness can be heightened by spending time in a wheelchair or on a scooter to see the world from the perspective of the child with physical impairments. Surely, time spent in a wheelchair will heighten awareness of how inaccessible the community is generally. For this to be a useful exercise for staff or children, it is important that all individuals understand the purpose of such exercises and that they are carried out for a sufficient period of time that the novelty wears off. Discuss the value of using exercises such as spending time in a wheelchair or standing frame and how you might use them.

Positioning the child requires a concerted effort to ensure that the child does not remain in one position for too long. This will help the child experience a range of activities to enhance motor development and prevent the development of other motor or health-related problems. The child's physiotherapist, medical professionals, and parents may be able to provide helpful information in this regard.

Children with physical disabilities may have delays in speech and language development. For example, in cases where muscle functioning is affected, as in cerebral palsy, the child may have difficulty controlling and developing the muscle movements required for speech. This may result in unclear speech, and some children will be hard to understand or may require alternative forms of communication, such as a communication board. The speech of some children with physical impairments may be affected as a result of the lack of interaction with the people and objects in their environment.

Cognitive development may be similarly affected. Children may experience delays in cognitive development due to associated conditions or to lack of interactions with their environment. This will likely be the case if a child has difficulty with fine-motor movements and control. For all children, it is important to ensure ample opportunities for them to interact with the people, objects, and activities in their environment.

Children who rely on others in their environment to provide the necessities of life, such as children with physical challenges, run the risk of becoming dependent, having difficulty understanding cause and effect, and having difficulty in problem solving because many tasks are completed for them. They may encounter people who are either too helpful or not helpful at all. Ensuring that children have opportunities for the development of these abilities is important.

SCENARIO

Tanisha was a 5-year-old girl with cerebral palsy. Her parents had been told repeatedly by doctors that Tanisha would develop the ability to walk, so they were reluctant to teach her other forms of mobility, which they felt might be easier than walking and thus become preferable for her. Tanisha was in a specialized program to meet her special needs, had regular physiotherapy, and was integrated into her community playschool program. She was unable to walk but could easily manoeuvre her wheelchair and needed assistance in transferring. Out of her wheelchair, she had limited movement.

Her level of mobility did not cause concerns in the preschool program because the setting was mostly accessible and because she was there for a relatively short time and did not require movement out of her chair. Her difficulties occurred in friendships outside of school. Tanisha lived in a newer suburb, where most of the houses were two-storey. Since the use of her wheelchair inside these houses was limited and she had little independent mobility, she needed to be lifted and carried through the house and up and down stairs in order to play at a friend's house. This did become a concern for her playmates' parents, who found the need to be constantly available to move Tanisha taxing and tiring. Over time, this led to Tanisha receiving fewer invitations to play.

As this scenario suggests, a consideration of the child's development and needs must be global in nature, considering all the possible contexts the child may be a part of.

The child's social and emotional development may be affected if he or she is not accepted or included by other children as a result of the disability. This may create a situation in which the child has fewer opportunities for peer interaction and experiences rejection or isolation. In addition, play experiences may be restricted by limited access to play areas and certain toys because of the child's limited fine-motor abilities. It is important to be aware of these potential barriers in the child's environment and to plan settings that will maximize play and social opportunities, which will in turn enhance the child's self-concept and self-esteem. Plan for the inclusion of the child with physical disabilities in activities with non-disabled children as well.

SCENARIO

Lucien had spina bifida and was integrated into a day-care centre. The caregivers were very open with all the children; they provided information about Lucien's condition and about the help he might need in the playroom. The children were very accepting and tried to help as much as possible. Initially this helpfulness almost became a problem because the children wanted to do everything for him.

After a short time, the children lost interest in Lucien and he became one of the group. At this point, Lucien began to accuse the children of avoiding him, not including him, and not liking him because he was handicapped and different. Some of the children then felt obligated to play with him because of this, although they still liked him and played with him. The caregiver was unsure if he should intervene or let the natural friendships and groupings continue.

This scenario highlights a dilemma that caregivers may face when including the child with special needs. How much intervention should you provide? When will you allow interactions and relationships to progress on their own? Again, the needs of the child with special needs must be balanced with the needs of all children within the playroom.

Delays in motor development occur not only in gross-motor areas but also in fine-motor skills. Typically, the finer and more precise the movement and co-ordination required, the more difficult the skill will be to develop. This will have an effect on the development of the child's personal care skills such as eating, dressing, and grooming. It may also be noticeable in play, where the child's manipulation of small toys and objects may be limited. Children with physical disabilities may require adaptation, more time to engage in these activities, and more practice to refine skills.

IMPLICATIONS FOR OTHERS

People typically believe that children with physical disabilities are also developmentally delayed, because the child may be slow to respond, have difficulty in self-expression, or interact awkwardly with objects.

SCENARIO

Miguel was a 5-year-old boy who was severely physically handicapped. He did not speak; neither did he have any consistent way of communicating his needs, and as a result he was dependent on adults to meet all of his needs. He was in a segregated program for children with special needs because of the high level of care he required.

The following year, Miguel began school in a segregated program. Within the first year, he was assessed and fitted with a new electric wheelchair that he could independently operate, which increased his mobility and independence. A communication therapist assessed him and introduced a symbol board that consisted of pictures and symbols of objects, places, and people, with the relevant word printed below. When Miguel pointed to the picture, the listener would say the word out loud. Miguel caught on to the board quickly, and soon it was discovered that he was reading the printed word, not using the picture or symbol. No one, including Miguel's parents, would have guessed that he possessed such skills and abilities.

Again, early childhood professionals must beware of stereotyped images and of making unwarranted assumptions about children. Attempting to learn everything possible about the child may be a key role for caregivers.

Other children are sometimes apprehensive about interacting with the child with physical needs. They too may think that the child has other developmental problems because of the child's speech, or they may become impatient with the child's slow movements.

Children without disabilities may notice differences but may not have the vocabulary to ask questions or ask them appropriately. As a caregiver, pay attention to these questions and comments. Notice not only the words, but also the non-verbal parts of the message — the child's facial expressions and tone of voice. These may tell you a lot more about what the child is thinking or feeling. It is critical to provide an explanation that uses concrete examples that the child will understand. Also acknowledge the child's underlying feelings and deal with them as well. Your actions will speak louder than words. The way you talk to and interact with the child with special needs will serve as a model for all children in the playroom.

SCENARIO

A student commented on the changes in her preschool-age son, Gideon, after he had attended day care with a child who had severe cerebral palsy. Gideon was the youngest of four children and not familiar with interacting with younger children. He typically kept to himself and was not a demonstrative child. When he began in the day-care centre, a 5-year-old girl with CP, Daria, began with her aide. The caregiver and the aide explained to Gideon about CP and made concerted efforts for Daria to be involved in the group.

One day after about a month in day care, the student was picking Gideon up early and Daria was waiting for the Handibus to pick her up. Gideon ran over to Daria and began to stroke her face, held her hand and massaged it in attempts to open it up, and talked to her in a quiet, calm tone. The student commented on how out of character this was for Gideon, but clearly he had noticed the actions and behaviours of the aide and caregivers working with Daria and had modelled his actions on theirs.

Values and actions will be noticed and modelled by children in inclusive settings, as this scenario shows. Caregivers should be aware of this at all times during the day.

Role of the Early Childhood Professional

Like many other members of the public, early childhood professionals must examine their attitudes regarding the child with orthopedic or other special physical needs. North American society idolizes beauty and bodily perfection. Children with special physical needs do not fit this image, and adults may have negative attitudes rooted in this.

Do you believe that children with physical impairments are developmentally delayed? Do you consider them to be a burden? Does their condition frighten or horrify you in some way? Do you feel sorry for the child, pity the child, or not see a future for the child?

Societal images and cultural and religious influences often affect our beliefs about children with physical impairments.

SCENARIO

A segregated preschool program for children with severe physical and developmental delays requested extra volunteer support so that the children could become more active in their community. A local Christian high school offered to establish a work experience program. The program was initiated with ten students who volunteered two mornings a week. The high school students were extremely attentive and helpful. Sometimes the caregivers thought the students were too helpful and did things for the children that the children could and should be doing for themselves.

When the director of the preschool program discussed this issue with the supervising high school teacher, his reply was, "We meet regularly to talk about our experiences with the children. We consider how fortunate we are to not be like those children and talk about ways that we can make their lives better." Although the director only partially agreed with the sentiment, she also could better understand the students' perspective and why they acted the way they did.

Similarly, your attitude as caregivers will ultimately affect how you interact with and include children with physical disabilities in your playroom.

STRATEGIES

With a little planning, early childhood professionals can provide children with special physical needs with a broad range of experiences. It is important to include children in first-hand experiences as much as possible and to provide a wide range of materials and equipment.

Accessibility is a key concern in playgrounds and other environments (Frost, 1992). An ever-expanding range of adaptive equipment, communication aids, and aids for daily living is available. Children's functioning and independence can be increased significantly by using these aids and adaptations. Funds for expensive adaptations may be available from funding organizations, or service organizations may be willing to help raise the needed funds.

There continues, however, to be controversy regarding adaptive aids. Some people think that children bypass learning important skills by using aids. For example, they fear that children will never learn to speak, walk, or tie their shoes because the adaptations are so easy to use. On the other hand, if children can communicate their needs, many behavioural problems may be avoided. If they can put on their own shoes, their independence is increased. Thus, adaptations can solve many dilemmas that children with physical challenges may not be able to solve without help. However, it remains important to remove the adaptations when they are no longer necessary or when the child is ready to learn the more complex skill.

SCENARIO

Tali was a 4-year-old boy with cerebral palsy. In his day-care centre, the caregivers were working on developing his motor skills, particularly his grasping and eye–hand co-ordination. One experience they introduced to develop these skills was self-feeding. They found a spoon with a built-up handle and had Tali feed himself thickened soup, yogurt, and pudding. However, the bowl often slipped because Tali did not yet have the co-ordination to use his other hand to hold the bowl. His caregivers then introduced a sticky mat to put under the bowl and hold it in place.

Tali continued to improve, but the caregivers found that unless the food was thick and stuck to the spoon, he lost most of it scooping it out of the bowl. They then found a special bowl with one side built up to reduce this problem. As Tali pulled the spoon up, the vertical built-up side would hold the spoon upright, so the contents did not spill out. This again helped. Tali's parents came in to observe him and were extremely pleased not only with his progress in these refined motor skills but with his ability to eat independently. "It's just too bad that he can't do this anywhere else but the daycare centre," his father observed.

It may be difficult to have adaptive aids available in all settings because of cost or availability. Would it be valuable to carry out the activity described in the above scenario at home? How could you as a caregiver promote this?

Children may become dependent on using the adaptive aid and not learn the required skill. For example, Tali may one day be ready to use his left hand to hold the bowl in place. To ensure that development continues, observe and regularly review the development of children with special needs.

In relation to the children's physical setting, the playroom may need to be rearranged to accommodate a wheelchair or a child who scoots around prone on a scooter board. Ensure that paths are kept clear of toys or obstacles so that the child can move more freely, that equipment doesn't easily tip when used, and that floor or ground surfaces do not inhibit movement (for example, plush carpet and thick gravel are difficult to move on). Provide ample space for movement, add temporary ramps if necessary, install rails in halls and bathrooms, and have a variety of chairs, wedges, and bean bags available so that children in a wheelchair can change their position regularly and not be wheelchair bound for long periods of time. The more that children are able to change their position and move around, the more activities and perspectives of the world they can experience.

It is likely that the child with physical impairments will present more needs for adaptations in the physical environment than in the social environment. The height of tables, sand tables, and water tables may need to be considered: can they be lowered so that the child can sit on the floor or made higher to accommodate a wheelchair, or is a special chair needed to ensure access? Similarly, the bathroom setup should be considered. Parents and therapists can give advice in these areas. Check local resources for available funding.

Toys and equipment may need to be reviewed to ensure that the child with physical disabilities can manipulate a range of toys and objects. Have a variety of different sizes and shapes for the child to manipulate. This may require searching for appropriate toys and providing a variety of choices to better suit the child's needs. Provide large crayons, chalk, markers, or paintbrushes, or push them through small rubber balls; tape paper to the table to prevent movement; build up spoon handles with foam rubber, tape, or a hair roller; use Velcro instead of buttons, zippers, or snaps; and provide bigger blocks that do not need to snap perfectly in place. All of these adaptations may be useful.

Attempt to include the child in a range of activities and experiences. Involve the child in experiences in which he or she is able to participate, since the child is likely well aware of things that he or she cannot do. This will enhance the child's self-concept and the ways in which other children see the child as well. Children with physical disabilities may need explanations and modelling to learn how to manipulate objects, and lots of practice to build and maintain their skills.

Planning in a Developmental Context
Motor

Enhancing gross- and fine-motor skills will likely be the focus of programming for the child with physical challenges. Physical therapists and occupational therapists are usually involved in the development of the child's abilities. In addition to providing specific skill-building programs, therapists may be extremely useful in giving advice about the playroom, equipment, and potential adaptations or skills the child may need to access them.

SCENARIO

Dietrich was a 3-year-old fitted with two prosthetic legs and one prosthetic arm. He was learning to walk with a walker and was gradually able to move about independently. Even though he could move independently he needed both arms on his walker, so he needed someone to move the toys or objects that he wanted. He was able to carry some objects in his mouth and others around his neck, but many others could not be moved.

The caregiver consulted the occupational therapist, who recommended hooking a bicycle basket to the front of the walker. After experimenting with several different baskets and several ways of hooking them on, Dietrich was ready and able to be much more independent in his travels and in his play.

The solution in this scenario seems simple, but early childhood professionals with limited experience may not be accustomed to thinking of such solutions. Therapists accustomed to working with children in diverse and varied settings have had different experiences and may be better able to make suggestions. Therapists who have little experience with young children may have fewer solutions. Parents, who have likely been in similar situations, may also have suggestions that are practical and economical. Collaborating and sharing ideas may be helpful.

Children must learn how to use equipment to transfer in and out, and how to fall and get back up. These skills are essential in developing the range of motor skills required to be independent. Thus, as difficult as it may be, caregivers should be careful not to rescue the children before they have had sufficient time to try on their own. Similarly, children with physical needs may require extra time to solve problems before adults intervene to do it for them.

A play-based environment in which children are free to move and manipulate a wide variety of toys provides the perfect setting to learn and practise gross- and fine-motor skills.

Attempt to ensure that a variety of skills are enhanced: eye–hand co-ordination, eye–foot co-ordination, using two hands, and so on. Often play experiences are well suited for this.

Play

Observe children with physical impairments to ensure that they are involved in a variety of play experiences. It is common for children to play almost exclusively alone as they learn to manipulate toys and practise skills, but it is important that they have opportunities to engage in social types of play as well. This may require actively teaching a child to engage in certain roles to provide the opportunity for him or her to be included. For example, ensure that the child has special skills or qualities to be the nurse or mother or vet in a play or suggest a role that the child may fill.

Social

If other children in the playroom see the child with physical disabilities in situations where that child is capable, co-operating, and included, it is more likely that the child will be included. You may need to explain how or why that child does something differently, but non-disabled young children will usually accept these differences with little explanation.

SCENARIO

Cinta was a 3-year-old girl with spina bifida. She was independently mobile in the playroom on her scooter board. One day, several children were playing in the housekeeping centre. Cinta waited and waited for an invitation, and then finally asked if she could play too. "No," Jillian replied matter of factly. "Moms have to be able to stand up to make dinner and be able to walk to clean the house."

The caregiver heard this and went over to explain that although moms usually stood and walked, Cinta could do all the things that a mom could do. She called Cinta over to demonstrate how she could cook on the stove, how she could get food from the fridge, and how she could vacuum. Jillian and her friends seemed satisfied that Cinta could do all the things that moms could do, so they invited her to play. The caregiver stayed close by to ensure that all the things that Cinta would need were accessible and that Cinta could successfully be the mom.

In this scenario, the caregiver is attentive to the child in the playroom and offers assistance where needed to include the child with special needs. It is carried out in a positive, valuing way for all children concerned. Can you think of other situations in which this type of intervention may be useful?

When the physical environment is conducive to inclusion, caregivers can play a major role in ensuring that the social environment is responsive as well. Young children are very accepting when adults model acceptance and create situations where children with special needs can be equally involved. This does, however, require attention and planning on the part of early childhood professionals; it will not happen on its own.

Emotional

Children with physical challenges often know, from a very early age, that they are different. Our society is filled with images of active, very mobile people. Very few positive images of children with physical impairments can be found beyond those of the poster children for organizations that serve children with disabilities. Last year, a major Canadian retailer, The Bay, included children with physical impairments in their catalogues and flyers. Children in wheelchairs and others with walkers and braces were included as a part of a group of children, not singled out to sell a particular product or advertise a special cause. It is likely that this small change in advertising strategy heightened awareness and positively influenced attitudes regarding children with physical challenges. However, these images are few and far between.

Children need opportunities to see themselves as capable, productive, and independent. They need experiences that highlight what they can do. Try to find some way for the child in your care to be meaningfully included. For instance, if the child cannot play a certain game, perhaps he or she can keep score or be the judge, or perhaps the child can use the tray on his or her wheelchair to help clear the tables after lunch. All of these experiences will not only affect other areas of development but also play a role in the development of children's self-concept and in the way they feel about themselves.

Language

Children with physical challenges may need to rely more on the use of speech and other forms of communication to ensure that their needs are met. This is why it is essential that children be able to communicate in a way that is understandable by others. Sometimes, although parents and caregivers are able to understand a child's efforts to communicate, other children and unfamiliar people cannot. This may limit the child's interactions, and the resulting frustration may affect comprehensibility even more. The child may need more practice, more time to speak or to learn a few key phrases, or an alternative form of communication. If the child requires an alternative form of communication, ensure that the other children are aware of how it works so that they can use it too. Children with speech delays may also need a means of signalling someone to meet their needs. A particular sound or adaptive aid may be useful for this purpose.

Sensory and Cognitive

Children with physical impairments will need to be involved and included in a range of activities to promote sensory and cognitive development. With planning, adaptations, and assistance, children with physical challenges can be included in most activities to some extent. Of course, the level of involvement and skill development will depend on the nature of the disability and the extent of the specific motor impairments. For example, a child who is severely physically disabled may be manipulating sand or water next to his or her peers, who are engaging in pretend play with objects. Children may be entertained by listening to others singing or playing, even if they cannot participate.

Summary

Children with physical impairments are a very diverse group of children. Some require minimal adaptations to fit in and will fit in well because of the limited problems their condition presents. Other children with physical impairments may require a higher level of support, care, and adaptation in order to function as part of the group. Although it is important to attend to the physical setting to ensure that inclusion can occur, it is equally essential to consider the social environment.

A child who is developing normally in all areas except motor skills will still likely perceive himself or herself as different, and other children may see the child as different as well. Such barriers, both physical and social, can reduce the possibilities for inclusion. When early childhood professionals are aware of this and make every attempt to foster acceptance, inclusion can happen more readily.

ACTIVITIES

1. Observe young children in a playroom. Consider ways that the physical environment might be adapted to meet the needs of a child with a wheelchair, a scooter board, or a walker.

2. Observe the toys and materials in a playroom. Can they be used by children with physical impairments? Which toys could be used? Which could not? Consider using other toys or adaptations to toys.

3. Consider adaptations that may be useful to the child with physical challenges in the area of personal care skills, health, and personal safety. Could they be used by other children? Think of ways that they could be used and the potential merit of doing this.

4. How will you explain the child's physical impairments to other children in the playroom? To parents?

5. Review the print media, television, and movies to determine the prominent images of children with disabilities. How are individuals with physical impairments typically |depicted? Find images of children and adults with physical disabilities who are included in "normal" daily activities and events.

DISCUSSION QUESTIONS

1. Discuss all of the behaviours and actions that might lead to the conclusion that the child with physical challenges is developmentally or intellectually delayed. What could you do to change this perception?

2. Discuss attitudes that people hold regarding children and adults with physical impairments. How do these attitudes vary across cultures?

3. Discuss how physical impairments are considered in various cultures and religions. Are people with physical disabilties valued, cared for, pitied? How might these values influence the care of children with physical challenges in a group-care setting? What would you do if a caregiver refused to interact with a child with special needs in the playroom because of that caregiver's religious or cultural beliefs? Which needs and values might have priority for these diverse individuals?

Children with Visual Impairments

CHAPTER 4

Introduction

Many changes have occurred in the area of visual impairments over the last few decades. The most significant change is the technological and medical advances in the diagnosis and treatment of visual problems. Many of these problems can now either be prevented or be treated much more extensively so that resulting concerns are not as severe.

The other major change has been a different approach to individuals with visual impairments. These individuals used to be called blind, which immediately suggests that they have either no vision or no useful vision. Common thought was that any residual vision a person might have would be diminished if it was used. Therefore, even though a child might have some vision, the child was treated as a "blind person" with no functional vision. Now, it is realized that residual vision can be enhanced. This is partly due to changes in technology so that it is now possible to determine how much vision is available, and subsequently children are taught how to use and capitalize on this vision. As a result of this shift, the term "blind" is less often used and the terms "visually impaired" and "low vision" are more commonly used (Winzer, 1990).

Children with visual impairments include those with problems that cannot be corrected, those who are reluctant or refuse to wear eye glasses or eye patches, and those whose visual impairments have not yet been detected. Early childhood professionals may be able to observe very young children in a variety of environments (indoors, outdoors, and on play equipment) where visual concerns may be more noticeable. In addition to determining ways of working with the child with identified impairments, early childhood professionals should understand how to recognize needs and then communicate these needs to parents.

After reading this chapter, you should have a better understanding of:

- types of visual impairments;
- the changes accompanying visual impairments;

- the impact of visual impairment on children's development;
- how others may be affected by the child with visual impairments;
- the role of the early childhood professional concerning attitudes, strategies, and planning in a developmental context.

CLASSIFICATION

Visual impairments can be classified legally, medically, or educationally. The legal and medical definitions focus on how clearly the child sees, or visual acuity. The educational definitions emphasize the ways in which children use their visual abilities.

Legal definitions of visual impairments are based on visual acuity — how a person sees an image, and from how far away the image can be seen. Children who are blind either have visual acuity of 20/200 in the better eye with the best possible correction or have peripheral vision of 20 degrees or less in the better eye with the best possible correction (Howard et al., 1997). A person with 20/200 vision sees at 20 feet what the person with normal vision can see at 200 feet. Children who are partially sighted have visual acuity of between 20/200 and 20/70 in the better eye with the best possible correction. It is important to remember that visual acuity varies with environmental conditions such as lighting, and personal conditions such as fatigue or age.

These classifications do not indicate how children may use their remaining vision or how readily they may learn to use that vision. Likewise, they do not tell us about other factors important to vision, such as seeing light and shadow, the field of vision, and so on. It is important for you as a caregiver to become familiar with the terminology and definitions used because this will most likely be the information available to you and to the parents.

Educational definitions provide information about the extent to which children are able to use their visual abilities to read printed material. Children who are blind are not able to read printed material and require alternative forms of communication, such as braille. Children who are partially sighted have sufficient vision to permit the reading of large print or regular print with some kind of mechanical assistance.

Since many definitions and classifications come from eye care professionals, they are medical and technical in nature and thus may not be very useful in the playroom setting. In addition, most educational information about visual impairments is oriented to older, school-aged children with a focus on developing academic skills through reading. As an early childhood professional, you must rely on your observation skills to develop an understanding of the child's experiences and then draw upon your developmental and planning knowledge to work with the child with visual impairments in the playroom setting. In addition, remember that children do not develop normal "adult" vision until the age of 5 years (Allen and Marotz, 1994). Accordingly, assessing the visual abilities of young children may be difficult.

The medical classification of visual impairments focusses on cause, type, and severity. There are three major types of visual problems:

1. *Damage to the physical mechanism of the eye*, including the cornea, lens, retina, or optic nerve, which affects how light passes through the eye. It may include cataracts caused by the clouding of the lens, which results in blurred vision; glaucoma, in which fluid around the eye does not drain properly and the increased pressure destroys sensitive

structures in the retina; cornea damage; a detached retina; and damage to the eyeball itself.
2. *Corneal impairments affecting visual acuity*, which affect the clarity with which children see objects at specific distances. These impairments are all refractive disorders, in which the length or shape of the cornea causes incoming light rays to focus in front of the retina (myopia) or behind the retina (hyperopia). Myopia is the technical term for being near-sighted, a condition in which children have more difficulty seeing objects far away than up close. Hyperopia is the medical term for being farsighted, in which the child is able to see objects in the distance better than those close by. Astigmatism is an irregularity in the curvature of the cornea so that light rays are refracted unevenly. This causes images to be out of focus. All of these conditions can be treated with eye glasses.
3. *Unco-ordinated eye muscles.* Normal vision requires the co-ordinated use of two eyes. Muscles work in harmony so that the images from both eyes are fused and one image is perceived. When the muscles controlling the eyes do not work together to produce a single, clear image, double or blurred vision may result. Three common problems are associated with muscle function. Amblyopia, sometimes called lazy eye, causes visual problems because the muscles in one eye are weaker than the other. Nystagmus involves the involuntary movement of the eye muscle, which results in blurred images. Strabismus, commonly referred to as cross eye, occurs when the eyes are not able to focus simultaneously on one object. These conditions can all be treated with exercise, corrective eye glasses, or an eye patch.

There are other visual problems, which are associated with diseases that affect the eye and with the transmission of the message from the eye to the brain via the optic nerve. If the message is interrupted, vision may be affected.

CAUSES

Visual impairments are caused by a variety of factors. They may be congenital; intra-uterine infections such as rubella and toxoplasmosis are the most common congenital causes of visual impairment. They may be caused by other prenatal factors, such as the use of drugs, or infections such as measles; prematurity; heredity factors, which may cause cataracts; disease, such as diabetes; and environmental hazards. They may also result from associated abnormalities of the central nervous system. Therefore, it is more common for visual impairments to be associated with developmental delays and physical handicaps (such as cerebral palsy) when the child is moderately or severely affected by these disabilities.

DIAGNOSIS AND ASSESSMENT

The assessment and diagnosis of visual impairments is most often done by eye-care professionals, including optometrists and ophthalmologists, who assess visual functioning and prescribe appropriate corrective measures.

Severe visual impairments or blindness can often be noticed in the first year of life because the affected child does not meet early developmental milestones such as looking at or reaching for objects. Partial vision losses are more difficult to recognize; often they are not identified until the child is in school, where reading the printed word in books and on distant blackboards may become problematic.

The assessment of infants, toddlers, and children with special needs is usually difficult and relies on observation of the child's response to visual stimuli such as light and movement and on the way in which the eye fixates on an object (Winzer, 1990). With the very young child, the early childhood professional may be one of the first persons to observe and notice differences in the way an affected child uses his or her vision. Issues to consider include the following:

- Does the child frequently bump into objects or fall?
- Does the child hold an item very close or very far away from his or her eyes when examining or playing with it? Does the child keep changing the distance?
- Does the child squint, rub his or her eyes, tilt the head, or close one eye when looking at something?
- Are the child's eyes often red, encrusted, or tearing?
- Do the child's eyes turn inward or outward?
- Does the child complain of headaches or stomachaches or have difficulty when standing because of dizziness?
- Does the child lose interest or appear inattentive when having to look at work that is at a distance from him or her?
- Can the child identify his or her parents or caregivers from a distance, especially in a new setting (where there are few other environmental cues, such as sounds)?

If you as a caregiver notice difficulties or changes in any one of these areas over a period of time, discuss them with the child's parents. This may help parents and professionals to assess and diagnose any visual impairments that the child may be experiencing. Again, the role of the caregiver as primary intervention agents is relevant here. It is difficult to diagnose young children, especially those with special needs, because they may not be able to articulate their problems.

SCENARIO

Nicky was 5 years old. He had always been a passive child who preferred not to take risks but liked quiet activities. He did not like rough play or playing out of doors. Everyone knew that this is what Nicky was like, and no one suspected that he had any problems. In preparation for grade one, Nicky's mother took him to the eye doctor. She and the staff were shocked when they learned that Nicky had less than 50 percent vision in each eye.

Nicky's reaction to his new eye glasses was incredible. He could not believe that things were "so big" and that there were so many things to see. His mother asked him why he never said anything about his eyesight. He replied, "I never knew you were supposed to see like this!" He soon became much more curious about his environment and more willing to try new things.

This scenario reminds us that if children do not have a basis for comparison, they may not even realize that they do not see or hear as well as other children. Further, parents may also not have a basis for comparison or a variety of opportunities to observe the child. A child may cope well in familiar environments like home or Grandma's house, but have more difficulty in new or unfamiliar settings or in settings where the noise level is higher, like a day-care centre.

Implications

IMPLICATIONS FOR THE CHILD'S DEVELOPMENT

Children with visual impairments are, again, very different and unique. They vary in the vision available to them and in the ways they use it. Most children with visual impairments can use some of their vision, but they may require special aids and lighting.

Visual impairments will likely have some effect on development. The more severe the visual problems, the more likely it is that developmental delays will occur (Allen et al., 1994; Howard et al., 1997). Much of what young children learn comes from observing their immediate world and from watching and imitating others. Children who are visually impaired will likely have a reduced range and variety of experiences and less freedom of movement. Their ability and opportunity to interact with people, objects, and activities will be limited. Thus, other delays may not result directly from the visual impairment but from the accompanying lack of experiences.

While visual impairments are not the cause of delayed motor development, they can have a negative influence. The greater the loss of vision, the more significant the delays in motor development. For example, many children who are blind do not walk until the age of 2 (Allen et al., 1994). Delays in motor development can be attributed to the restriction of experiences (Saracho and Spodek, 1988). Imagine what it would be like to manoeuvre through your playroom if you had little vision to guide you. Imagine this at the beginning of the day, when everything is orderly, and then again when the room is full of other children moving themselves and other objects around. Imagine how you would find the toy you wanted to explore and play with if you could not see it.

It is easy to see why children with visual impairments may be hesitant to move and have difficulty orienting themselves to new environments — it is a lot safer and more manageable to stay in a familiar spot, especially when the room is filled with activity and noise. Thus, delays in physical development may result as the child becomes mobile, and difficulties in developing body image may occur as well. Children with visual impairments tend to develop body awareness and image more slowly, perhaps because they have difficulty in emulating others and making judgements related to direction and distance.

It is commonly thought that people automatically compensate for sensory disabilities. For example, many believe that children with visual impairments will have enhanced hearing and that children with hearing impairments will have better vision. This is not true; children with visual impairments must learn to use other senses to their best advantage. The use of hearing alone will never give people the same information as using sight and hearing together, but it may assist children in developing skills when they learn how to use their residual vision and hearing together. Since they use texture, sounds, and smells to learn about the world, children with visual impairments require many experiences with a lot of variety to develop an understanding of the world.

Children with visual impairments often have difficulties in free play. Infants and toddlers may not reach out for toys and remain passive. Young children who are affected tend to engage in solitary play more frequently and receive fewer invitations to play. As a result, many of them are content to be left alone or engage in repetitive self-stimulatory behaviours (Frost, 1992). Older children with visual impairments may spend more of their time in fantasy and dramatic play (Saracho and Spodek, 1988). Often, this too is done in isolation. These visual impairments affect the development of not only play abilities but also social skills. Accordingly, children with visual impairments often experience difficulties in interacting and forming relationships.

Difficulties in social interactions may be partially due to difficulty first in initiating social interactions and then in maintaining them, since the child with visual impairments cannot use visual cues. For example, we often signal our desire to be included or left alone with visual cues like making or not making eye contact. These cues cannot be used or received by the child with visual impairments and may pose difficulties in developing social abilities.

The acquisition of language skills is largely dependent on interactions with the environment. If the child is limited to interacting with things that can only be touched or heard, opportunities for language may be reduced, and language development may be affected in turn. Language development may be delayed, but with experience, children with visual impairments usually catch up by school age (Allen et al., 1994).

On the other hand, it is sometimes assumed that children with visual impairments have higher vocabularies or enhanced speech and language skills. In a sense this is true, since the child relies on verbal communication to attain and maintain social contact. Rather than "seeing" that someone has entered the room, the child with visual impairments will listen to sounds to determine if someone is there and then use language to make contact. Children with visual impairments do tend to ask more questions in order to gather information (Winzer, 1990) and talk more frequently.

SCENARIO

Mohammed was a 4-year-old visually impaired boy in a day-care centre. Early in the day and at the end of the day, his ability to use sounds and his voice to attract and maintain attention was evident. Mohammed could identify people before they reached the room and sometimes would start to call his greeting before the person was in hearing range. He readily identified staff, parents, and children and was the official welcomer each day.

We see here how Mohammed is able to use his other sensory abilities, especially when the environment is less crowded and noisy. How can you facilitate the development of sensory abilities for the child with visual impairments?

Similarly, delays in cognitive development have been noted as a result of children's limited interactions with the environment. It has been noted that children with visual impairments have difficulty orienting to space and time and in separating reality from fantasy (Frost, 1992). However, with early intervention, gains can be made.

IMPLICATIONS FOR OTHERS

Many of the delays in development for children with visual impairments may not be a direct result of the impairment but rather a consequence of people's beliefs and reactions. There may be an assumption of the child's helplessness, and adults may encourage this by assuming the child cannot learn or by not providing a stimulating environment (Frost, 1992). For example, if adults are unaware of the child's hesitancy to be mobile and explore his or her environment, they may provide fewer opportunities for the child to explore and learn about that environment. Further, caregivers can help a great deal by ensuring that children have a range of experiences and receive information in various ways. For instance, if the child cannot see the toy, tell the child where it is so that he or she can use hearing and tactile senses to locate it. If the child is not initiating social contact, help by providing the verbal and social skills needed. Children may require encouragement and stimulation to develop their curiosity and interest in the world and the people around them.

It is quite common for people to assume that the child with a visual impairment has other impairments as well. Most commonly, it is assumed that the child is developmentally delayed, has behavioural concerns, or has physical impairments. Although this may be true for some children, it is certainly not a direct result of the visual impairment. For instance, the child who has not learned an effective means of getting attention may develop inappropriate behaviours like swinging his or her arms, grabbing others, or yelling. Paying attention to the child and his or her needs in the surrounding environment may be helpful.

It is not uncommon for others, children and adults alike, to assume that the child is disinterested or uninterested in social contact. Babies with visual impairments often will not hold up their arms for parents or caregivers to pick them up; rather, they may become very still to try to determine who is near, instead of becoming excited. Parents and caregivers, unfortunately, may attribute this behaviour to the child not wanting to be picked up or not liking contact with them. Similarly, the child who is visually impaired may not initiate social contact or may be hesitant to join in established groups. Other children may interpret that passivity as disinterest or as an indication that the child does not like them. It is easy to see how the child's social development may be compromised by other people's misinterpretation of the child's actions.

It is also typical for others to do things for the child, assuming that the child is incapable of doing them. Other children will bring toys, parents will bring jackets, and caregivers will lead the child to the bathroom and outside. This may be easier (and less frightening) than teaching the child to navigate independently and may even be necessary on some occasions. However, it is important to balance these opportunities at least some of the time.

SCENARIO

An adult college student who was visually impaired commented that his attempts at independence and mobility were often hampered by "boy scouts and little old ladies" who always felt obliged to help him cross the street. He related several different occasions on which he was turned around and confused by the helpful actions of others and his self-admitted inability to say no to the kind gestures of others.

This scenario illustrates that we must always be aware of occasions when children or adults need assistance but also be sure that we provide opportunities for children to explore and problem solve on their own.

Similarly, it sometimes becomes easier to allow children to remain passive and not explore their environment. This may reduce safety concerns and may be easier for staff in a playroom full of children, but caregivers should encourage children to develop new skills and to use abilities that they already have.

Role of the Early Childhood Professional

Attitude

A good starting point for you as a caregiver is to consider your attitude regarding children who have visual impairments. Do you believe that they are necessarily delayed in other areas? Do you think they cannot learn and will eventually become delayed in other areas of development? Do you think they have no potential to use residual vision? Will you consider these children a burden in your playroom? Will you have to reorganize your room and schedule for children with visual impairments? Will these children make extra demands on you to meet their needs?

It is common for people to fear blindness more than other disabilities. They cannot imagine the world without sight. This personal fear can be transferred to the child: the adult may become overly protective of the child with visual impairments and may not permit the child to explore.

Strategies

One of the most notable things you can do for children who are visually impaired in their group is to remember that they too require a range of experiences and activities to grow and develop. They may need some adaptive aids and particular means of coping in the environment, such as a way to get the attention of others in an appropriate and effective way, ways to explore and find their way around an ever-changing playroom landscape, and ways to initiate and maintain social contacts with their peers.

Remember that many of the concerns and problems that develop are not due to the disability itself but to the way that others in the environment react and treat the child. Children with visual disabilities may require extra support, but they will develop most skills and abilities when given the opportunity. Get to know the individual child's abilities and concerns and include the child in regular activities as much as possible.

SCENARIO

Marilyn began her practicum in an integrated day-care centre. Although she had worked with children with special needs in a high school work-experience program, she had never worked with a child with visual impairments. Two-and-a-half-year-old Bjorn had just begun in the day-care centre. He cried for the first two weeks; when he arrived he would place himself in the middle of the room and not move until someone moved him. He did not speak or interact with others; he just cried.

After two weeks, the crying stopped but Bjorn did not move. The staff began to help him move around the room — to the lunch table, to the diaper changing area, to the door. After several weeks, Bjorn appeared settled but was extremely passive and only interacted with objects if someone gave them to him or moved him. Marilyn tried to get Bjorn to move to different parts of the room, but each attempt was met with tears so eventually people stopped asking Bjorn to move. Was Marilyn ever surprised when she went for a home visit and saw a chatty, curious, mobile little boy.

Caregivers must be careful to consider the child's individual needs, interests, and abilities. It seems apparent in this scenario that Bjorn's needs and desires at home are different from those when he is in group care. How would you attempt to support Bjorn in this environment?

Find out what resources and resource people exist in their community. For instance, most communities have an association such as the Canadian National Institute for the Blind (CNIB), which houses a variety of experts, resources, and adaptive aids suitable for children. Often other agencies exist that can assist in finding and funding necessary equipment. Determining which resources the centre and family can benefit from can be very beneficial.

Children with visual impairments must be provided with a variety of stimulating activities and need information about what is happening in their world. As a caregiver, tell the child when you are there and when you are leaving. Call other children and adults in the area by name as often as possible. All of this provides children with information about their environment.

Try to create an environment conducive to play and exploration by removing clutter and confusion in the playroom as much as possible. Eliminate unnecessary obstacles like chairs, for example, by pushing them under tables. Attempt to keep items, especially large pieces of equipment, in a consistent location. Inform children of changes in the arrangement of the room. Consider safety issues as well. For instance, tables that are round or padded may prevent unnecessary bumps and bruises. Paint the edges or borders of bookcases, tables, and door frames a different colour so that they are easier to see. Consolidate items if possible; for example, have one large garbage can rather than several small ones. Children and adults alike will feel more secure about moving around when safety issues have been taken into consideration.

Paying close attention to how the environment is set up may be particularly meaningful for planning for children with visual impairments. Marking the different areas of the playroom may be useful. For example, the book corner could be carpeted with plush carpet, the art and eating areas could be floored with tile, and mats could mark the entrance to the gross-motor area. If the room arrangement is consistent and children can manoeuvre in order to make independent choices, the likelihood that they will be mobile and more independent will be increased.

Planning in a Developmental Context

Once caregivers have considered the potential implications of the impairment for the child's development, it is important to plan for all developmental domains.

Emotional

Children with visual impairments may not actively explore their world and may, over time, become dependent upon others to assist them. That is why it is important to expose them to a variety of activities and situations. It may be necessary to provide them with extra support and to explain things to them, providing all the extra information that they may not be able to pick up visually, such as telling them that you are there or that you are leaving.

Before play begins, outline the various play options available — playmates, toys, materials, and so on. Encourage independence by giving children a coat hook or cubby hole that is easy to locate so they can locate items on their own. Help them find things on their own by marking the objects with textured labels. Include as many sensory cues as possible to alert and guide children. Having this exposure and information may help them to feel less fearful in new situations. They will need a balance of new, challenging activities and familiar activities over the course of the day. Like all children, children with visual impairments need the opportunity to make mistakes in order to learn from them and to experience success.

Sensory

It is sometimes assumed that if a person lacks one sensory ability, other sensory abilities will compensate. Although this is not true, children will need to learn to use their other senses and how to get and use information from them. Through continued and meaningful practice, these senses may become more acute. Help children to get information in other ways. For example, guide their hands to the bottle when being fed, and encourage them to smell the food they are eating. Expose them to different smells, objects, and sounds, and provide explanations so that they understand how this information fits into their world.

On the other hand, some people assume that children who lack skills in one area will also lack skills in another sensory area. So, for example, these people will speak loudly and slowly to the child with visual impairments, assuming that the child cannot hear. Again, ensuring that other people are aware of and understand the child's needs may alleviate such misconceptions.

Since children with visual impairments are more dependent on hearing to cope with their environment and to ensure personal safety, they should be taught to identify and discriminate between sounds. Children need opportunities to locate sound and then identify what or who made the sound. In the playroom, attempt to keep background noise to a minimum and noise levels low because children will need to rely on their hearing.

Attempt to use information gathered from the child's other senses as much as possible. Emphasize characteristics that can be felt, heard, and counted rather than just seen, such as smelling the lunch, hearing the lunch cart.

It may also be necessary to foster visual skills by encouraging children to use their vision. This may be problematic: how will you ensure that the child wears eye glasses or an eye patch throughout the day? How will you explain this need to the other children? How can you ensure that the child wants to wear these aids? Will you become the "bad guy," who makes the child wear them and who polices? In addition to considering corrective devices, you may need to consider light levels and other factors in your environment. For example, try to have books and other materials available that have bright, high-contrast colours and clear, simple pictures.

Play

It is not uncommon for children with visual impairments not to be included in play activities with their peers. This may occur because these children do not initiate interactions or because the other children feel unsure about how to include "different" children in their play. Model for all the children how to lead, guide, and talk to those with visual impairments. Let the other children know that they can assist by telling children with visual impairments about objects or activities they cannot see, and praise children when they follow through. If children see this behaviour occurring and are rewarded when they attempt it, they may feel less hesitant about involving children with visual impairments in their future play.

Physical

Fear of injury may prevent children with visual impairments from being given opportunities to participate in activities that promote physical development and contribute to their overall fitness. Early childhood professionals and other adults should address this attitude by attempting to find activities that they and the children are comfortable with or by finding people who may be able to assist. Children usually will take risks only when they have developed a sense of safety (Hayslip and Vincent, 1995). Instilling this sense of safety and developing good motor skills may be the prerequisite to more difficult or riskier experiences.

Children may not develop fine-motor skills either because of their difficulty in seeing or because other people perform these tasks for the child. Children need the opportunity to explore and attempt a variety of tasks in their environment. They must be free from fears of spilling or being messy. Learning will occur as children experiment and attempt these tasks. Manipulating objects using a variety of materials may help them develop a range of concepts, such as size, shape, and the physical arrangement of objects (Saracho and Spodek, 1988). Try to ensure that children have easy access to various objects and materials, know where they are, and do not accidentally spill or knock them over. It is important to allow children to experiment with objects and at least try to manipulate objects on their own. Always correcting children or taking over may lead them to cease trying or experimenting. Children will then need ample opportunity to practise these basic skills.

Cognitive

Some children with visual impairments may develop conceptual confusions, and other people may assume that these children have developmental delays when they fail to understand certain concepts. This may happen when children have not been provided with the required information.

> ### SCENARIO
>
> An elementary school teacher was attempting to teach Sharma, a 7-year-old girl, how to operate a brailler. Although Sharma usually learned new tasks quite quickly, she was hesitant and had difficulty understanding this particular task. After several attempts, the teacher placed Sharma's hands on the brailler and the paper. Sharma burst into laughter: "I thought you meant a sheet — like the sheet on my bed."

In this scenario, Sharma's behaviour could have been interpreted in many ways. Her reaction to learning this task was based on her understanding of her world. Once the meaning of "sheet" was clarified, her learning could continue.

Verbal information should coincide with concrete experiences in order for children to make the connection between symbols and the related ideas or objects. Create practical learning opportunities, and don't forget to talk about the obvious. Give children explicit instructions. People often avoid using the terms "look" and "see" when speaking to those with visual impairments, but these words are very much a part of our normal vocabulary and should not be avoided.

Use teachable moments throughout the day. For example, name body parts as the child is dressed; name the different parts of clothing and where they go on the body; name the different areas of the room and what happens in each. If the child does not yet know left from right, identify them in some way for the child. For example, the hand with the bracelet or watch on it may be the left hand. Everything bears description and explanation so that the child can begin to understand his or her world. When early childhood professionals engage in this kind of teaching consistently and regularly, other children may model and do the same, thereby increasing the amount of information the child with visual impairments will receive.

Social

Other children may consider this child helpless and always needing adult assistance. From their perspective, the child will often need someone to feed him or her, assistance in toileting, help to move from area to area, and so on. The other children may then come to think of the child as mentally impaired or handicapped and incapable. It is important for caregivers to find ways for the child to be considered competent and capable. Including the child where possible, promoting independence, and highlighting the child's unique characteristics or equipment may be helpful.

Some children may need to be given reasons why others wear eye glasses or eye patches. Other children may need to understand these aids and how they work. Try to make these aids as attractive as possible so that the child will want to wear them, or accentuate positive experiences when the child wears such corrective devices, by saying, for example, "You climbed much better with your glasses on." Keeping the other children informed and part of the child with special needs' life will promote an understanding of these unique features.

In addition, children with visual impairments may need opportunities to talk about their feelings and to learn to express them ("I don't like being called four eyes."). Other children may need to learn that it is not okay to say disparaging things about others.

Summary

Children with visual impairments are as diverse as their impairments. They may fit into your playroom with ease, or they may require adaptations to your physical and social environment. Early childhood professionals should familiarize themselves with the child's particular condition and how it may affect not only how the child sees but also any other areas of their development. They should then consider how they may facilitate the development of the child in their care.

ACTIVITIES

❶ Examine your own playroom from the perspective of a child with visual impairments. Can the child move around easily? Are toys accessible? Has personal safety been considered? Look at the playroom at various times during the day. Does accessibility, manoeuvrability, or safety change? In what ways? How can the needs of the child best be met in this environment throughout the day?

❷ Check your playroom to observe whether it has toys suitable for children with visual impairments. Will they attract the child's attention? Will they hold their attention? Do they promote development in some way? Do they promote a variety of different types of play? Will they promote interactions with other children? Are a range of play materials available?

❸ Investigate the community resources available for children with visual impairments. What is available in terms of equipment, adaptive aids, funding, and professional development opportunities?

❹ Some people feel that they are better able to understand the perspective of the child with special needs by experiencing the world as the child would. Other people feel that such an exercise can never simulate the experience of being visually impaired but is a mockery. Discuss the benefits and concerns of this type of activity. How would you use it with young children?

If you feel that this would be a beneficial approach for the staff or children in your care, set aside a block of time in which individuals can simulate a visual impairment in your playroom. This may be useful in determining how the physical environment should be changed or how routines may need to be altered. Remember to carry out the activity long enough for the novelty to wear off and be sure that everyone (including parents) understands the purpose of the activity.

DISCUSSION QUESTIONS

❶ Discuss the legal, medical, and educational definitions of visual impairments. Consider how each definition affects the way you look at the child. How does this view of the child influence your attitude toward or approach to the child?

❷ Discuss ways of adapting your environment: what sounds, textures, and smells can be used to enhance vision? What can be done to enhance the child's use of vision?

❸ Discuss how you would explain a child's visual impairment to other children. What words would you use? How would you help them to understand? What could you do to demonstrate the child's abilities?

❹ Discuss the warning signs that you might look for to suggest that a child might be having difficulty seeing. Be sure to consider these indications in relation to the child's age. For example, how infants and toddlers look at or interact with books may not give you a lot of information about vision. How children watch for and locate familiar people in their usual and in non-familiar environments may give more of an indication.

❺ Think about attitudes that people have toward individuals who are blind and visually impaired. Is there a difference? Consider books, media, and television. What do these media say about people with visual impairments?

Children with Hearing Impairments

CHAPTER 5

Introduction

The primary area of concern in the care and education of young children with profound hearing loss is language. Hearing loss has been referred to as the "invisible handicap" because children affected with it have no obvious sign of disability and because they develop in ways similar to hearing children in all other areas, including physical and cognitive development. Since these children tend to participate less in communication exchanges, their language skills tend to be delayed. Problems related to language and communication are more severe for children who experience chronic hearing loss before they have heard and developed verbal abilities than for those who experience a hearing loss after language development has begun.

It is crucial that the environmental opportunities of children with hearing impairments are as broad as possible to compensate for their lessened auditory learning opportunities; otherwise they may have delays in other areas of development due to loss of life experiences. Some children's hearing losses are mild and/or temporary. These children may be assumed by others to have low motivation or lack of ability. Thus is important for early childhood professionals to look for signs of undetected hearing loss. Undetected impairments may cause affected children to slip further behind and not realize why they are not developing like their peers.

Communication between children with hearing impairments and adults or other children with hearing can be difficult. Children whose hearing loss is such that they are unable to use verbal language as their main mode of communication may need to learn other systems. Few early childhood professionals are proficient in the use of sign language, so it is important for them to work closely with other professionals who can assist them in maintaining communication with children who are non-verbal and hearing impaired.

After reading this chapter, you should have a better understanding of:
- sensorineural and conductive hearing loss in children;
- the impact of a hearing impairment on a child's development;
- how others may be affected by the child with hearing impairments;
- how the early childhood professional may include the child with hearing impairments in the playroom setting and provide experiences that are worthwhile and developmentally appropriate.

Causes

The causes of hearing difficulties in young children are many, varied, and, in some instances, complex. For the purposes of this chapter, we consider the causes of two primary hearing impairment categories: conductive hearing loss and sensorineural hearing loss.

Conductive Hearing Loss

A conductive hearing loss is characterized by an obstruction to sound waves in the external or middle sections of the ear. In young children a common obstruction is the excessive buildup of ear wax pushing against the eardrum. Another is objects that have been inserted into the ear canal. Such obstructions normally cause mild hearing losses that may be detected by parents, early childhood professionals, or others in routine hearing-screening programs.

The most common cause of conductive hearing loss is ear infection, which most young children suffer from at one time or another. The Eustachian tube, which extends from the middle-ear cavity to the back of the nose and throat, is often the conduit along which infection spreads from the nose and/or throat to the ear. Eustachian tube congestion (leading to a buildup of fluid in the middle-ear space [otitis media]), which may occur when the child has a cold, also restricts the flow of air through the middle ear and may cause poor balance as well as reduced hearing. Exposure to excessive environmental noise may cause temporary, and in some instances permanent, hearing loss. Many of us, for example, have experienced a temporary loss in the sensitivity of our hearing as a result of exposure to very loud music or loud machinery.

A conductive hearing loss is often a partial hearing loss and is usually temporary. However, repeated ear infections may affect the child's capacity to hear over longer periods of time. Typically, some speech sounds — often those at a high frequency — are more muffled or faint, and the affected child may have difficulty in hearing sounds of lesser intensity. Treatment is often unnecessary because the problem clears up on its own. Infections may require medications such as decongestants or antibiotics to clear the infection.

Although antibiotics are traditionally prescribed to help clear infections, there is increasing concern that overprescribing these medications may cause additional problems. For example, repeated doses of antibiotic medication may be less effective in clearing infections and leave the body more vulnerable. Continued or chronic ear infections may require tubes to be inserted into the ears (through the ear drums) to help with ear flow and normal Eustachian tube functions. These tubes are surgically inserted and remain in place for up to two years. Usually they are helpful in solving the problem.

Sensorineural Hearing Loss

Hearing loss that occurs as a result of damage to the inner-ear structures, including the inner ear, the auditory nerves, and brain damage, is classified as sensorineural. There are myriad causes of sensorineural hearing loss, which is characterized by injury to or the poor development of nerve fibres and hair cells in the inner ear. First, children who suffer from conductive hearing loss through frequent infection and who either do not receive or do not respond to medical treatment may show characteristics of sensorineural damage. Second, a range of diseases, such as meningitis, measles, influenza, and mumps, can cause damage to nerve fibres in varying degrees. Third, although less is known about the effects of maternal infections while the child is in utero, it is well established that rubella (German measles) can seriously affect the hearing (as well as the vision, cognition, and cardiac health) of the unborn child. Fourth, frequent exposure to high-intensity noise may cause sensorineural damage. Noises that may cause such damage include cap guns, snowmobiles, music played at high volumes, and various pieces of machinery, including tractors.

Sensorineural hearing loss (inner-ear disorder) is usually more severe and chronic than conductive hearing loss and is more difficult to treat or correct through medical procedures. Terms such as "deafness" and "hard of hearing" usually refer to children who have significant and chronic hearing difficulties resulting from a sensorineural hearing loss.

In working with children who have permanent and severe hearing loss, it is important to know when the condition started. Children who are born deaf or who are seriously hearing impaired at birth, and those who acquire these conditions in the first year of life ("pre-linguistically," that is, before language) are at a significant disadvantage in learning language. Others, whose deafness or hearing impairment is acquired at later ages, are at a lesser disadvantage.

DIAGNOSIS AND ASSESSMENT

A child's ability to hear is measured in terms of loudness (that is, how loud a sound needs to be for a child to be able to hear it accurately) and in terms of pitch or frequency. Tests for intensity or loudness and for pitch or frequency are normally measured by a pure-tone audiometer administered by an audiologist.

Loudness is measured in decibels (dB), and although children may hear a wide range of sounds, the focus of the audiologist is on the range normally associated with speech. A whisper from a distance of 5 feet would normally measure about 20–25 dB, and normal conversational speech at the same distance would measure about 65–80 dB. Frequency of sound is measured in cycles per second (cps) or Hertz (Hz) and refers to the highness or lowness of the pitch of the sound. Most conversational speech sounds fall within the range of 500–2000 Hz, although non-speech sounds may be heard at frequencies both lower and higher than those used in speech.

Early childhood professionals have important roles to play in identifying and including young children with hearing difficulties. Spending time with young children in social play settings allows the caregiver to focus on individual children and to notice subtle differences in their responses. Throughout the preschool years, many children experience temporary periods of reduced hearing. It is important for you as caregiver to remain sensitive to this possibility and to discuss your observations with parents, your co-workers, and other professionals. Your observations may help the speech pathologist, health nurse, or doctor to diagnose and treat the condition.

Other children may have more permanent and severe hearing loss that has not been detected before their entry into the early childhood program. Again, your vigilance in observing and noting children's auditory responsiveness and language development is important in the early detection of any problems.

Some of the more common observable examples of children with hearing difficulty include:

- a child who is unusually attentive (watches your face and lips very closely) or unusually inattentive (ignores most of what is going on and spends a lot of time daydreaming or choosing activities that do not require interaction with others);
- a child who is noticeably slow in speech development so that it interferes with the ability to make his or her needs known or to communicate with peers;
- a child who has frequent colds and ear infections;
- a child who turns her or his head in an attempt to hear better;
- a child who suffers from allergic reactions or who recently experienced measles or mumps.

If you suspect a hearing loss and this is confirmed by others in a position to observe the child, promptness in referring the child for a thorough assessment is very important.

It isn't uncommon for young children who are deaf to develop a typical language pattern. Babies will cry in differentiated ways, and they may coo and babble in the same sequence and time frame as all babies. This seemingly normal sequence in babies may hinder the identification of a hearing problem because affected children make a wide array of sounds. However, children who are deaf will likely not develop spoken language, partially because of the lack of feedback they experience when verbalizing. It is not until children fail to talk that difficulties may be suspected.

The ability to hear is crucial to learning and development, and the sooner problems are identified the more effective the intervention. Similarly, the younger the child, the more effective intervention will be. This is true of all handicapping conditions but is of particular importance for hearing because of its impact on language development. The role of the early childhood professional and other adults is crucial because this condition is not easily noticeable. When it is noticed, it may be identified as a behavioural problem or developmental delay.

● ● ● ● ● ●
Implications for the Child's Development

Children with hearing impairments may be affected in many ways. For those with a conductive hearing loss, the effects may be temporary, especially if the problem is identified early and appropriate treatment is provided.

SCENARIO

In a day-care centre, 3-year-old Marcia was beginning to cause problems in her interactions with other children and with the adults in the room. She went from being a generally content child who played easily and became engaged in various activities to becoming a child who wandered and had little to do with other children other than pushing them or trying to take toys from them. At times she seemed to ignore the requests of the caregivers. They became frustrated with her behaviour and began to question her mom about how she was behaving at home and whether there had been a significant change in her home environment. Mom was also concerned and took Marcia to see her doctor.

The examinations indicated ear wax and a heavy buildup of fluid in Marcia's Eustachian tubes, resulting in pressure on the inside of her ear drums. Marcia was referred to an ear, nose, and throat specialist at a local hospital and had small plastic tubes inserted in her ear drums to reduce the pressure on them and to allow the wax and fluid to escape.

Almost immediately, Marcia's hearing ability improved. She returned to using spoken conversation, interacted appropriately with other children, and responded to the requests of her caregivers.

Conductive hearing loss may be intermittent. That is, the child may change from being able to hear well to not being able to hear at all from one day (or even one minute) to the next. It is important to provide the child with an immediate medical examination (by a doctor or health nurse) and to avoid making premature assumptions about the child's behaviour and motivation. It is also important to remember that each time the child suffers from a cold or ear infection, his or her ability to learn may be affected. The cumulative effects of intermittent losses during the months when language learning is so rapid have a great impact on language development.

SCENARIO

When I entered the kindergarten program I did not immediately identify Tim. He was busily engaged in building tunnels and mountains in a sand box with another child when the teacher pointed him out. In spite of having a profound sensorineural hearing loss that resulted from a severe attack of measles when he was 25 months of age, Tim continues to use spoken language as his main method of communication. In addition to *wearing a hearing aid, Tim is fitted with a frequency modulation (FM) training device to augment his hearing aid and to reduce problems of noise, distance, and reverberation.*

The FM auditory trainer consists of a microphone worn by the speaker (in this case, Tim's play partner), and a receiver worn by the listener (in this case, Tim). It amplifies the speech of Tim's playmate, to compensate for Tim's hearing loss, and lessens the impact of other noise in the room. It creates a listening situation comparable to the playmate's voice being only 6 inches (15 centimetres) away from Tim's ear at all times. Later during the morning the caregiver took the microphone from Tim's play partner and wore it herself as she gave some directions to the children, settled them down, and read them a story.

Most children with chronic hearing loss may be helped with technological aids. In the above scenario, Tim, whose permanent hearing loss occurred after he had acquired verbal interactions was able to work with an FM auditory training device. Other children may be fitted with hearing aids.

Although technological aids may be helpful to those with hearing impairment, they can create problems of their own. They may amplify all sounds, including background noises. This may prove distracting for the young child who has not developed the ability to screen out extraneous sounds. In addition, children may be reluctant or refuse to wear a hearing aid because the aid sets them apart.

The careful maintenance of technical aids is extremely important. Early childhood professionals should ensure that they understand and can complete simple "trouble-shooting" maintenance and that they know who to go to for fast and precise service. Rudimentary knowledge for early childhood professionals includes battery maintenance, understanding how moulds fit into the child's ears, awareness of problems that may arise through microphone and receiver proximity, and familiarity with switches and tubes.

Whether the sensory deprivation of hearing is conductive or sensorineural, or temporary, intermittent, or permanent, the major barrier it presents to young children is in relation to language development and language learning. Up to the age of 7 years, children learn to understand verbal messages, to speak, and to read. Within a few weeks after birth, they begin to perceive sounds in the environment and associate these sounds to meaning. At the same time they begin to imitate vocal sounds, which emerge as words by about 1 year of age. By the time children start school a few years later, they learn to read. This learning is based on a well-established foundation of experience in hearing and producing words.

The basic tenet of this hierarchy of language development is that language input precedes language output. Thus, children understand more than they are able to convey. For example, a young child may understand and follow a three-step set of directions, such as "Close the door, bring your coat, and give it to me." However, the child may be unable to state this set of directions in words. Any interruption in this process, through loss of hearing, will affect children's ability not only to receive information but also to express themselves verbally.

The extent to which hearing loss affects children's ability to use language depends on such factors as the age of onset, the promptness of the medical intervention, whether the loss is temporary or permanent, and whether it affects one ear or both ears. Again it is critical to recognize warning signs and detect concerns early in the development of all children.

Children's social and personal development depends heavily on verbal communication. It is through social interaction with others that we learn about ourselves and the world around us. Hearing children not only hear, they overhear much of what goes on around them and so benefit from this informal education. Children with hearing impairments do not have these benefits. In the most extreme case, a child with a total and profound hearing loss may be cut off from communication with others both at home and in the early childhood program and live in relative isolation. Young children take in new information at an incredibly rapid rate. Interference in this learning process, even for a few months, can create a serious problem in terms of not developing understanding, misunderstanding the social environment, and social isolation.

Children with hearing impairments may show a number of responses that may lead us to make erroneous assumptions about their ability. A child who responds more slowly to verbal requests, or whose responses indicate that he or she does not fully understand what has been requested or what is expected, may mistakenly be considered to have intellectual impairments and to be developmentally delayed. The child who does not listen, especially to an adult, may be considered to have behavioural problems.

It is important for adults working with young children to be alert to the possibilities of hearing loss and to ensure that the child is assessed for this possibility before looking into other reasons for the child's behaviour. There may be no noticeable effect in other areas of development, such as fine-motor and cognitive development. Gross-motor development may be affected by difficulties with balance, but other concerns may not be noticeable.

Role of the Early Childhood Professional

ATTITUDES

Attitudes toward individuals with hearing impairments are diverse. Some people believe that these children should be treated as "normally" as possible because they will have to live in a hearing world. Thus inclusion, using technological aids, lip reading, and speech, are promoted. Others promote a "deaf culture," which include the use of sign language, art, and theatre. Here, the skills required to cope in a hearing world are considered secondary to the ability to communicate in the deaf community. Thus it is important for early childhood professionals to understand the various settings and therapies available for children with hearing impairments.

SCENARIO

When Julia was hired as a special-needs assistant to work with 5-year-old Travis, she was both excited and nervous. She had enjoyed her college classes that looked at children with special needs and spent a part of one practicum in an integrated day-care setting. Travis had no recognizable language abilities. He was born deaf, and although he had made normal sounds as a baby, by the time he was 2 years of age these had decreased. Now he made only harsh throat sounds. For the past 2 years he had received help from a speech pathologist, who was just beginning to introduce Travis to sign language.

Julia did not know any sign language. At first she taught herself a few signs by reading manuals and watching training videos. She then taught them to Travis. While this worked well for a few weeks, she soon realized that Travis's ability to integrate with and play alongside other children was not improving. In fact, as he learned to sign he became more dependent on her because she was the only person who understood him and who could respond to him.

To encourage the inclusion of Travis and reduce his isolation, Julia started to gather a small group of children with Travis to learn one or two new signs each day. The hearing children loved the experience — learning a "secret" language that their parents and some others did not understand — and Travis found support and inclusion in play with others.

Gradually all the children in the room learned to sign, and Travis was given a few minutes each day to teach new signs to the whole group. As the children completed their year in kindergarten and moved into grade one, many of them moved together with Travis, taking with them attitudes of acceptance, inclusion, and cooperation.

This story of Travis's and Julia's experiences in kindergarten point to the importance of the attitudes brought by the adults toward the child with a hearing disability. Julia's realization that Travis's need was not merely to learn the technical aspects of a language, but to integrate and socialize with peers and to decrease his isolation and dependence on her, are commendable and important attitudes that help the child with special needs and his or her peers.

Some people have assumed that teaching young children to sign is not beneficial, especially when they are learning spoken language. The literature and our experiences suggest, however, that language development will continue and that the learning of sign language will not interfere (and may even promote) the development of spoken language and other communication abilities.

Other children's understanding and attitudes may be affected by their interactions with the child with hearing impairments. For instance, if that child does not respond, grabs toys that others are using, and attempts to interact in rough ways or in ways that are not accepted by others, the other children may not want to interact with him or her. As well as developing social abilities in the child with hearing impairments, it is important to provide information and explanations to hearing children so that they do not actively isolate the child with hearing impairments.

Whether the child is already diagnosed as having a hearing loss or is identified during the time he or she is attending the early childhood program, the caregiver should build and maintain a relationship of co-operation and collaboration with the child's parents. It is the parents who know their child most thoroughly and who can provide information about his or her development, interests, and idiosyncrasies. It is also helpful for the child to know that this relationship exists; this knowledge will ease the child's transition from home to early childhood programs. Working with a child who has a hearing loss, both as a parent and as an early childhood professional, requires co-operating with others and providing mutual support. Relationships between parents and the child's other caregivers are essential for the well-being of the child with a hearing loss.

This need to co-operate and work collaboratively extends to other professional personnel. As a caregiver, get to know the agencies, associations, and professional personnel in your region who may be able to offer help to (1) you, in your daily encounters with the child; (2) the parents, in their search for more knowledge, information, and support; and (3) the child, in his or her need for assessment, technical assistance, and emotional and social support.

STRATEGIES

For the inclusion of children with chronic hearing loss to be truly beneficial and not merely token, the caregiver must prepare thoroughly. This preparation requires you to know the child and his or her family, to give sensitive thought to the needs of all those involved (including the hearing children), to provide adequate professional support, and to identify ways to increase the information and knowledge base relating to the condition of the child, its implication for his or her development, and implications in the playroom. Following are some of the strategies to consider and adapt to the child's particular situation.

In preparing a physical environment to include children with hearing impairments, there are several issues to address. First, the environment should include both quiet and active areas. For many children with a hearing aid, background noise can be a major interference in their ability to focus on and hear language and the sounds that are most important.

Second, the environment should be conducive to the use of technical aids such as FM auditory trainers. This will involve preparing hearing children to use these devices in order to communicate with the child with hearing difficulties and making sure that technical support is readily available to make adjustments and repairs. Children with hearing impairments may need to be encouraged and supported in consistently wearing technical aids until they have adjusted to hearing so much sound.

Third, many children with reduced hearing ability use visual clues to gain understanding. The environment should, therefore, contain various and well-organized visual displays that will help the child. These visual aids may include ensuring that stories have visual supplements such as computer animation, flannel-boards, picture books, and pictures that demonstrate how to complete particular self-care tasks, such as hand washing. Make sure that the child is paying attention before you speak and that you give directions so that he or she can see and use contextual clues.

Sign language and finger spelling are two approaches to communication that are traditionally known as the manual method. Auditory training (teaching children to use whatever hearing they have) and speech reading (using visual cues, including lips and facial expressions) are alternative approaches known as the oral method. For many years, these approaches to teaching communication to those with a profound hearing loss were considered radically different and oppositional. Parents and professionals took a strong stance in favour of one or the other. Thus it was not uncommon to have a program based on the oral approach, in which lip reading and learning speech were primary, and another program based on manual approaches, in which sign language was provided.

More recently, the "total communication" approach has attempted to combine the two traditional approaches to better meet the needs of children with hearing impairments. In this approach, the child's particular strengths are assessed and the most suitable methods of communication are taught. The emphasis is on maximizing the child's ability to communicate in all ways — not necessarily speech.

Planning in a Developmental Context

Planning must consider the developmental abilities and interests of all the people in the playroom and not simply target one area of development for one child. The process of planning, which includes preparation of the environment, the people, and the materials, should include all those involved in working with the children, including the special needs assistant.

Play

Play is the vehicle through which young children learn a great deal about themselves and the world around them. While traditional approaches to working with children with hearing impairments tend not to stress the importance of play (they more typically stress teaching language by use of oral, manual, or finger-spelling methods), in inclusive settings the children's ability to engage with the environment and with peers is essential to their success and to the effectiveness of the program.

One experience in working with children with hearing loss is that they tend to continue in isolated or parallel play and appear reluctant or unable to participate at associative or co-operative levels. Of course, much of the reason for this is their reduced ability to understand and express ideas to others. An important role for the caregiver, therefore, is to engage the child with hearing difficulties in a playful way with materials and with others. For younger children, this probably means that you will spend time each day as the play partner for the child.

By playing alongside and with the child, you can both model and engage the child in such essential play skills as using materials for fantasy and make-believe purposes; for example, a block becomes a car, chairs become an airplane. You may take on roles of being a nurse, an astronaut, or a horse! When appropriate, encourage the child to engage in these make-believe play experiences with you. Another part of this experience for the child is that of choice and control. As a skilled and sensitive play partner, you will be able to follow the child's lead, thus allowing him or her to experience notions of decision making and control.

As the child grows older and other children show interest in your co-operative play, you may want to invite one or two other children to join in the play. This may be especially helpful if the hearing children you invite in have good play skills and are able to engage themselves co-operatively with others by taking either "leadership" or "follower" roles in the play. You may extend your participation in helping the child with hearing difficulties if you tell and model for the hearing children skills that may enable the experience to be successful for all. These skills include ensuring that a method of communication is established (perhaps by using sign language or an FM auditory trainer), providing hearing children with the ability to understand the responses given by the child with hearing difficulties (for example, informing them that the child may respond more slowly or may need to be prompted when it is his or her turn), and following the lead (interests) of the child.

It is important for caregivers to remember that play is not instruction or a method of teaching. It is rather a process by which children freely choose and control activities and roles, and it normally involves the suspension of reality and engagement in a make-believe world. It is through such experience that children understand themselves — their abilities and limitations — and the world around them and how they can manipulate and interact with it. It is as important for the child with a hearing difficulty to experience and re-experience playfulness as it is for children without hearing difficulties.

Social

Because hearing is essential to learning spoken language and communication skills, children with a hearing loss experience difficulties in communicating verbally and consequently in their social development.

From the earliest age, children with a hearing loss may miss many of the formal and direct explanations about social behaviour. They may also miss many of the informal conversations from which children with hearing learn many of their social skills (such as the conversations that occur when children in play take on roles and practise talking from various perspectives).

Encouraging social skills for children with a hearing impairment is very important. Hearing impairment is often confused with behavioural disorder, and children who are affected may act with indifference or aggression toward others. Helping them to engage with others and to make friends with peers is a critical role for the caregiver.

It is important to ensure that any verbal requests, instructions, or directions are completely understood by the child with hearing difficulties. The child's participation in informal conversations may be more difficult to encourage. As with the suggestions for play, however, the role of the early childhood professional is to help other children to understand and behave sensitively to ensure the inclusion of the child with hearing difficulties. Specific suggestions include:

- telling and modelling for hearing children;
- speaking naturally (not exaggerating movements of the mouth or shouting);
- facing each other when talking, whenever possible;
- showing (modelling) for the child to clarify understanding.

Many of the skills required for positive social development are those learned as part of verbal language. For instance, when we engage in conversations with others, we follow the lead of the other and recognize when to take turns and speak and when to listen and allow the other person to speak. Such social skills are used in many other situations, not only in conversation, and hearing children learn them through play and interaction with others from an early age. It is important for the caregiver to provide opportunities for children with hearing difficulties to experience these skills. They include imitation, taking turns, and prompting.

Very young children learn imitation through games such as peek-a-boo, mutual smiling, and hand-clapping, and through the imitation of vocal sounds. Turn taking — learning when to take your turn and when to allow others to take theirs — is learned through sharing materials and playing games. The caregiver, as well as the hearing children, can engage the child with hearing difficulties in playing catch, baking cookies together (stirring the batter or putting cookies on the baking sheet), and taking turns at stacking blocks instead of watching the child talk about what he or she is doing.

The aim of turn taking is balance, so that the child with hearing difficulties neither dominates and takes all the turns nor retreats and takes no turns. Sometimes children with hearing difficulties need to be prompted either to take their turn (in a conversation or activity) or to stop and let someone else take a turn.

Emotional

The personal emotional development of children with a hearing loss largely depends on the level of acceptance of those around them and of their efforts at communication and support. Children who are unable to make their needs known to their peers or who are rejected in their efforts to engage in play with others will suffer from a sense of low self-esteem. A primary goal of the inclusion process is that all children, including those with profound hearing disabilities, should experience a sense of belonging and security. The attitudes of the hearing children toward the child with hearing difficulties will be largely determined by the attitudes modelled by the caregiver. Encouraging the child's independence, looking for improvements in communication, and supporting friendships are three important ways to foster the emotional development of the child.

Cognitive

Differences, and often difficulties, in speech and communication models among children with hearing difficulties can create the misconception that children with hearing difficulties are somehow less intelligent. (There are some theorists who believe that the ability to think is dependent on spoken language.) This is not accurate: intelligence is distributed normally among children with hearing difficulties, and children who use alternative forms of language (for instance, sign language) are clearly able to demonstrate their ability to think. Because our world is so dependent on verbal language, however, children with a hearing loss may miss concepts and ideas available to their hearing peers. As a result, they may not always understand, and in late years (grade school) many children with hearing difficulties do not achieve as well as their peers.

The implication of this for the caregiver is to ensure that the child with hearing problems has an opportunity to experience and gain knowledge from exposure to many situations alongside and with hearing peers. Concepts missed in verbal language may be learned through physical practice or visual exposure. This makes it even more important for you to ensure that children have the opportunity to interact and be understood. It is also important, however, to continue to explore avenues of communication with the child and to use them frequently.

Sensory

One of the myths associated with sensory disabilities is that children with visual or hearing difficulties either develop a "sixth" sense (a type of radar) or have extraordinary abilities in another sense that compensate for their loss. For instance, misconceptions regarding children who are deaf are that they see better and cannot appreciate music or dance. These are false assumptions about children with hearing loss and may limit what can be done to meet their needs as healthy, active, curious children. At the other extreme, some people assume that if hearing is impaired, then other senses are as well. Thus, they reason, if the child cannot hear well, then he or she probably cannot see well either.

Children who cannot hear well will become more dependent on other senses to understand their world. It is important for to provide opportunities for children with a sensory hearing loss to learn from their other senses. However, an overabundance of visual or tactile stimuli, intended to supplement verbal learning, may only be confusing. Other sensory stimuli — whether tactile or visual — should be well organized and arranged so that they help children to clarify their understanding.

Children with hearing impairments may need some help in learning how to integrate and use various pieces of sensory information. If they can integrate sensory information, understanding will follow; if not, they may be more confused than ever. This may occur when children are first fitted with technological aids. All of a sudden their world may be bombarded with sound, much of it extraneous. The child needs to learn to select what sounds to pay attention to and what sounds to tune out. This will take time and practice and, in the case of hearing aids, the support of an understanding adult who will be aware of minimizing background noises, such as a furnace fan, a radio, or an air conditioner.

Summary

A major theme of this chapter has been the impact of a hearing loss — whether chronic, temporary, or intermittent, and whether mild or profound — on language and communication. Receptive language (the ability to hear and understand) always precedes expressive language (the ability to speak and communicate effectively with others). Children who are unable to hear and understand the sounds that are going on around them (spoken language and other environmental sounds) will have difficulty expressing their needs, interests, and understandings.

The primary efforts of the caregiver in working with young children with hearing difficulties are to help create and build on communication skills. These tasks should not be undertaken in isolation or without knowledge. Support from the parents, speech pathologists, audiologists, and others familiar with the development and needs of the hearing impaired is essential.

Children with hearing impairments may either fit into a preschool program or cause major frustrations there. It is important for early childhood professionals to understand hearing loss and the impact on the child's development, particularly in the areas of language and social behaviour.

ACTIVITIES

1. Children with chronic hearing loss may use other means of communication, such as American Sign Language (ASL). In groups of two or three, learn to sign a simple action song or story that you can then communicate to the remainder of the class. Make this the beginning of your efforts to learn ASL. Set a goal to learn three or four new signs each week, and spend time sharing them with others in class.

2. Invite a local audiologist or other expert in the use of hearing aids to show you how these aids operate and demonstrate straightforward maintenance procedures that you can perform.

3. Invite an early childhood professional who works with a child with a hearing impairment and the parent of a child with a hearing impairment to talk to you about the development of the child and the provisions they make to ensure the child's inclusion in other groups.

DISCUSSION QUESTIONS

1. Some people in the "deaf" community argue that inclusion for a deaf child is necessarily in a segregated program in which everyone else is using sign language or lip reading. Do you agree? Why or why not?

2. Children who experience difficulties in hearing may be wrongly thought to be exhibiting behaviour problems. Why do you think this occurs? What can you do to prevent yourself from making such a judgement?

3. What environmental and play provisions would you consider in preparing to include a 3-year-old child with a history of hearing problems into your preschool program?

Children with Communication Difficulties

CHAPTER 6

Introduction

Communication is a complex process that serves many functions. It allows us to learn about the past, dream about the future, understand abstract concepts, and share all these experiences in social interactions with others. This chapter considers three components of communication — speech, language, and non-verbal communication — as well as conditions that interfere with communication development in young children.

The development of speech and language in children follows an orderly sequence that is closely connected to physical, cognitive, and social development. As a result, it is possible to provide a broad timetable that points to the sequential acquisition of important indicators in the development of speech and language (see Box 6.1), although it is not always possible (or helpful) to attach specific ages to the sequence.

Oral language may be thought of as the ability to express and understand ideas. For instance, the child who says "I see the house" has demonstrated expressive oral-language ability by arranging words in an order that expresses a meaningful idea. If another child, the listener, understands the meaning of this arrangement of words, he or she has demonstrated receptive oral-language ability.

Speech is the primary method used to express language. The utterances that make up words are usually known as phonemes. Throughout the first eight years of life, children learn to pronounce the sounds of language, beginning with vowel sounds (by the age of about 12 months) and culminating with consonant blends such as sh, ch, th (by the age of 7 or 8 years).

Children may have problems with expressive and/or receptive language and/or with speech production that make it difficult to be understood by others. According to Van Riper (1978), "Speech is defective when it deviates so far from the speech of other people that it calls

> **BOX 6.1 SEQUENCE OF SPEECH AND LANGUAGE DEVELOPEMENT IN YOUNG CHILDREN**
>
> **BIRTH**
>
> 1. Cooing-crying: Random vocalizations, not intended to communicate anything in particular.
> 2. Babbling: Repetition of sounds for their own sake. Often in response to the speech of others. Includes intonation patterns that approximate mature speech.
> 3. Approximations or echolalia: Duplication of sounds. Repetition of words without giving them (understanding) meaning.
>
> **12 MONTHS**
>
> 4. First word: Use of single words with accuracy (usually to name objects or people).
> 5. One-word sentence (holophrase): Use of a single word (usually a noun) to convey larger thoughts (e.g., "milk," may mean "I spilled my milk" or "I want more milk").
> 6. Pivot-words: Combination of single nouns with another phrase to convey a thought more accurately (e.g., "all-gone" is a typical pivot phrase: "doggie all-gone," "daddy all-gone," "milk all-gone," "cookie all-gone").
>
> **2 YEARS**
>
> 7. Two- and three-word sentences: Use of telegraphic speech (e.g., "Mommy gone work"; "Teddy go bye-bye").
> 8. Expanded grammatical form: Use of four- or five-word sentences. Expression of many concepts with words. A vocabulary of about 1000 words, perhaps some speech disfluency, self-talk, and imaginary speech. Use of sentences to tell stories that are understood by others.
> 9. Complex sentences: Use of negative forms of verbs, but sometimes in error (e.g., "I swimmed with my friend at the pool").
>
> **6 AND 7 YEARS**
>
> 10. Sophisticated speech: Accurate use of grammatical rules. Ability to learn to read. Articulation of all alphabet sounds. A vocabulary exceeding 2500 words.

attention to itself, interferes with communication, or causes the child to be unstable." Identifying speech problems in young children is difficult because they are still learning to articulate sounds and it is both normal and acceptable for them to make mistakes. Thus, a 10-year-old child saying "I see duh wed cah" (I see a red car) might indicate a problem with speech. However, the same statement produced by a 4-year-old child would cause less concern and would be more acceptable.

Disabilities of speech fall into several categories: (1) insufficient articulation, in which speech sounds are left out (such as "mato" for "tomato," "ju" for "juice," "po-y" for "pony") or replaced by a substitute sound (such as "won" for "run", "tate" for "cake," and "wikes" for "likes"); (2) voice problems, in which the loudness, pitch, or quality of the voice is affected; and (3) lack of fluency (interruption in the flow of speech), including stuttering.

In addition to using language and speech, children learn to communicate non-verbally through facial expression, use of hand and body gestures, and contact with others. Very young children soon learn the power of holding out their arms in order to be picked up (long before they are able to ask to be picked up) or pointing to a picture of a cookie to let a parent know what they want. When a little older, children express their intentions through physical action. It is not unusual for a 3-year-old child to show her lack of interest in a story by simply getting up and walking away.

Sophisticated communication, which includes clear pronunciation and the well-organized articulation of ideas, also includes the use of gesture, physical proximity, and facial expression. Difficulties in these areas may lead a child to send incongruent or confusing messages to others. For instance, a child may be too dependent on gesture as a means of communication and so expect that merely pointing to or looking at a cookie is sufficient to convey a message.

After reading this chapter, you should have a better understanding of:

- difficulties that children may experience in the areas of speech, language, and non-verbal communication;
- the primary causes of communication difficulties in children;
- the impact of communication difficulties on children's development;
- how children's communication difficulties may affect others;
- ways in which early childhood professionals may provide inclusive and developmentally appropriate experiences for children with communication difficulties.

CAUSES

There are four major reasons for the disruption of the learning of good communication skills in children.

Sensory Deprivation

Children who have hearing difficulties almost always have problems in communication. Hearing difficulties always imply that children cannot receive sounds as well as their hearing peers, and consequently they will have difficulty expressing their needs and interests. Children with profound hearing loss from birth may develop communication skills that are very different from those of other children with language difficulties. For instance, these children may not babble for long because they cannot hear their own voices. They use gestures frequently and watch attentively for facial expressions, movements, and other visual cues. Not only is sensory input affected by hearing impairment, but the output of speech sounds becomes a laborious, if not impossible, task, depending on the degree of loss. Even for children who suffer a temporary, conductive hearing loss as the result of an infection or cold, the ability to communicate verbally and to express themselves clearly through oral language is impaired.

Experiential Disadvantage

In order for communication to develop, children need certain types of experiences. In general terms, they must live in a verbal-language environment, in which the activities of listening, talking, and remembering surround the child. Children deprived of these opportunities may not learn appropriate communication skills. For children who live in a language-rich environment, in which stories, conversation, music, and verbal explanations are a regular part of everyday life, the chance of communication problems is much reduced.

Perhaps most damaging of the potential areas of experiential disadvantage is the environment in which conversation is limited. Children who are consistently ordered to behave in particular ways are more limited in their opportunities than are children who receive reasonable explanations for behavioural expectations.

Compare the communication advantages and disadvantages in the following scenarios.

> ## SCENARIOS
>
> When Leslie and her mother got on the bus, her mother immediately told her to sit down. As Leslie continued to walk down the aisle of the bus, her mother repeated a stern "Sit down." When she continued to walk, her mother took her firmly by the arm and repeated, "Sit down. You sit down when I tell you."
>
> When Walt and his mother got on the bus his mother immediately said, "Come and sit by me before the bus starts to move." As Walt continued to walk down the aisle of the bus she repeated, "You need to sit down. The bus is about to start moving." When Walt continued his journey down the aisle, she took him firmly by the arm and repeated, "You need to sit down now. The bus will start to move and you might fall."

Children learn the basic skills of conversation from a very early age — long before they use verbal language — by playing games that involve imitation, turn-taking, listening, and responding. Children who play games such as peek-a-boo, mutual smiling, rolling a ball back and forth, and imitation hand-clapping with others who are older develop basic skills of communication.

Emotional and Social Difficulties

Children with severe social and emotional difficulties may exhibit a range of communication disorders. For example, children diagnosed as having "autistic" tendencies may not talk at all, talk very little, use words repetitively (echolalia), have problems of articulation, or use verbal language only for self-talk and not as a way of establishing interpersonal communication.

Children with emotional difficulties less severe than those associated with autism may also have communication difficulties. Those who are afraid or who are very anxious may respond differently to communication from others — as though they did not hear or understand what was said — and they may express themselves differently, perhaps by using less mature speech and language. An everyday example of this phenomenon is the behaviour of a 4-year-old child who has recently become the older brother or sister to a new baby. It is not uncommon for the child to revert to some less mature behaviour and language, perhaps as a way of drawing attention away from the baby to himself or herself, or as a way of expressing anxiety about his or her position in the family now that a baby has arrived.

Central Nervous System Impairment

Impairment of the central nervous system (CNS) may result in many types of conditions. Children with cerebral palsy, for example, typically have difficulty in speaking due to the mouth, tongue, and breathing apparatus not functioning easily; limited ability to move; and associated perceptual problems.

Physical or organic impairments of the mechanisms required for speech, such as a misalignment of the jaw or teeth, a cleft lip and palate, and problems associated with the tongue or larynx (voice box), may cause temporary or permanent language and speech problems that should be identified and dealt with.

Children who are unable to use symbols to communicate language are described as aphasic. Their disability is not due to hearing difficulties, severe emotional difficulties, or mental retardation. They may not be able to understand speech (receptive aphasia), use speech (expressive aphasia), or use language for any purpose (central aphasia).

Children who are developmentally delayed may have communication difficulties that include receptive and expressive language, speech production, and non-verbal communication.

DIAGNOSIS AND ASSESSMENT

The communication problems of children are identified through a careful observation of children's attempts to communicate. The early childhood professional plays an important role in the identification and referral of a young child with communication problems. Often the identification of a problem begins at an instinctive level: you begin to notice that a girl is not playing and interacting comfortably with her peers; perhaps she is domineering, not joining in enough, or maybe other children are having difficulty understanding what she is saying.

The early childhood professional can watch for several indications of possible communication problems:

- The child does not play easily with other children and usually chooses isolated activities.
- The child is domineering in conversations with others: he or she takes over conversations and does not allow others to participate.
- The child is quiet and withdrawn and does not take a turn in play or conversation.

Specific observations for possible receptive language difficulties include the following:

- By 18 months, the child does not respond to his or her name, "no-no," "bye-bye," or "bottle."
- By 24 months, the child does not understand or point on request to his or her mouth, nose, eyes, and hair.

- By 36 months, the child does not understand and demonstrate the concepts of in, on, under, front, and back.

Specific observations for possible expressive language difficulties include the following:

- By 18 months, the child is not saying at least six words with appropriate meaning.
- By 24 months, the child is not using simple two- or three-word phrases such as "Go bye bye," "Want cookie."
- By 36 months, the child has not begun to ask simple questions such as "What's this?"
- By 48 months, the child is limited to telegraphic sentences, or the sentences are confused; for example, "Me go car," "Candy me want."
- By 60 months, the child consistently uses past tenses incorrectly; for example, "he throwed a ball").

Specific observations for possible speech problems include the following:

- At 24 months, less than 50 percent of the child's speech is understandable.
- At 36 months, there are *many* consonant omissions.
- After 36 months, the child omits many initial consonants.
- The child is concerned or teased by peers about his or her speech.
- The child has had disfluent speech for more than 6 months.
- The child fears situations in which he or she is required to speak.
- The child's voice is difficult to listen to; for example, it is too nasal, too loud, pitched too high or too low, a monotone.

The early identification of speech and language disorders is important. The majority of children's communication problems fall into the speech category. Fortunately, these problems tend to be the least serious and most receptive to help. The early childhood professional, together with the parents, may be involved in referring the child for further assessment and treatment with a speech and language pathologist.

Implications

IMPLICATIONS FOR THE CHILD'S DEVELOPMENT

The ability to communicate with others, to clearly articulate ideas, and to express wants, needs, and feelings is highly regarded in our society. We gain our initial impressions of other people through their efforts to communicate, whether through verbal language or through non-verbal body language, gestures, or even dress. The development of the ability to communicate with others occurs primarily during the preschool years and is possibly the most important area of development for young children. The ability to communicate affects the child in all areas of development — socially, emotionally, cognitively, physically, and creatively.

Since problems in communication are many and vary from one child to another, and since it is during the first 7 or 8 years that children's communication competence is being developed, identifying problems or potential problems in this area may be difficult. Young children are not generally rejected by their peers because of speech or language problems alone. However, they may receive enough messages — both subtle and direct — from peers to cause increased sensitivity and affect their social development. A child who is conscious of speech or language impairments may choose not to participate in play with others but engage in isolated play or "onlooker" play behaviours, thus missing not only the development and learning that occurs spontaneously in play, but also the specific opportunity to practise and improve communication skills. The emotional "overlay" that some children develop as part of their communication difficulties merely increases the problem. Children who receive messages of impatience from peers or adults may become very self-conscious in their communications and become shy and awkward in language situations.

IMPLICATIONS FOR OTHERS

In the playroom's "formal" language situations, such as group time, children with speech and/or language difficulties may find that other children become inattentive or disruptive when they talk. At other times, especially in a room full of busy, demanding children, the early childhood professional may find it difficult to listen to children who are disfluent. It may seem easier to finish their sentences or correct their pronunciation.

The quiet, well-behaved child who chooses to play alone most of the time may be considered shy and as a result be easily overlooked and not included or engaged by others. The child who talks a lot, who initiates and dominates conversations and play, may be regarded as a leader or as "outgoing," and that child's communication difficulties may not be easily recognized by the early childhood professional.

Role of the Early Childhood Professional

The early childhood professional has a varied role in working with communication disorders. First, since communication ability is largely determined through imitation, it is important for the caregiver to engage in imitative behaviour and to encourage the child with communication difficulties to do the same. This may involve formal interactions, such as teaching finger plays, songs or poems, or less formal "playing" with sounds or words.

Second, the early childhood professional should regard all behaviour in the child as communication and to respond to it appropriately. For instance, if a toddler begins to cry, the role of the caregiver is to respond to the crying in an appropriate and sensitive way — not necessarily to stop the child from crying, but rather to find out what the child is attempting to communicate by crying and then responding. While the mode of communication may not be as sophisticated as that of the other children (for instance, a 4-year-old child who uses two-word phrases as the major means of communication), it is important to respond to the child's efforts positively and with encouragement, listening and responding to the content of the message, and engaging the child in a conversation in which turn-taking practice may occur.

Third, the caregiver should engage all of the children, including those with communication difficulties, in "real talk" at least once every day. Real talk is not restricted to giving directions, making statements of guidance, or engaging in small talk. Communication is first and foremost about exchanging ideas and thoughts; each child needs to feel sufficiently cared about to engage in an authentic conversation about something that concerns, interests, or challenges him or her.

Fourth, the early childhood professional should provide a rich communication model for the child, and should encourage all other children and adults to do the same. This involves many foci, including story-telling, singing, playing games that require imitation, joining in play, and making and maintaining face-to-face contact with the person with whom one is communicating.

Attitude

It is too easy to judge people on the basis of their ability to communicate. A child whose vocabulary does not seem as extensive as that of his or her peers, whose speech is not clear, or who responds to requests or conversations in an unsophisticated way may be prejudged to be slow learning, disinterested, a behaviour problem, or simply too difficult to attempt to talk to. The attitude of the early childhood professional toward children with communication difficulties is critical for the children's well-being in general and for further development in the area of communication in particular. Children who have difficulty making themselves understood or who experience isolation because peers and adults avoid communicating with them receive messages that may not only damage their self-esteem but that also prevent them from practising and improving their communication skills.

The early childhood professional must be sensitive to the child's difficulty. A child going through a period of disfluency (stuttering, for example), should not be pressured to speak publicly in front of a group of peers at a circle time or similar event. Nor should the same child have the disfluency pointed out or corrected each time he or she is in conversation with the caregiver. It is important to listen and watch for the message that the child is attempting to convey and to respond to it.

An example of this technique may be seen in the response of a mother to her young toddler who is beginning to learn to talk. The boy, looking out of the window, may say, "Daddy gone brrrm brrrm." The mother's typical reply may be "Yes, Daddy's gone brrrm brrrm. Daddy's gone to work in the car." She listens for the message and responds to that. She does not correct the child's language or laugh in a hurtful way at the unrefined manner in which he talks; in fact, she may repeat his words and sounds, thereby sending the message that she has heard and understood his communication. She then repeats what he has said in a more sophisticated way, not expecting that he will instantly correct his attempts but that he has heard this slightly more "correct" way of communicating the message.

The sensitivity of the early childhood professional extends to projecting an attitude of acceptance and belonging to the child. Van Manen (1988) suggests that the purpose for seeing a child is that the child knows he has been seen. In the area of communication, this may be interpreted to mean that all children need to experience belonging and to communicate comfortably and meaningfully about their concerns, interests, and challenges. The early childhood professional should not only respond to these communication attempts in an authentic and interested way but should also initiate and engage the child in "real talk" or meaningful conversation whenever appropriate, but at least once every day.

Acceptance of the child's communication attempts has been referred to as "recognizing all behaviour as communication." Adults generally are very good at recognizing the behaviours of infants as attempts to communicate — sometimes even when the baby doesn't intend to communicate. So, when the baby smiles, big brother may smile back and say, "Are you smiling at me?" Or when the toddler says "mamamama" as a part of her babbling routine, Grandmother may respond "Mommy mommy, yes, mommy will be here soon." When the 3-year-old falls from his tricycle and comes crying to the kitchen, saying "Owie, owie," Mom may respond with a hug and "Poor you, did you fall and hurt yourself? Let me see. Shall we put a Band-Aid on it?"

As children increase in size and physical maturity, we expect their attempts to communicate to become more sophisticated, and it may be more difficult to recognize and respond appropriately to a 5-year-old child who uses vocalizations or gestures as her primary mode of communication. It is, however, important for the early childhood professional to accept the child's communication mode and speech patterns as the starting point for future communication development.

The attitude of the early childhood professional is especially meaningful for the child whose development in communication is delayed. First, it is important to provide an environment in which communication is expected and encouraged. A language-rich program in which views are openly expressed, feelings and emotions are described, interests are discussed, and new information and knowledge are actively pursued is important for all children.

Second, early childhood professionals need to use all of their expertise in observing and monitoring the communication development of each child in their care. This includes maintaining records to ensure that each child is making progress in his or her development toward sophisticated adult communication. For children who appear to have some difficulties, it is important to identify what these difficulties might be — are they in the areas of receptive or expressive language, speech production, or non-verbal communication?

Third, it is important to remember that children may have communication difficulties that are not always obvious. For example, the "leader" who dominates interactions with others, not permitting them to take turns in conversation or in play, may have difficulties in basic conversation skills that are easily overlooked. Similarly, the child who selects quiet play, often engaging in solitary play activities, who appears shy and well-behaved, may have difficulties in communication not unlike those of the "leader." Possibly neither of these children understands the importance of maintaining a balance of receptive and expressive language (turn-taking) in conversation and communication with others.

Fourth, the early childhood professional needs to work closely with the parents of a child with communication problems, both to help determine the nature of the problem and to develop strategies to help the child's development. Working with parents may also extend to working collaboratively with other professionals. In the case of communication, the professional who will be most involved is the speech and language pathologist (speech therapist). Other professional personnel may include psychologists; ear, nose and throat specialists; and occupational therapists or physiotherapists.

STRATEGIES

This chapter has discussed a number of strategies for the successful inclusion of a child with communication difficulties into an early childhood group setting. This section will articulate these strategies clearly and concisely and add other suggestions.

Strategies that provide an environment that promotes communication include:

1. those providing physical environments in which the setting, materials, and schedule of activities set the stage for communication; and,
2. those providing social environments in which conversation and non-verbal interactions occur constantly and comfortably and in which there are responsive adults and children.

Both types of strategies require the early childhood professional to remain aware and sensitive to each child's communicative attempts — especially those of children who appear to have some difficulty in this area — and to maintain careful records of language and speech development. Becoming comfortable with techniques such as paraphrasing helps to create communication dialogue for children and may lead to conversation attempts. For instance, when a child gestures that he wants to be held by raising his arms, you might respond with "You want up?" or, when a child makes a long statement about a confrontation she has had with another child, you might respond with "Mabel took your toy and you are upset at her?"

Perhaps the most important strategy, however, is to construct the total environment — physical, social, and emotional — around the needs, abilities, and interests of the children within it. A play-focussed setting, in which children choose topics or areas of play that interest them and partners with whom they wish to play, provides opportunities for interactions with materials, people, and settings. In this natural world you as caregiver may use any number of strategies to encourage the child to communicate: become a play partner with the child, take turns with him or her, provide physical or verbal clues about when to take a turn, and respond to all communication efforts in ways that encourage a continuation of the communication.

SCENARIO

Cheryl found that working with a group of 4-year-old children was both challenging and exciting. She was, however, worried about Martin, whose attempts to communicate with her and the other children were difficult to understand. Often he made no attempt at all beyond pointing at or simply taking what he wanted. Cheryl decided to try a number of strategies to put some pressure on Martin to communicate more. First, she identified some of his favourite toys and materials and put them in view but out of reach (on a high shelf). Second, she started to give him fewer materials than he needed (for instance, she provided paints and paper but no brushes or sponges). Third, she began to arrange "silly" situations for Martin (for example, she put modelling clay on his plate at snack time instead of giving him a cracker).

Cheryl then watched what happened to Martin and his communication efforts. One or two of the strategies she modified because they were ineffective or because they appeared only to cause frustration for Martin and for other children. Other strategies, she found, brought a response from Martin, and she was able to engage him in meaningful dialogue as he asked for additional materials or laughed at silly situations.

The physical environment we invent for young children is very important in creating an atmosphere conducive to healthy development and learning. Typically, early childhood professionals consider a number of important variables in setting up such an environment, including traffic flow, safety, public and private space, noisy and quiet places, and soft and hard areas. Often the overriding factor in making such decisions is to encourage independence in children. We look for ways for children to be able to choose materials from shelves that are easily accessible, to be able to toilet themselves without needing to ask for help, and to be able to move materials around the room in order to make play ever more complex. The above scenario illustrates one child-care practitioner's attempts to also consider ways of creating an environment that encourages a certain level of dependence or interdependence and especially stresses the need to communicate with others.

A second planning strategy involves planning specific social interaction strategies that encourage the child's communication efforts. These strategies include identifying the child's communication abilities through careful observation, identifying the child's primary mode of communication, setting up play situations in which joint turn-taking can occur within the child's mode of communication, and "teaching" other children how to communicate and play with the child who experiences communication difficulties.

Planning in a Developmental Context
Play

Play involves interaction. Children interact with materials, their environment, and play partners in make-believe ways in order to learn about themselves and their relationship to the world they live in. These interactions generally involve communication with others. To be successful players, children learn both to associate and to co-operate with others to determine the topic of the play, the various roles they will play, the direction the play will take, the materials to be used, the space and time in which play will occur, and the rules that will govern the play. The skills that are basic to successful play with others are the same as those that form the structure of good communication: balanced turn-taking, sometimes taking the lead and sometimes following the lead of others, authentic engagement with materials and people, and interest in the topic.

Children with communication difficulties may experience problems in developing play skills. They may choose isolated play activities, such as making puzzles or painting pictures, or spend long periods watching others play together, but always remain just outside the play itself. When they do engage in play with or alongside others, they may be subject to comments from other children who experience problems with their communication. Other children with communication difficulties may attempt to engage in play with them but may get into trouble with them because they take over the play or conversations so that the others do not have the opportunity to take turns.

It is important for caregivers to provide play experiences for children with communication problems in which they interact with materials and other children in pretend play. A starting point for such development is that the adult becomes the play partner to the child, following the child's lead and taking turns in the activity, rather than sitting on the outside watching and commenting on the child's play.

SCENARIO

Four-year-old Martha was diagnosed as having Down Syndrome. She had difficulty in areas of communication that resulted in her spending a lot of time playing alone or looking at books. Trent, her primary caregiver, decided to attempt to improve her inclusion in play settings. One day, when Martha was standing by the water table and pouring water from a cup, Trent approached Martha, held out his hand, and said "My turn." At first Martha just looked at him and stopped her play. Trent gently took the cup from Martha and repeated, "My turn." Martha looked as though she might cry. Trent quickly dipped the cup into the water, poured some out (imitating Martha's actions), and gave the cup back to Martha. "Your turn," he said, and indicated that she should pour the water again. Although Martha was uncertain at first (she probably expected Trent to take over the play or to change it to a formal teaching situation), she soon realized that Trent wanted to play with her and was willing to follow her lead. She was delighted and engaged in turn-taking play. Sometimes she took more turns than Trent, but generally they achieved a balance of give and take.

Some weeks later, Trent and Martha had established several good joint-attention routines in which they imitated each other's actions, took turns, and made brief verbal comments to each other. At this point Trent decided to introduce other children to the play. To begin, he identified three other children who had good play skills and who were comfortable playing with other children and adopting different roles in their play. He then suggested to Martha that they invite someone else to play with them. Again Martha was reluctant and unsure, but Trent continued and invited Patricia, one of the three children he had previously identified. Trent and the two girls continued with turn-taking play for a few minutes, with Trent taking slightly fewer turns and encouraging Martha and Patricia to play together.

After playing a few games in this way, Trent invited another child to the play. He gradually built up a small social group for Martha. These children were willing and able to play with her, to encourage her to interact in playful ways, and to introduce her to more advanced play and communication.

Social

Social development depends on interaction with others, and this may be difficult for many children with communication disorders. Some children may exhibit behaviours that are difficult to interpret or that present problems for the adults and children around them. Children, with profound problems such as autism may exhibit behaviours that appear antisocial and bizarre, and regular forms of speech and language may not be a part of their communication repertoire. It is important to seek help from other professionals when working with children with these problems.

An important strategy in working with all children with communication disorders is to provide other children with the skills to communicate. If a child has delayed speech and language, for instance, it may be necessary to teach other children to begin a conversation, stop, wait, and prompt or signal to the child that it is his or her turn to talk. Language provides avenues through which all children get to know and understand themselves and their world, to identify their feelings, emotions, and behaviours, and to mediate them. The child with communication difficulties requires additional help in these areas.

Emotional

As is the case with children who have a hearing loss, children with communication difficulties may have problems in relating to others and in fully understanding what is occurring around them. They may also receive messages of non-acceptance by peers who do not know how to respond to their unsophisticated communication attempts. As a result, they may be isolated by peers or may remove themselves from social-interaction settings. Without peer interaction, in particular, children with communication difficulties may develop a distorted view of themselves, possibly as not belonging or as unacceptable. Developing a healthy and positive self-image for each child is an important aspect of the work of early childhood professionals; the child whose communication is delayed may require extra attention.

Cognitive

Although several theories attempt to explain how and why children learn language as their primary form of communication, we do know that speech and language development are related in a general way to physical maturation, cognitive development, and socialization. As very young infants, children communicate without any particular intent or understanding. Others who see their actions or hear their cries interpret the communication. When the baby starts to cry, the mother may say, "Oh, he must be hungry. That's why he is crying," and then proceeds to feed the baby; or she may say, "Maybe the baby is tired. That's why she is crying," and then cuddles the baby until she falls asleep. Over time, the baby communicates his or her needs more precisely, and adults concerned with everyday care may learn to differentiate what the crying means.

As children grow older and begin to learn that the sounds others make have meaning and that language provides an efficient way to structure concepts and assist with memory, they begin to approximate the sounds of others as a way of communicating with them. However, initial vocalizations (babbling) only have meaning when others interpret the sounds; so, when the toddler says "dadadada," the mother may say, "Dada, Daddy. Where is Daddy?" As children's concepts become more refined and they understand their world more precisely, their expressive language reflects their thinking. Thus at the age of 15 months, children may say "Doggie" when looking at a sheep, intending the word to convey the concept of "animal"; at the age of 5 years, however, they are unlikely to make this error because they now classify animals into many subcategories.

A child with receptive language difficulties may miss many of the concepts important to cognitive development, and a child with expressive language problems may make errors in explaining these concepts to others. Language provides the framework for thinking and memory. It provides a powerful "short-hand" for complex thoughts and for seeing connections between ideas. It is no coincidence that early memory and language development occur at about the same time in a young child's life. In these ways cognition and communication are closely linked, and the child with communication difficulties may be affected cognitively.

Summary

Children with communication difficulties may have difficulties in areas of socialization, maintaining self-esteem, and cognitive development. It is important to work sensitively with these children, whether their difficulties are temporary, as in the case of most disfluent speech, or more permanent, as in the case of a child with expressive aphasia. Learning to accept all behaviour as communication, to respond appropriately to the content of children's communication, and to use a mode of language to which the child can respond are important factors. The provision of a language-rich, interactive play environment, in which they belong and know that they are welcome, goes a long way to support children who have communication difficulties. Children without communication difficulties may be encouraged or taught to interact with children who are experiencing difficulties and to include them in their play and other activities.

ACTIVITIES

1. Describe the stages through which language and speech change to eventually become social speech.

2. Invite a local speech and language pathologist or therapist to talk to you about the work he or she does with young children who have communication difficulties.

3. Practise "turn-taking" with a colleague: one plays the part of the child with communication difficulties, and the other plays the early childood professional. Try to take turns with the child in the language mode that she or he uses, such as single words, simple phrases, and physical gestures. How successful were you? What was difficult about this exercise? What did you learn about communication?

DISCUSSION QUESTIONS

1. How does modern technology help and/or hinder the development of communication abilities in young children?

2. A parent tells you that the reason her 4-year-old son cannot talk in understandable sentences is because his father and uncle were also late talkers, so there is no need to worry. What would you say? What would you do? Why?

3. List and describe ten ways to ensure that you provide a language-rich, inclusive environment for all young children, whatever their communication abilities.

Behavioural and Emotional Challenges

CHAPTER 7

Introduction

Children with behavioural and emotional challenges can be the most interesting and challenging group of children to work with. Conversely, they can be also the most frustrating. This is due, in part, to their diverse range of behavioural challenges. These behavioural challenges may exist on their own, that is, some conditions have a strong behavioural base; or they may result from other conditions. For example, a child's severe language or speech delay may indirectly result in problem behaviours. Behavioural challenges may also be considered as a part of normal growth and development, for example, "the terrible twos." As children develop a sense of autonomy and independence, they are often thought of as difficult.

It may in fact, be the case that children display inappropriate behaviours because of two or all of these factors. Although the literature never specifically discusses the topic, a child may have a condition that causes behavioural problems and still strive for autonomy in his or her early years. Although this might just be seen as an extension of the "behavioural problem," it may also be due to other factors such as development. This constellation of interacting factors is important for early childhood professionals to be aware of in identifying and planning for children's needs. This chapter considers the variety of interacting factors and some of the conditions specific to behavioural concerns.

After reading this chapter, you should have a better understanding of:

- the varying contexts of behavioural challenges: conditions may exist on their own, they may co-exist with other conditions, or they may be the result of normal development;

105

- behavioural challenges within a developmental context, including a review of temperament;
- specific conditions, such as attention deficit disorder, pervasive developmental disorders, autism, fragile X syndrome, and fetal alcohol syndrome;
- implications for development;
- the role of the early childhood professional.

TEMPERAMENT

Although information about the concept of temperament is familiar to most early childhood professionals, it may not be familiar to other professionals or parents and may never have been reviewed in the context of children presenting behavioural concerns.

Temperament refers to differences in the quality and intensity of individuals' emotional reactions (Berk, 1996). Thomas and Chess (1977) conducted a longitudinal study suggesting that children are born with different types of temperaments. These temperaments are inborn and can be seen in very young children. This explains why some babies are very passive and calm while others are loud and active, and why some infants seem to develop a schedule for eating and sleeping readily while other children struggle for years to achieve this. Temperamental traits tend to be stable over time, but this does not mean that they are unchangeable — traits may change as a result of growth and development and parenting practices (Berk, 1996). It is these traits that parents often recognize early in their children as personality, especially when they have other children to make comparisons with. The key temperaments are shown in Box 7.1.

Each of the temperamental characteristics has a continuum from low to high. Children may fit anywhere between the two extremes and may differ from one temperamental trait to another. For example, a child may have a high activity level but a very low regularity level. Sometimes, some of the traits coincide; for example, a child who is distractible is often active as well and may not persevere at tasks. When the child tends to display a number of characteristics at the high end of the continuum, he or she may be referred to as a difficult child (Turecki, 1989).

The assessment of these characteristics tends to be subjective. A parent who does not have a particular characteristic (for example, who approaches new settings readily) may be concerned about and influenced by a child who has the opposite temperament (for example, who withdraws in new or unfamiliar settings). When parents or caregivers see some of their personality and traits in the child, they are not as likely to label the child or have as many concerns. For example, if the father was a picky eater and picky about which clothes he wore, he is more likely to understand his son's complaints and needs than the father who does not have this trait. This tendency has been referred to as goodness of fit (Berk, 1996; Thomas and Chess, 1977). A good fit between the characteristics of the child and of the parent or caregiver may promote development, whereas a poor fit may lead to interferences in learning and development.

BOX 7.1 KEY TEMPERAMENTS

Activity Level The amount of time spent in active movement. Some children are very active; other children are not.

Adaptability The ease with which one adapts to changes in the environment. Some children adapt quickly and quietly to the routine changes of the day, whereas others have more difficulty and require more support.

Rythmicity The regularity of bodily functions such as eating, sleeping, and eliminating. Some children are predictable in terms of when and how long they sleep and when they eat; others never seem to develop a routine.

Distractibility How easily stimulation from the environment changes one's behaviour. Some children remain absorbed in an activity no matter what else is happening, whereas others are easily distracted by something new or novel.

Attention Span and Persistence The length of time one is engaged in an activity. Some children will spend long periods of time engaged in activities such as eating or play. Some children persist at an activity until it is complete or done, whereas others pay attention for only short periods of time.

Approach/Withdrawal The way in which one responds to new objects or people in the environment. Some children will shy away or withdraw from new things, whereas others will join in on their own.

Threshold of Responsiveness The degree of stimulation required to get a response. Some children react to the slightest noise or movement in the room while other children seem not to notice.

Intensity of Reaction The strength of one's reactions. Some children react intensely, whether happy, sad, or upset. Some just seem to be loud and always noticeable. Others react very mildly and quietly.

Quality of Mood The dominant attitude or feeling. Some children seem naturally happy and friendly, whereas others appear unhappy or sullen by nature.

SCENARIO

Marcie, an extremely picky 3-year-old girl, ate only certain foods of certain consistencies and wore certain clothing most of the time. If her mother tried to get her to wear different clothes, Marcie would cry and have a tantrum. If her mother succeeded, Marcie was miserable the whole day. Marcie's mother soon learned to let Marcie choose her own clothes.

Marcie's mother had difficulty in understanding what pleased and displeased Marcie since she herself was a very adaptable person. Because she did not understand Marcie's needs, it was difficult to understand what to do to keep her happy, and Marcie and her mother often battled over clothing and food choices.

Marcie's father, on the other hand, was somewhat more like Marcie. He too only wore certain fabrics and restricted his diet to certain foods. He was better able to understand Marcie's complaints and needs and allow her to make choices for herself. He very infrequently battled with Marcie over these matters. Marcie's mother felt that he was indulging Marcie rather than teaching her to be adaptable.

In this scenario, we see a good fit between the characteristics of Marcie and her father and less of a fit between Marcie and her mother. The degree of fit leads people to see and interpret the child's behaviour in very different ways. This difference in fit need not interfere with development and learning, as long as people are aware of the differences and accommodate them.

Children with special needs also have unique temperamental characteristics, although the developmental literature does not openly acknowledge this. Each child has a unique personality and temperamental traits that account for some of the variation among individuals; the same is true for children with special needs.

Consider the following situations and decide if the situation is one in which the child could be identified as a behavioural concern or if it illustrates a temperamental characteristic:

SCENARIO

Three-year-old Jason becomes agitated whenever the caregiver tells him it is time to clean up. He will typically have a tantrum, throw toys, and cry.

Two-year-old Shameek clings to his mother each morning when she arrives and cries for a long time after his mother leaves. He is very hesitant to join in with the group and usually needs a caregiver to accompany him.

Five-year-old Gisela is considered the pickiest eater in the day-care centre. She will not touch food that is mushy and always gags on foods that vary in texture. She drinks only liquids that are at room temperature and will not drink anything carbonated. Mealtimes tend to be an unhappy time for Gisela and the group.

Four-year-old Sheldon is always ready and looking for action. He seems to feed off of the emotions of the other children. If another child is upset and crying, Sheldon cries too. If a group of children are loud and boisterous, Sheldon is usually right in the middle of the action. Loud voices, music, and excitement always get him going.

Two-year-old Fatima can be quiet and charming, but when she decides that she wants something, she can be very different. Yesterday, all the children were at the sand table playing for quite a long period of time (for toddlers). Out of the blue, she swung a pail into Cal's face and yelled, "Go away, mine!"

As you read these scenarios, if you have been thinking about children with special needs, you may consider each child to have a behavioural concern and, accordingly, treat each behaviour as a behaviour problem. If you have been thinking about typically developing children, you may see the behaviours as indicating a temperamental trait (such as withdrawal, adaptability, activity level) or as a normal stage of development (for example, autonomy). As a result, your approach to each of these children will be different. It is important to remember that the way you view the child is a result of your own perspective. If you see the child as delayed, you may view all behaviours as a result of the delay and treat the underlying behavioural problem. If you see the behaviours as a part of normal development, your practices will reflect this.

SCENARIO

In a playroom for 3-year-olds, a mother came in and left a bright blue box with a birthday cake on the side counter. Shortly after, Gunder walked over and tried to pull the box down. He almost succeeded, but when the caregiver noticed what he was doing she gently removed his hands, explained what was inside, and asked if he would like to see. She showed him the cake and explained why he couldn't take it off the shelf. She then suggested that he could help when the time came, but that he should now join the group for story time.

A short time later, Derek went to explore the box and almost tipped it over the edge before the caregiver noticed. The caregiver darted across the room and gently pulled Derek away, saying, "No, don't touch. Don't pull things off the counter." She led him to the story telling and sat him down in the group.

You can see in this scenario how differently the caregiver responds to and deals with behaviours, depending on the child and her perception of his behaviour. The difference between the two children is that Derek has Down Syndrome and Gunder does not.

Again, it is essential for caregivers to consider that behavioural or emotional concerns may result from a variety of factors or from an interaction of those factors. Considering each child in a developmental context in which all aspects of development and behaviour are taken into account may be a good starting point.

Causes and Etiology

Most of the conditions associated with behavioural concerns do not have a known cause or etiology. Over the years, much research has been conducted and many factors have been put forward to explain emotional problems. Some recent studies suggest a biological base, and research in this area continues. Others have posited an environmental base, which may include parenting, discipline issues, the weakening of family structures, substitute caregiving, and stress. Although it is likely that some combination of biological and environmental factors contribute to behavioural problems, it is still commonly thought that lack of parenting and discipline is the key contributing factor.

SCENARIO

Thomas has been coming to the day-care centre for two years. He has been on a program to monitor his behavioural outbursts. His mother and father separated last year, but Thomas seemed to handle it well as a result of some support and structure added to his ongoing program. Now, he is distracted, sleepy, and generally irritable. The behavioural program has recorded a marked increase in all inappropriate behaviours. His caregivers have mentioned this to his mother on several occasions, but she too seems preoccupied and distracted. She has begun dating again and Thomas is being left with a baby sitter, so his programming and sleeping routines have been neglected. His caregivers assume that this is the root of the change of behaviour and believe that if his mother would just spend more time with him and re-establish his routines, Thomas would be his old self again.

Thomas's caregiver finds the opportunity to talk to his mother. As soon as she states that she has concerns and suggests that Thomas's mother needs to focus on his ongoing programs, his mother breaks down into tears. The last four months have been miserable; the only job she can find is split shifts, and finding child care to fit in around her working hours has been impossible. On top of that, Thomas's dad has been attempting to gain custody of him, so he has interfered with baby sitters and taken Thomas to his home on occasion, called their lawyer, and filed reports of neglect.

"This is as much as I can manage to do to keep Thomas and myself going at this point," Thomas's mother explains. Rather than lecturing her about Thomas's need for rest and routines, the caregiver decides to find some local resources for respite care and potential child-care services.

This scenario illustrates the difficulty of determining one cause for particular behaviours. Typically, several factors coexist and may even interact. For example, we may surmise that

Thomas's mother has been living under a lot of stress and perhaps has not been as able to parent and discipline consistently. All of the factors and the interrelationships between factors need to be considered. Can you think of ways to best deal with Thomas and his family?

Determining the cause of behavioural problems usually seems to be related to the conceptual model applied. Thus, Freudian psychologists attempt to determine the subconscious phenomenon underlying the inner turmoil. Behavioural psychologists are more apt to look at factors in the child's environment and ways for the child to learn new ways of interacting. Others will consider organic or genetic causes. However, there seems to be little empirical evidence linking behavioural problems to particular causes (Winzer, 1990). The emphasis seems to be on treatment.

DIAGNOSIS AND ASSESSMENT

The assessment and diagnosis of behavioural problems also is based on the conceptual model used. The identification of behavioural problems does not seem to cause concerns — children who behave differently and do not conform to the group are often easily identified by early childhood professionals and parents. This usually appears to be a product of informal judgements, which seem to be fairly reliable (Winzer, 1990). However, early childhood professionals must maintain an air of caution in making informal judgements.

SCENARIO

Jalid was a 5-year-old boy who attended a day-care centre and kindergarten within the centre. The centre was in a fitness club, so it provided many opportunities for all of the children to be active both indoors and outdoors. The day began with physical activities, the children then spent extensive periods of time outdoors, and the day ended in the gym with free activities. Jalid fit right in. He was active during all of the active times but was able to settle and concentrate when the group was not active, such as during circle time, table activities, and lunch. If asked, the caregivers would say that Jalid was an active little boy, but they rarely expressed concerns about his behaviour.

The next fall, Jason started grade one. The teacher had just returned from a leave and had taught high school biology before making the change to elementary school. Moving into a grade one class was her desire, and her leave had been used to prepare for the transition. Nothing, however, had prepared her for Jalid. Jalid did not sit, could not concentrate, and was judged by her to be unruly and not ready for school. By the end of November, she suggested that the parents review the placement and hold Jalid back one year. Jalid's parents were shocked because reports from his kindergarten teacher and day-care staff had been much more positive.

Even though professional judgements tend to be reliable, these observations usually are subjective and may vary, depending on the environment. In this scenario, Jalid's behaviour did not seem active in the day-care centre but looked very active in the classroom.

Observations about behaviour may depend on the people making them and on their particular expectations. If you are a parent of a quiet little girl, you may find little boys very active and very loud. Personalities may also play a role. For example, some children's behaviours just seem to get on the nerves of some parents and caregivers; whining is a good example. Other adults are not as bothered by the behaviour, so they may judge it differently or not notice it as frequently.

Many factors interact and play a role in our perceptions of behaviours and behavioural problems. Therefore, it is important to observe the child carefully in all environments and discuss these observations with others, particularly parents, to ensure that all information is considered.

SCENARIO

Bernice was 4 years old and her brother Bernie was 5. Both attended the same day-care centre. Bernie was considered to be very active and highly distractible. Although he was never diagnosed, his caregivers had a lot of difficulty with him and assumed that he would have major difficulties in kindergarten and school. Bernice, on the other hand, on some days appeared to be bright, following along with the activities of the group and participating openly. On other days, she seemed lethargic and confused. On one day she could recognize her name on her locker, but on the next day she could not. The caregivers assumed that she was like her brother, although not as active.

Bernice's mother had Bernice's eyes checked. It was found that Bernice had less than 30 percent vision in one eye and 100 percent vision in the other. Although she was very good at compensating and using her good eye, that eye tired very quickly because she relied on it so much and her behaviour would change.

It seems that Bernice behaved the way she did not because she was like her brother, but for another reason. Caregivers must remember to consider the unique characteristics of each child and not to rely on easy assumptions.

Classification

The terms "behavioural disorders" and "emotional disturbances" have defied a clear definition or classification. Their definitions appear to be related to the particular perspective or discipline used to assess them, and many factors have interfered with developing clear definitions. For example, it is difficult to determine what is abnormal when the meaning of normal is unclear. Behaviours and emotions have a vast range and vary from situation to situation, making it difficult to categorize them as normal or abnormal. Similarly, behavioural expectations vary from one situation to the next. While it may be acceptable to yell and run in the gym, it may not be appropriate in a church.

In addition, the judgement of a behaviour as deviant may be based on an individual's interpretation of the rules. What may be judged as inappropriate for one person may not be so for another, because of cultural or social expectations. For example, some cultural groups have a much lower tolerance for respecting adults than other groups do. Thus, their expectations and judgements of inappropriate behaviours may vary. Also, it is important to remember that all people engage in a range of behaviours. Just as 'normal' people engage in abnormal behaviours, it is possible for children diagnosed with behavioural problems to engage in appropriate behaviours. All of these factors make it difficult to arrive at a definition of what an emotional or behavioural concern may be.

All children exhibit behavioural or emotional problems at some time, but it is the length, severity, and unacceptability of the behaviour that determines whether it will be determined a problem or a disorder.

Social emotional disabilities are characterized by difficulties in developing and maintaining interpersonal relations, inappropriate feelings or behaviour, depression or unhappiness, and physical symptoms or fears related to personal problems (Dunlap, 1997b). These aspects are generally difficult to identify and are typically assessed subjectively. Some may be transient because they are reactions to environmental events, whereas others are more permanent.

Emotional and behavioural problems can be categorized as externalizing and internalizing (Deiner, 1993). Externalizing behaviours include aggressive behaviour, destructive behaviour, temper tantrums, hitting, and biting. Internalizing behaviours include withdrawal, anxiety, crying, unresponsiveness, shyness, and isolation. Some of these behaviours occur as a part of normal development; for example, hitting is common for older babies and biting is common for toddlers. When the behaviours persist beyond the expected ages or increase in intensity or frequency, however, they are considered behavioural problems.

Specific Conditions

PERVASIVE DEVELOPMENTAL DISORDERS

Pervasive developmental disorders (PDD) are characterized by difficulties in communication and social interaction and by stereotyped and ritualized behaviours that lead to poor play behaviours (Mauk, Reber, and Batshaw, 1997).

The most severe type of PDD is autism. Communication for children with autism is typically delayed, often echolalic, and idiosyncratic. These children may require alternative systems of communication to communicate in a meaningful way. Social interaction concerns may include lack of eye contact, little interest in the feelings or thoughts of others, indifference to people, and lack of friendships. Related to this, is the inability to imitate or engage in pretend play. In terms of behaviour, children with autism engage in stereotypic patterns of behaviour, such as rituals and routines, and are resistant to change. They often engage in stereotypic movements such as hand flapping, rocking, spinning, or head banging. Their play often involves stereotypic patterns focussed on one aspect of a toy (for example, repeatedly spinning wheels). Children with autism may overreact to environmental sounds and odours. Autism is typically associated with mental retardation (Mauk, Reber, and Batshaw, 1997).

Rett syndrome is a progressive neurological disorder that affects girls primarily. These children progress normally during the first year of life, but then their behaviour, language, and cognitive abilities deteriorate. Rett syndrome is characterized by autistic behaviours (for example, stereotypic behaviour), seizures, mental retardation, and progressive spasticity in the lower limbs.

The classification of PDD is used when either of these two conditions is not clearly diagnosed and when there are abnormal patterns of communication, social interactions, and behaviours too brief or too insufficient to be called autism. These behaviours are often called autistic-like behaviour.

Fragile X Syndrome

Fragile X syndrome results from an abnormality of the X chromosome. It results in children having a characteristic appearance — elongated face, a prominent jaw and forehead, large ears, a high-arched palate, and flat feet. These features tend to become more prominent with age. In addition, children with fragile X syndrome experience developmental and speech delays and demonstrate stereotypic behaviours such as hand flapping, making little eye contact, tactile defensiveness, and disciplinary problems, as well as characteristics typically associated with attention deficit hyperactive disorder (Batshaw, 1997). Although fragile X syndrome affects boys and girls, it is usually more severe for boys than for girls.

Attention Deficit Disorder and Attention Deficit Hyperactive Disorder

Attention deficit disorder (ADD) and attention deficit hyperactive disorder (ADHD) are some of the most common neurological disorders of childhood and have been called by a variety of names over the years (Blum and Mercugliano, 1997). Children with ADD or ADHD tend to have persistent difficulty with their attention span, impulse control, and organization. As a result they dislike waiting and following rules, have low frustration levels, bore easily, are unable to recognize consequences and learn from mistakes, and have difficulty in reading cues associated with social behaviour (Blum and Mercugliano, 1997). These symptoms may or may not be accompanied by hyperactivity. The significant difference between the two conditions is the level and amount of excessive motor activity; ADHD children exhibit more motor activity. The difference, however, is sometimes difficult to actually distinguish.

The difficulties associated with ADD and ADHD become more noticeable at school age, when distractibility and the degree of activity are more noticeable and disruptive. Associated problems of learning, behaviour, and emotion become more noticeable in school settings as well. However, ADD and ADHD are being diagnosed more and more for preschool-aged children. This sometimes results from the child's environment and sometimes results from people's expectations.

SCENARIO

Mario was in a day-care centre where he was in kindergarten for half of the day and in day care for the other half. The kindergarten program was in the morning and was highly structured and had a circle time, French class, and computer class scheduled for each day. The day-care portion was very unstructured; free play and outdoor play dominated the schedule. The kindergarten consisted of one teacher and one assistant. The day-care component had two caregivers. The four staff met regularly to share and exchange observations of the children and program.

After the end of the third month, the early childhood professionals met to discuss the program and the children. The kindergarten teacher began by stating that she had requested a referral for Mario and was going to call a case conference with his parents because she felt that he displayed characteristics associated with ADHD. She described him as disruptive, impulsive, not able to wait his turn, and unable to listen. The two caregivers from the day care were surprised, to say the least. They described Mario as active, energetic, curious, and creative. They did agree that, like all 5-year-olds, he did not like to wait or listen.

This scenario shows how observation of the same child in different environments led to a very different description of the child and, potentially, to a very different approach to his behaviour.

Although the diagnosis of ADHD or ADD is based on clinical judgement, it cannot be denied that children with these characteristics are difficult to manage in group-care settings. In particular, health and safety are ongoing concerns because children with ADD or ADHD often do not anticipate the consequences of their actions and because excessively active children are at a high risk for accidents.

FETAL ALCOHOL SYNDROME (FAS)

Fetal slcohol syndrome (FAS) is a relatively new term. The disorder has been known for some time, but typically children with FAS were considered learning disabled or behavioural problems. The incidence of FAS ranges from 1 in 1000 in Canada and the United States generally to 1 in 8 in northern reserves. FAS usually results in developmental delays, growth deficiencies, particular facial features, and emotional and behavioural concerns. Children with FAS have characteristics similar to those of ADHD — hyperactivity, impulsiveness, and attention problems. They often disregard rules and authority figures, may experience difficulties in transitions, and may have difficulty in peer interactions.

All other problems that children with special needs exhibit are typically categorized and labelled as behavioural or emotional problems. These categories are open-ended: they include almost any and all characteristics of any and all degrees.

Implications

IMPLICATIONS FOR THE CHILD'S DEVELOPMENT

The characteristics of behavioural concerns are as varied in type and degree as is imaginable. Behaviours may range from outbursts to disruptive behaviours to withdrawal. The most troubling and noticeable are actions that involve injury to self or others or the destruction of property. Unco-operative behaviours, non-compliance, attention seeking, distractibility, and poor relationships with others are also common. All of these behaviours may be seen in children from time to time, but the child will likely become a concern when these behaviours occur over and over. The child may also demonstrate lags in other areas of development or difficulty in learning, even though there are no identified reasons for delays or learning difficulties.

Often children with behavioural difficulties display more than one problem. For example, it is not uncommon for children to exhibit inappropriate feelings, for example, to cry when laughter is expected or to get unusually excited over insignificant events. These children may have difficulty in developing social relationships with others in their environment, particularly with other children, who may not understand their actions. Their relationships with caregivers may also be strained, although adults are generally better at understanding their behaviour and attempting to assist. These difficult behaviours may continue and even escalate until intervention occurs.

Behaviours do not exist in isolation but interact with all other areas of development. Predictably, the child with behavioural concerns will likely have difficulties in forming and maintaining relationships with others, especially other children. At first, the difficulties in forming relationships are a friendship issue: "They won't play with me" or "He's being mean." Over time, as the behaviour continues, other children may neglect or reject their peer and children with a behaviour problem may begin to see themselves differently: "I am bad." Alienation, feelings of worthlessness, and lowered self-esteem may follow and interfere with the further development of social skills.

Children with behavioural difficulties often have communication difficulties, and there is a higher prevalence of behaviour disorders in children who have delayed language abilities (Winzer, 1990). This makes sense: if a child wants a toy, food, or attention but is unable to gain it by using words, he or she may then attempt to attain the desired item by using physical actions that have been successful in the past. Thus, the child comes to use and rely upon trusted methods of getting things and may not attempt to use language. This is particularly true when the child's efforts are successful. For example, if the child is successful at grabbing toys from other children, the motivation to learn a new way to get that toy may not be evident. The child continues to act in this way because it works.

Older children with behaviour problems may be seen to use language too much or in inappropriate ways. In normal development, children around the age of 4 to 5 go through a stage in language development in which they realize the power of language, particularly ways in which words can hurt. For instance, children will use words such as "hate." Just ask a parent whose 4-year-old has screamed "I hate you" for the first time — the message is very powerful indeed. Children may then learn that words can be used to hurt, to disrupt, and to control situations. The child then incorporates words and language as another means of acting out.

Studies suggest that most children with behavioural problems will experience cognitive and academic delays (Winzer, 1990). Often, people consider the child's behaviour problem to stem from the academic or cognitive problem rather than considering that cognitive difficulties may stem from behavioural problems. When the child is engaged in inappropriate behaviours and has strong emotions and strong needs, he or she may not be receptive to learning in cognitive areas or in other areas like language or social skills.

Other areas of development are typically affected by behavioural concerns, so caregivers may need to pay special attention. A child who is very active and distractible may have no developmental concerns in physical abilities, but if the child frequently "sits out" of structured learning activities because of his or her behaviour, the opportunities for learning may be minimized. This may occur in any area of the child's development and thus impair development in other areas.

IMPLICATIONS FOR OTHERS

SCENARIO

A practicum supervisor went to a day-care centre to visit one of her students. The group of 4-year-olds were in the playground when she arrived. She was met at the gate by three of them, who informed her not to come in. When she asked why, they told her that Jimmy was out and that he would bite her and scratch her and kick her. They pointed to Jimmy, a lone, solitary figure in the corner of the playground.

Jimmy noticed the new person and started to move in her direction. When the children saw him approaching, they ran and began to yell "Jimmy's coming, watch out, watch out!" One child grabbed her hand and tried to get her to move to the caregiver too.

Jimmy's behaviour in this scenario is irrelevant; it is the behaviour of the other children that is important to note. It is difficult to know what Jimmy's intentions were in approaching the new person, but his behaviour was probably dictated, in part, by the response and expectations of the other children. How would you deal with Jimmy and the other children in this situation?

Children will take measures to protect themselves and others from being hit or hurt. They may avoid the individual, try to get assistance, or retaliate by using words and actions. Any of these actions will then affect the behaviour of the child with behavioural problems, who may now also be feeling rejected, different, or disliked. Thus, it is critical to be aware of a behaviour's impact on all children and to include the children in dealing with the problem as much as possible.

Adults may also find themselves attempting to arrange the environment to circumvent difficulties. Caregivers must be cognizant of how these attempts are made and why.

SCENARIO

Aten was a very active and disruptive 3-year-old. He was constantly getting into trouble by grabbing toys, hitting, pinching, and occasionally biting, if he felt the situation warranted it. Robyn was one of three caregivers in the room. She interacted well with Aten, and he appeared to listen to her most of the time. Over time, Aten became Robyn's charge more regularly. She was comfortable with having him in her group, and the other caregivers were happy to have a group without him. Eventually the same children tended to be grouped with Aten and Robyn, and as a result other children never had the opportunity to interact with him.

After many weeks of this arrangement, Robyn became ill and was off work for a week. All hell broke loose in the playroom. Caregivers who had not had to deal with Aten's behaviour now had to, and Aten had to interact with adults who typically ignored or avoided him. Children who were not accustomed to his behaviour were now fresh targets for him.

This scenario illustrates how the environment was arranged very comfortably for the staff and children. It is evident, however, that the caregivers were not really dealing with Aten's behaviour but managing it. How would you attend to Aten's needs while at the same time meeting the needs of the other children in this group?

Role of the Early Childhood Professional

The early childhood professional must remain cognizant of the needs of all the children in the playroom in relation to the needs of the individual child with problems. This is especially true in managing groups that include children with behaviour problems. Children do not like to get hurt, and their parents like it even less; thus, the role of the early childhood professional is central in ensuring that all children feel protected and are safe.

ATTITUDES

Early childhood professionals again should examine their attitudes toward children who present behavioural concerns. Some adults find these children a worthwhile challenge and are willing to take them on, while others resent the time and attention these children take from the group. Their attitudes may include sentiments such as: "The only thing this child needs is a firm hand and more discipline at home. Poor parenting is the cause of the problem." Caregivers need to observe the behaviours in context, both in terms of the development of the child and in the context of the playroom. It is also useful to be aware of cultural perspectives and the effect that these may have on the child's behaviour. With awareness will come understanding.

STRATEGIES

The most common interventions are behaviour management methods. These methods have been tested for many years and found to be effective in dealing with inappropriate behaviours, so they are likely to continue to be used. Caution, however, is in order. Caregivers must remember to consider the whole child, including the child's desires, needs, wants, likes, dislikes, the home environment, and what's happening in all areas of development, rather than just "the behaviour". Following are some issues to consider.

The first issue is that behaviour management is based on the idea that behaviours are caused by a stimulus. The stimulus and the behaviour should be observable and measurable, especially if adults want to deal with the behaviours. Behaviour management, however, neglects to account for unobservable and unmeasurable stimuli that may cause the behaviour, namely, feelings such as loneliness and internal states such as hunger. These stimuli may play a role in actions or behaviours.

Thus, it is important not only to stop inappropriate actions but also to determine why they occurred by talking to and observing the child. Young children are at a stage of development in which they are just beginning to understand feelings and emotions. Early childhood professionals can ensure that this development occurs by attending to and naming some of these feelings for children. The first step in anger management may be realizing that anger is the emotion that one is feeling.

Next, the child needs to learn ways to deal with this emotion. Hitting may be one way to solve the problem and may be effective (because it works), but the child must learn that there are other ways to solve the problem. It is common for adults working with children with behavioural problems to become attuned to impending difficulties and to stop behaviours when or before they occur. Although this is necessary, it is also important to use these occasions for teaching the child an appropriate way of dealing with a difficult situation.

One way to consider the whole child is provided by the following example of the vicious cycle, in which many different behaviours by various people can work together to create or perpetuate problems. This cycle is typically seen in parent–child interactions, in which there is an emotional bond that makes it difficult to deal with the behaviour objectively.

The child engages in inappropriate behaviour. The adults deal with the behaviour as they deem acceptable. The child continues engaging in inappropriate behaviours. The adults may begin to think of themselves as incompetent ("Why can't I control this child? Why does a 2-year-old run my life?"). The adults may then begin to deal with the behaviour on a more personal level ("This child hates me"), and may begin to punish the child because of the feeling invoked in the adults ("You embarrassed me. You made me look incompetent"), rather than dealing with the behaviour itself.

Adults often are dealing with their own emotions regarding the child's behaviour problems. These emotions may include feelings of incompetence, loneliness, or loss of control. They may also be inconsistent in dealing with recurring behaviours because of their feelings. For example, one day they may tolerate very little, but the next day they may be exhausted and let the child behave in any way. The child may be getting very mixed messages and may begin to think of himself or herself as bad. In conjunction with this, the adults may be receiving advice from professionals and other parents about how to deal with the problem. This advice may create more negative emotions about themselves, but the adults may follow these new suggestions. The adult tries a new approach and the behaviour, more often than not, increases before it decreases.

From the child's point of view, this pattern makes sense. The old behaviour is met with a new response, so the child tries again to get it to work. For example, if the child demands something and the parent yells, the child continues and the parent eventually gives in (this may take a long time; children can be extremely persevering). Now, all of a sudden, the parent does not yell but responds by asking the child to leave the room. The child tries again, but more loudly, and the parent responds with the same request. The child responds again by being louder and adding some physical behaviour. The parent thinks that this is not working and abandons this technique, resorting to the old behaviour, in which the yelling was not so loud and not so long. The behaviours continue and may escalate, and the parent may one day lose control.

Although the parent hasn't planned it, he or she may react aggressively toward the child. However, the bigger surprise is that it works. Punishment often temporarily stops behaviour, so it is immediately reinforcing to the parent who uses it, although the child doesn't learn anything from it. Because it works when nothing else does, the likelihood that it may be used again is increased. Thus, it is possible to understand where the parent's behaviour comes from and to understand how the behaviours of adults and children interact and escalate together. Early childhood professionals need to understand this, not only in their own practices with children, but also to understand the methods that parents may use with children.

Another example to illustrate this is that of the child who is labelled as attention seeking. This label seems particularly sad, for two reasons. First, it is sad to think that the child must seek out attention and that sufficient attention is not given to the child to meet his or her particular needs. This has always been a particular problem with behaviour management strategies in general — children can only receive attention and praise when they act in an appropriate manner and children should need the reinforcement in order for it to become meaningful; there are no mechanisms to reinforce children for just being children, being cute, being kind, or being themselves. Second, it is even sadder that the child desperate for attention has learned, at a young age, that the only way to get attention is to act in inappropriate ways. The message here is clear. Early childhood professionals must consider the whole child and provide ways for the child to express those needs in a more appropriate way.

After carefully observing the child in the context of group care, caregivers must decide how to help that child manage his or her own behaviours. They can begin by outlining the problems and then considering each problem in the context of the child's development and the context of the situation. Could the child's behaviour be a product of developmental delays? For example, has the child yet to develop the necessary language skills or social skills to act? Can these skills be taught? Is the child experiencing some stress or difficult life situation that may be causing the behaviour? For example, is the family experiencing stress at this time? Is the behaviour a result of development? For example, is the child attempting to demonstrate independence or determine cause and effect? It is well known and often joked about that 2-year-olds live by the creed "No," "Don't," "Mine" — could this child with special needs be engaging in the same autonomous behaviours?

One strategy is to create an environment in which the child with behavioural problems can better cope. Children need a warm, relaxed environment that is consistent and predictable, so it is important to make rules for the playroom, set limits, and stick to them. Be sure that these are clear and that children understand both the rule and the consequence for breaking it. This is often a difficult balance for early childhood professionals who dislike the idea of rules or limits, but when children know what is expected of them and the limits on their behaviour, they often feel secure and cope better.

Try to keep waiting times to a minimum. Waiting can be hard for all children, but inevitably children with behavioural or emotional problems use this time to engage in inappropriate behaviour. In addition, provide children with ample warning prior to transitions. Telling some children that you will be cleaning up for lunch in five minutes may be sufficient. Other children may need more time and warning.

Check the physical setting of the playroom to see if changes can be made, such as rearranging the traffic flow so that it does not disrupt play, eliminates running through play areas, and allows for choices. Be sure to give the child with behavioural or emotional problems choices. The tendency is often to eliminate choices, believing that the child cannot handle making them. But, when the child feels empowered to make choices, he or she may feel less need to engage in disruptive behaviours.

Attempt to catch and deal with problems early, before the child gets too involved or before other children get hurt. This sounds easier than it is, but the careful observation and monitoring of the child with behavioural or emotional concerns is necessary.

In dealing with specific behaviours, observe the child to acquire some preliminary information that may become useful in managing the behaviour and catching it early. Following are some issues to be aware of:

- When does the behaviour occur?
- Does the behaviour have a pattern? Is it random?
- Does the behaviour occur at a particular time of day, such as arrival, departure, lunchtime, or naptime?

- Does the behaviour occur during particular activities or routines, transitions, waiting time, or free play, or in large group activities?
- Does the behaviour occur in a particular place, such as outdoors, indoors, or at a particular centre?

Planning in a Developmental Context

After considering these perspectives, the early childhood professional can view the concerns from a developmental framework, not only in relation to the particular problem, but to ensure and enhance the child's development in all areas. Following are some examples of points to consider. It is hoped that these will serve as a catalyst to the early childhood professional considering different perspectives for each child.

Emotional

Children may experience difficulties in managing their impulses. The resulting loss of self-control may lead to feelings of low self-esteem and feelings of incompetence. Before they can learn to control their feelings, they must become aware of their emotions and of how they respond to them. Children also need consistent guidelines for behaviour explained clearly to them. Early childhood professionals can further help children to deal with their impulses by acknowledging their feelings and then providing them with ways to deal with these feelings or frustrations by, for example, redirecting them to an experience that helps them to express their feelings in a more positive way.

It is also important to let children know when their actions are positive and acceptable. Adults often tend to see and acknowledge bad behaviour, but they must be aware of when children do good things and let them know that these are desirable behaviours. Children should be provided with opportunities to feel good about themselves and to be acknowledged by adults and other children. This may be very difficult to do for children who have behavioural problems and never seem to engage in positive behaviours, so caregivers should be extra attentive.

One of the most important things caregivers can do is help children see themselves as "good" children. When children feel valued and liked, they may engage in behaviours that reflect the perception. To achieve this, early childhood professionals may want to ensure that children are provided with playroom experiences at which they will succeed, teach them to control their own behaviour, and ensure that other children in the playroom provide feedback.

Play

Children with behavioural problems may not have the ability to organize their play and maintain their involvement. They may move from activity to activity, disrupting the play of other children, and being easily disrupted in their own attempts. From time to time, caregivers may want to get involved in these children's play to settle them in and model a more satisfying play experience by giving suggestions for extending play.

Expecting children with behavioural problems to play for long periods of time may be unrealistic. As a caregiver, you may want to plan progressively longer free-play times for these children, beginning at a point where the children experience some success (such as five minutes) and expanding from there. Consider the length of time for sitting and listening activities as well. Praise children for their attempts at extended play, and build from there. Consider the children's toys and equipment, and remove those that cause problems to erupt. Some day-care centres have policies forbidding guns or action figures in the centre, thereby lessening opportunities for aggressive behaviours.

Social

Children with behaviour problems often have difficulties in social interactions with others, especially children. Holding them back from engaging in social experiences will not help, since doing this removes the opportunity to learn new behaviours. As a caregiver, you need to explain clearly to these children what your expectations are, what the limits are, and the consequences to the children of engaging in inappropriate behaviours. Likewise, reassure other children in the playroom that they will be safe and encourage them to be supportive of engaging children with behavioural problems back into play.

Again, when children engage in positive behaviours, praise them and ensure that the other children are aware of the behaviours also so that they just don't see children with behavioural problems as bad. When children engage in inappropriate behaviours, either follow through as you started out or use the opportunity to teach children a more appropriate way to act.

Language

Children with behaviour difficulties may have short attention spans and may not attend to what others are saying or catch only parts of the message. They may be easily distracted and over-stimulated by visual and auditory activities. Thus, although the background noise level may not be a concern for you or other adults, it may be overwhelming for children who are not able to tune out certain stimuli. Ensure that you have the children's attention before issuing directives. It may also be necessary to give children directions one at a time, rather than giving a whole string at once. This will help children to understand what is expected of them.

Children may need to learn vocabulary associated with expressing their needs, wants, and feelings. Teach children words they may use, such as "I'm angry" or "I feel like hitting you." This applies not only to children with identified problems but all children in the playroom. Children with behavioural problems typically hear mostly negative comments about themselves and their behaviour. When talking to children, try as much as possible to phrase things in the positive: tell children what to do, not what not to do (for example, "Paint on the paper"), praise the good part of the action (for example, "Thank you for trying to help"). Stating things in the positive provides more feedback for their behaviour and models good language.

Cognitive

Children who have a short attention span and are easily distracted may have difficulty making connections in their world. This, in turn, may hamper their attempts to translate their ideas into appropriate actions and sequences. Observe children to better understand their interests so that meaningful, functional experiences can be set up for them to learn. They will, for the most part, learn concepts about their world that are meaningful to them; for example, counting out treats for lunch is more meaningful than counting out beads. Break long tasks into shorter steps that can be accomplished in shorter time blocks. Providing experiences that are functional and that promote success will help to create an environment in which children will continue to learn.

Sensory

Some children react negatively to sensory information and are overloaded very easily. Their reactions may include withdrawal (for example, to get away from the noise) or aggression due to the frustration they may be feeling. Carefully observe children to determine if certain events or sensory cues seem to irritate them, calm them, or are conducive to coping. Creating these circumstances may help in dealing with children's behaviour. For example, if a child is the only child in their family, the noise and activity in a group-care setting may be overwhelming and cause inappropriate behaviours such as crying, withdrawal, or aggression that the parents have never seen at home. Creating a quiet area or quiet times for this child may be helpful. In addition, the child may need extra support to learn to cope with feelings of frustration in large, noisy groups.

Physical

Children with behavioural concerns may not stay with activities long enough to learn and practise large and small motor skills. This may occur for two reasons: the child is easily distractible, or adults constantly remove the child from activities because of his or her behaviour. In either case, caregivers need to define and enforce limits for the protection of all children participating. Help children with behavioural concerns to find ways to use their energy in meaningful ways that promote the development of a wide range of skills and teach the children to respond to what their bodies are telling them. For instance, children can learn to run to work off frustration. If children endure a long bus or car ride to day care in the morning, perhaps their day at the centre should begin with physical activity.

Children with behavioural problems may not wish to engage in fine-motor activities because it is too difficult for them to sit for extended periods of time or because fine-motor skills, which often require concentration, are difficult to perform. Caregivers need to be aware of all areas of development and foster opportunities for children to develop such skills. For example, many fine-motor activities can happen in the context of personal care.

Pay attention to the types of activities children are given. For example, children may avoid an activity requiring careful cutting or engage in inappropriate behaviour to avoid the task, thereby also avoiding learning this skill. Perhaps a different art activity, in which free cutting is more acceptable, may be used on occasion. Schedule fine-motor activities for times when children are less likely to become frustrated and for short blocks of time.

Children with behavioural and emotional concerns may need to develop body awareness so that they become more aware of their feelings and what their body does. For instance, they may need to learn what their body does when they are tense and how it feels. This awareness will help them to control their actions.

Summary

Children with behavioural concerns present ongoing challenges for early childhood professionals. Caregivers must be ever vigilant, observing these children in all areas not only for their sake but to ensure the safety of other children in the playroom, who may not be able to defend themselves. It is likely that caregivers will find children with behavioural concerns the most demanding and taxing of all children; thus caregivers must be aware of their abilities and their limitations. They should request assistance if needed, and try to find resources that may help. Although parents may be helpful here, parents see their children in a very different environment: biting, not sharing, and aggression may be concerns that they never see. At the same time, parents may understand the particular child's temperament or sensory needs and know ways to calm or soothe the child.

Early childhood professionals need to be cognizant that the source of their stress will come not only from a particular child and his or her needs, but also from that child's interaction with other children who may be the target of the child's actions or encourage the child's behaviours. Accordingly, caregivers must remember to consider the needs of all children in the group.

ACTIVITIES

1. Observe a group of preschool children. Record the actions and movements of three or four children in the group in different settings: outdoors, indoors, free play, circle time, and lunch time. Compare what you saw in each setting for each child. What are some of the similarities and differences?

2. Observe children interacting with a child who has emotional or behavioural problems. When do they interact with the child? When do they avoid him or her? What is their reaction to him or her? What do they say about this child (to you or to other children)?

3. Talk to parents and others from diverse cultural and religious backgrounds about their view of behavioural and emotional problems. What behaviours would they tolerate? What behaviours would they not tolerate? Are certain behaviours that we might call "problems" not considered as such from their perspective (or vice versa)?

4. Observe a child who has behavioural problems and determine if there is a sequence leading up to the behaviour: are there any warning signs that the behaviour will occur? Can this information be used by caregivers or the child to manage his or her own behaviour?

5. Spend a long block of time observing children playing in your playroom. Are there aspects of the environment that contribute to behavioural concerns? Are certain parts of the room or play centre the setting for problems to occur? Are there times of the day or particular experiences when behavioural concerns are more evident?

DISCUSSION QUESTIONS

1. Discuss ADHD or ADD and what it means in your playroom. What behaviours would you see, and how could you manage them?

2. Discuss feelings that the child with behavioural or emotional problems may need to learn and how you might teach those feelings.

3. Discuss how you would talk about the child with behavioural concerns to other children in the playroom. What should they do when they get hurt? What should they say to the child who hurt them?

4. Discuss what you would say to the parents of other children who go home bruised or bitten or with stories of how mean the child with emotional problems is. Parents will undoubtedly hear about the child and will expect to know how their child's safety is being guarded.

5. What characteristics of FAS might you see in young children? How is its identification hampered? How would the identification of FAS help you in the context of the playroom? How would you talk to the affected child's parent about FAS?

6. List the rules that apply in your playroom. Do these rules apply to all children? Are there exceptions? Why do these exceptions exist? What are the typical consequences of breaking the rules? Do these consequences apply equally to all children?

7. Observe a group of young children, paying particular attention to their temperamental traits. Include children with special needs in your observations. Consider the traits of specific children and discuss how these traits are manifested, when they may be considered problems, and how they are typically managed.

Children at Risk

CHAPTER 8

Introduction

This chapter considers the needs of those children who have thus far not been discussed. "Children at risk," also known as disadvantaged or vulnerable children, are children with medical or health concerns, children at developmental risk, and children experiencing stress in their lives. Many day-care centres have children who are not "labelled" but who come with a range of needs that makes inclusion in a group-care setting extremely challenging. Child care may be the primary intervention agent for most of these children. Thus, early childhood professionals who have a strong background in child development and interact with a diverse range of children are the first to recognize and identify relevant concerns.

After reading this chapter, you should have a better understanding of:

- the needs of three groups of children:
  - children with health or medical needs
  - children at developmental risk
  - children experiencing stress;
- health concerns of children including:
  - allergies
  - asthma
  - cystic fibrosis
  - diabetes
  - epilepsy
  - hemophilia
  - heart problems;

- concerns potentially facing children considered at risk;
- concerns potentially resulting when children and families live in stress;
- the developmental implications of and planning strategies for each group of children.

Children with Health Needs

Advances in medical science and technology have increased both the survival rates of infants and the number of children with special health needs (Norton, 1997). Thus, it is likely that more and more children with health needs will be included in child-care programs.

Health impairments can be defined in the following way: "limited strength, vitality, or alertness due to chronic or acute health problems" (Allen et al., 1994, p. 210). Children may live with a vast range of medical and health conditions. Some of these conditions may be minor and affect children in group care minimally, whereas others may require a higher level of support and care. Children with health impairments may present more challenges in a group-care setting. It would be a daunting task to list and define all possible disorders, so this chapter considers the most common disorders encountered in day-care centres.

ALLERGIES

Allergies are the most common health impairment of young children (Deiner, 1993). They account for one third of all health conditions that occur during the early years.

An allergy is a heightened sensitivity to some substance or agent that normally does not cause a reaction in other individuals. Allergenic substances may be one of four types:

1. airborne substances that are taken in through the nose or mouth, such as pollen, dust, and animal dander;
2. food consumed, most commonly peanuts, chocolate, citrus fruits, fish or shellfish, milk, eggs, tomatoes, and food colouring;
3. substances that come into contact with the skin, such as wool, starch, soap, or detergents;
4. drugs or chemicals such as penicillin or the venom from insect bites or bee stings.

Symptoms of allergies include a runny nose, a dry cough, puffy eyes, a skin rash, swelling, or redness of the skin. More severe reactions include difficulty in breathing and more severe bodily reactions. Caregivers should ask parents about their children's allergies in order to know what to watch for and to be prepared to treat the child if necessary.

SCENARIO

We were discussing allergies in a class on children with special needs in day-care centres. When we discussed allergies, the topic of epipens arose. One student commented that a child in her day-care centre required the use of the pen for a severe allergy to peanut oil. The student admitted that she thought she knew where the kit was

> located and she had read the instructions once when the parent brought it in, but she had not considered the matter since.
>
> Several other students related similar stories from their own work experiences. They all agreed that they would be totally unprepared in case of an emergency. After the discussion they realized the importance not only of being informed but of being prepared for an emergency in which time would be of the essence.

It is important to be aware of allergy symptoms and reactions generally because it is common for a child's first allergic reaction to occur when the child is in care. For example, bee stings may occur in day care because children are typically out of doors during the day. Further, caregivers must know how to respond when an emergency does occur.

ASTHMA

Asthma is a respiratory problem caused by an obstruction of the airway resulting from the narrowing of the bronchial tubes. This may be caused by swelling in the tubes, contraction of the muscles around the tubes, or the tubes becoming plugged with mucous.

Asthma attacks can be brought on by allergies, overexcitement, physical activity, or overexertion. They typically occur without warning and come on quickly, which can be frightening for both the child and the adults present.

Regardless of the cause, the symptoms of asthma are generally the same. The child experiences shortness of breath, wheezing, coughing, and/or choking. It is important to be aware of these signs and to develop an understanding of the factors that may trigger an attack so that you, as a caregiver, are prepared to intervene before the onset of an asthma attack. Working with parents may be helpful in gathering this information. You may need to be prepared to administer medication, usually in the form of an inhaler, and to be aware of when an asthmatic child may require further assistance.

CYSTIC FIBROSIS

Cystic fibrosis (CF) is a genetic disorder that affects the digestive and respiratory systems. Children with CF will produce a thick, sticky mucous that interferes with breathing and the release of digestive enzymes so that they are unable to metabolize fats and proteins. Chronic symptoms include persistent coughing, wheezing, frequent bouts of pneumonia, excessive appetite, and poor weight gain (Howard et al. 1997).

Children with CF typically require intense medical and therapeutic intervention, including diet management, physical therapy for respiratory concerns, and medications. In group care, children with CF may require close monitoring of their activity, diet, and medications. They may frequently be absent.

DIABETES

Diabetes is a metabolic disorder in which either the body produces insufficient insulin or the insulin produced is ineffective. Insulin is a hormone made in the pancreas that helps the body use glucose. Children with diabetes are managed by developing and balancing their diet, physical activity, and medication, usually insulin injections. In addition to receiving regular injections of insulin, children often need to have their sugar levels monitored regularly by either blood or urine testing. For some children, finding and maintaining this balance is relatively simple; for others, constant supervision and monitoring are required. Some children with diabetes are very aware of it and play a role in managing it from a very young age, while others see it as something that makes them different. As is the case with many childhood conditions, adults can play a key role in determining how the child deals with the disease itself and with the resulting feelings.

SCENARIO

Seth was diagnosed as a diabetic at the age of 2 years. He required daily insulin injections and careful monitoring of his diet and activity levels because it was difficult to balance them. Seth's mother quit her job and stayed home with him to ensure that his diabetes was under control before he started school. At home, his diet was fairly easily controlled by not having forbidden foods available in the home. This diet was considered normal for the entire family. Physical activity was also easily monitored because there were three children in the home.

When Seth started kindergarten, however, neither he nor his parents were prepared for the changes and the implications for his health. Snacks of all kinds, usually containing sugar, were readily available, and Seth's physical activity was more frequent and intense than it had been with his younger siblings at home. This new environment initially caused major health problems for Seth, and he missed a lot of time in kindergarten. Seth also experienced difficulties interacting with his peers. He suddenly felt different — the normal diet and routines of home were not normal for most of the children in day care. The other children did not understand why he was always sick and why he sometimes acted "funny" and ate "weird" foods.

As his health concerns were addressed and brought under control in the day-care centre, Seth's parents realized that there was more to the problem. They could not protect him from what normally occurred outside of their own home; Seth needed to learn to cope with his disease in all settings. They began to explain these things to Seth: what he needed to eat and why; why he needed medication and the other children did not. In turn, Seth began to explain these things to his peers, who began to understand why he ate the foods he ate, why he could not share their snacks, and why he had to have needles all the time. Not only were the children understanding, but they became helpful to Seth in managing his diabetes.

This scenario illustrates how the attitudes of various people can affect the management of a particular condition. The attitudes of the child, the family, and all others involved with the child may have an impact. In addition, the scenario points to the importance of keeping all children, including the child with the special health-care need, informed. Is there a way for the early childhood professional to play a role in promoting awareness and well-being?

Common symptoms signalling the onset of diabetes include extreme thirst, constant hunger, weight loss, frequent urination, frequent tiredness, changes in vision, and the slow healing of open wounds. The severity and number of the symptoms vary.

In addition, it is important to recognize the symptoms of being out of balance. Children who have too much insulin in their system may have an insulin reaction. The warning signs include dizziness, shaking, trembling, or emotional outbursts. Children experiencing an insulin reaction need sugar, which is tempting, easy to take, and fast burning. Sweet snacks include orange or apple juice, a sugar cube, or a piece of chocolate. Again, remember that not all diabetic children will exhibit the same symptoms, and some children may exhibit none.

SCENARIO

Tithi was a quiet, 5-year-old child with diabetes who was in full-time group care. Her diabetes was controlled most of the time, but when she was out of balance her reactions came on quickly. Her caregiver and mother noticed that prior to an insulin reaction, she would get loud and then disagreeable with both the children and the adults in the area. If the adult waited too long, it became increasingly more difficult to get Tithi to take sugar in any form, no matter how tempting.

After the caregiver and her mother had discussed Tithi's situation, they tried to ensure that Tithi received a sugar intake when she got loud but before she got too disagreeable; this seemed to work. They also attempted to make Tithi aware of this warning sign so that she could learn to tell when she might be out of balance.

This scenario provides a good example of a caregiver and parent working together to ensure the best care for Tithi. The observations of behaviour, shared by the two adults, will assist them in managing her diabetes now and may be used by Tithi herself in the future.

The other possibility is for children to have too much sugar in their body in relation to the amount of insulin. This may happen when the child with diabetes has eaten too many forbidden foods (those containing sugar) or when the child has been inactive or ill. The symptoms of having too much sugar include the need to urinate often, thirst, hunger, drowsiness, and weakness. If this is left untreated, the child may lapse into a coma. Treatment, therefore, is necessary.

It is very important to work closely with parents in order to recognize symptoms and understand the treatment of diabetes. When their diet, activity, and insulin intake are regulated, children with diabetes can manage very well in a group-care setting.

Epilepsy

Epilepsy is a neurological disorder characterized by repeated unprovoked seizures (Brown, 1997). Seizures occur when abnormal discharges of electrical energy occur in the brain. They may last only a few seconds and make the child appear to be daydreaming, or they may last for several minutes and involve more motor activity. Epilepsy may occur on its own or may be associated with other disabilities. Approximately half of the children with epilepsy are considered to be normally developing; the other half may experience developmental delays (Brown, 1997). Most seizures can be controlled by medication, but seizure management may be affected by illness, rest or lack thereof, and other factors.

Several types of seizures are common in young children. Tonic clonic, or grand mal, seizures begin with a sudden loss of consciousness during which affected children may fall and injure themselves. These seizures progress with rigid muscular contractions followed by a rhythmic jerking of the body. They usually end with lethargy or the need to sleep and may involve the loss of bladder control. Children may be disoriented after a grand mal seizure and typically will not remember the seizure.

Absence seizures are also known as petit mal seizures. In this type of seizure, the affected children stop all activity, assume a glazed look, and stare, for one to fifteen seconds. They maintain normal muscle tone, so they do not fall. During the seizure, they are unresponsive to verbal and tactile cues, unlike the case during an episode of daydreaming. Due to the brevity of petit mal seizures, they may go unnoticed or be interpreted as a behavioural problem (for example, the child may be assumed not to be listening to requests).

Young children frequently experience febrile convulsions. These typically occur between three months and five years of age and are associated with a fever. The seizure is usually brief, is tonic clonic, and typically does not reoccur after the fever subsides. There is no evidence that there is any greater risk for later problems or epilepsy.

When a child has a seizure, caregivers should remember several points. A seizure cannot be stopped once it has begun, so it is critical to remain calm and ensure the child's safety. Because there is a loss of consciousness during a grand mal seizure, it is important to first consider the child's safety. If necessary, move the child to the floor and remove any objects close by so that the child does not get hurt. Turn the child's head and or/body to the side so the child can breathe and doesn't choke on saliva or anything else in the mouth. The child should not be otherwise moved or interfered with; for example, nothing should be placed in the child's mouth.

Children may be disoriented when a seizure ceases, and they commonly want to rest. Remain with them until they are awake and alert; they require reassurance and comfort. You will need to discuss with parents if and when medical intervention may be required. It may be necessary to document seizures for the agency or the child's parents.

Seizures can be frightening for others, particularly children, to witness. For this reason, it is important to stay calm and explain, in a matter-of-fact manner, what is happening: "Tithi is having a seizure. She needs to rest. She will be okay."

HEMOPHILIA

Hemophilia is a genetically transmitted blood disorder in which the blood lacks one of the essential ingredients for clotting. It typically affects only males.

Many myths and fears surround hemophiliacs. For example, it is a common belief that if they are cut, they will bleed to death. A recent treatment involves using a clotting agent isolated from blood plasma. Although this treatment eliminates the imminent dangers of hemophilia, over the long term, bleeding into the joints can lead to other problems.

It is essential for all caregivers involved with children who have hemophilia to understand how to provide treatment when necessary. Although children with hemophilia can fit into group-care settings, they require constant supervision and monitoring. Caregivers may have to be careful to avoid creating a situation of dependence and overprotecting the child.

HEART PROBLEMS

Heart problems may be the result of rheumatic fever or various types of heart defects. The symptoms most commonly associated with heart problems include shortness of breath and/or faintness as a result of physical activity, frequent respiratory infections, and a bluish colour around the lips. Over time, the child's physical development may be affected. Children with heart problems may require monitoring and some limitations of their activity but otherwise fit into group-care settings relatively easily.

This review provides only a brief sketch of some of the most common conditions. Numerous other conditions have not been discussed in any detail. Several resources can be used to access more thorough and current information (Batshaw, 1991; Deiner, 1993).

Implications

IMPLICATIONS FOR THE CHILD'S DEVELOPMENT

Each of the health concerns described above has its own pattern of symptoms and most can be managed medically, although none can be "cured" at this time. Over time and as a part of their development, children must learn about their particular disease — how its symptoms are triggered, and how to monitor and manage it. This may take years, but children should be involved in all aspects of their care from an early age and have as much explained to them as possible.

In addition to understanding and coping with their specific medical problem, the affected children typically feel different, isolated, and insecure about it. These feelings affect not only the way that children feel about themselves, but the condition and its management as well.

SCENARIO

Andrei was a 5-year-old boy with asthma. His asthma attacks were commonly triggered by overexertion. Although Andrei and his caregivers were well aware of this, he was extremely competitive and constantly challenged his peers to running, climbing, and chasing activities. One of the caregivers suggested that this competitiveness seemed like his way of proving to his friends that he could do what they could do, and that he was no different from anyone else.

Children's feelings about their disorder may affect the disorder itself. If they feel ashamed or different, they may attempt to hide their symptoms or avoid treatment. If they feel okay about themselves and about the condition and accept it as part of their life — as difficult as this may be — they may live with their condition more easily.

IMPLICATIONS FOR OTHERS

Other children typically treat the child with health concerns differently because they do not understand. (Why does he get a snack and we don't? Why does he need to nap and we don't? Why can't he play on the climber with us?) It is common for other children to fear, exclude, or tease the child with health concerns because they have not been told why the child eats certain foods, can't play outdoors, takes special medication, or has needles every day. Explaining the child's condition and the procedures taken to counteract it may enhance their understanding and lead to a better acceptance of the child.

SCENARIO

A nursery school teacher reported that one fall a boy with severe allergies to a variety of items, particularly peanuts, enrolled in her program. The child's mother provided information to all the parents regarding diet, including what foods to avoid and special recipes to avoid forbidden products. The boy's mother and teacher explained to the children what allergies were and why the boy could eat only certain foods. Not only were the children helpful in determining what was a safe food, but many of them reported that they too had allergies. Many of them appeared to have severe allergies to broccoli and liver!

Again we see how the attitudes of others, adults and children alike, can shape their attitudes to the child with special needs and affect their ability to cope. Children can often be quite accepting of differences, especially when adequate information is provided.

A common reaction from adults — parents and caregivers alike — is to try to protect the child as much as possible. This sometimes leads to overprotecting the child by limiting his or her activities or cleaning up for the child because it may be too tiring for him or her. It may not take long before the child comes to use the medical condition as an excuse for avoiding responsibilities ("I'm too tired to clean up"). Adults must learn to be responsive to the child's special needs within a framework that promotes responsibility and independence.

In addition, adults often take total responsibility for monitoring and managing a child's special condition. Although this may be necessary, especially in the early years, when children are not ready to independently care for themselves, it is important that children learn to accept and manage their condition as much as possible within these developmental parameters. This is not as easy is it sounds — just ask any parent whose child has even a minor health concern — but it is important to work at striking a balance between protection and overprotection, dependence and independence.

SCENARIO

Darlene had been an early childhood professional in an inclusive day-care centre for 16 years. During that time, she had worked with children who had a diverse range of special needs. She was, however, unsure of how to handle the situation when 4-year-old Sudha entered her playroom. At first Sudha's seizures were well controlled, but as time progressed her seizures increased in frequency and she required constant supervision to ensure her safety.

Sudha's parents were adamant that the other children in the playroom should not be told about her epilepsy. It was extremely difficult not to inform the children, so Darlene was unsure about what to say. She believed that the other children should understand the situation, but she realized that Sudha's parents' request needed to be respected as well.

Although caregivers and parents need to work closely together, this may not be easy. Individuals have different beliefs about privacy, responsibility, and independence. All these beliefs must be respected while meeting the needs of the child in a group-care setting.

Role of the Early Childhood Professional

Whatever the day-care setting, early childhood professionals will work with children who have diverse and special needs. Regardless of the child's particular condition, you as a caregiver will be able to cope with the child better if you consider the following issues.

Ensure that you have good communication with the child's parents. Typically, the parents and family will be your best source of information about the medical condition both in general and in relation to the child in your care. Ask parents the following questions to gather information, but also make your own observations, because the home setting and the day-care setting may be very different and some of those differences may cause different reactions.

For example, large numbers of children, noise, or excitement may trigger seizures or an asthma attack. Note your observations and share them with parents. This sharing may help both you and the parents to develop a better understanding of the complexities of the disease and its management.

Ask the following questions to gain an understanding of the child's health concerns.

1. *What sets the condition off?* For example, will lack of sleep, diet, or overexcitement trigger an attack or seizure? Are attacks or seizures most likely in the morning, afternoon, or evening?
2. *Does the child display any warning signs before developing difficulties?* Does the child have difficulty in breathing, appear disoriented, or want to lie down? Are there changes in the child's behaviour? These warning signs may be noted by parents and through your own observations of the child.
3. *How should you cope with the medical situation?* Will the child require immediate medical intervention or monitoring? As a caregiver, you may need to learn how to handle seizures, diabetic comas, asthma attacks, or allergy reactions. Ask parents to provide this information or find a local hospital, clinic, or association that may assist. For example, in some communities, the local health clinic may provide seminars to staff regarding allergies and what to do in emergencies. Other special-interest groups may provide similar services. Again, remember that parents may be the best source of this information.

    Another factor to consider is how to manage the individual child in case of an emergency. When do parents need to be informed? When will medical intervention be required? How will this decision be made and who will make it? Who will administer medication?

    Children with special medical needs often exhibit difficulties randomly and infrequently. On most days they function well as part of the group and perhaps require only medication and monitoring. However, sometimes they require one-to-one observation and assistance. A prearranged plan may be beneficial in coping with these days. You may also find that you may not necessarily have to deal with the health condition itself but with the aftermath. For example, children typically experience asthma attacks at night and may be recovering from the resulting lack of sleep and increase in medication the next day. The child's frequent absences may be a concern as well.
4. *What precautions should be taken on the child's behalf?* For example, how much exercise should the child engage in, how often? Should the child's diet be increased or decreased in relation to his or her activity? Will medications affect the child's functioning (for example, will he or she be tired)? Will the child need to be out of the sun? Will he or she require more fluids? Are there ways to prevent attacks, for example, by avoiding certain foods or limiting activity? Discussions with parents and other professionals may assist in avoiding problematic situations.

SCENARIO

Jans was a 5-year-old child with a severe eating disorder who was starting kindergarten. Due to the disorder, Jans' diet was extremely restricted in regard to both the *quantity of food he could eat and what he was able to eat. The classroom, which was in a day-care centre, was set up so that the lockers were outside in the hallway. In this centre, children were allowed to bring their own snacks.*

One of the goals the teacher had was for children to be as responsible as possible for their age, within the confines of the school. Accordingly, she allowed children to move back and forth between the room and their lockers freely so that they could decide what they wanted for a snack and had access to the bathroom facilities. Although the teacher was aware of Jans' condition, she was not aware that he had noticed that the other children brought yummy snacks that were routinely stored in their lockers.

Jans became very independent in finding other children's snacks and eating them on his way to the bathroom. This caused concern not only for Jans, who had not previously been in environments where a range of foods was so easily available, but for the other children, who often lost their snacks.

This scenario underscores the importance of understanding both the environment and the child's condition in order to know what to watch out for and how to avoid potential hazards.

In summary, children may bring a wide range of health and medical concerns to a group-care setting. Some may require minimal adaptation, some may require observation and monitoring, and others may create great difficulties for caregivers. Try to ensure that information is forthcoming from parents, support groups, and resource centres. When you have access to information, you may feel better able to meet the very individual needs that children with special needs bring to the group-care setting.

Children at Developmental Risk

This group has had many labels over the years, including environmentally delayed children, socially disadvantaged children, and children in poverty. What is common to this group is that its members are considered to be at risk or more vulnerable to developmental delays because of the environment they live in. Some family situations and environments are more conducive than others to developing delays or patterns of behaviour that can make learning difficult (Deiner, 1993; Dunlap, 1997b). Potential detrimental environmental conditions include poverty, low socioeconomic status, teenage parents, a dysfunctional family, prenatal exposure to viruses, drug abuse, alcohol abuse, malnourishment during pregnancy, prolonged difficult labours, low birth weight, prematurity, and an emotionally unresponsive mother, often as a result of an unwanted pregnancy or chronic illness (Dunlap, 1997b).

Often these factors do not occur in isolation but are compounded. For example, children growing up in poverty face many risks from birth. Women living in poverty may be less likely to receive prenatal care and eat properly. These factors are associated with a lower birth weight for the child and an increased chance of birth defects. Early deprivation resulting from poverty has long-lasting effects on children's development (Phillips, et al., 1994). Children who live in poverty are more likely to receive inadequate nutrition and to suffer more illness and emotional and psychiatric difficulties (Offord, 1991). In addition, they typically endure interruptions in learning and live in situations of overcrowding, hunger, stress, and illness, all of which contribute to poor performance at school.

Children from single-parent families have been characterized as being less compliant, more antisocial, more likely to experience school difficulties, and more likely to have psychological concerns (Ward, 1994). The literature suggests that father absence has an effect on the development of children. Children from father-absent homes experience higher levels of school failure and delinquency (Shimoni and Baxter, 1996).

Children exposed to abuse may experience long-term developmental effects (Osofsky, 1994). The ways in which they think about themselves and their world may be affected; for example, they may experience feelings of guilt, worthlessness, shame, or isolation (Wallach, 1995). Studies have suggested that abused children show more aggressive and negative behaviours, withdrawal, depression, fearfulness, disruptions in routines, nightmares, and difficulty in controlling their emotions (Osofsky, 1994; Vanier Institute, 1994).

Similar effects are apparent for children who live with violence, who are homeless, and who live with drug- or alcohol-dependent parents. Generally speaking, the literature suggests a bleak picture for their development. All of these situations have a common theme: children who live in these environments are more vulnerable to, or experience developmental delays and have a diverse range of special needs, all of which contribute to difficulties in group-care settings.

Two points about these studies must be made to put the information into context. First, they do not present direct relationships or correlations. Thus, it cannot be said that father-absent homes cause school failure or that living in poverty creates behavioural problems. There is, however, a much higher likelihood that children in these circumstances will experience developmental delays and associated concerns. Second, many of the situations described in these studies are not unidimensional. The problems they discuss are created over time and are caused by a number of factors. For example, a child living in a single-parent home may have recently experienced a divorce; the child may now be living in poverty; the custodial parent may now be employed outside the home, so the child may feel abandoned by the custodial parent as well as the non-custodial parent; and the child may have been forced to relocate and have lost the companionship of family and friends as part of that transition. Given the multiple factors at play, it is difficult to assume that one factor — father absence — is the sole factor. Rather, the child's problems may result from any one of the myriad of factors or from the relationship between several or all of them.

Implications

IMPLICATIONS FOR THE CHILD'S DEVELOPMENT

It is important from the outset to remember that children at developmental risk may be living in circumstances not of their choice and not under their control. They may be victims of the circumstances they live in.

SCENARIO

Faith was 4 years old and lived in a blended family. Both her parents worked full time and she was in day care. On some days, she was the first child to arrive and the last child to leave; on other days, she arrived late and left early. On most days, she had difficulty separating from her mother. Faith often dissolved into tears over something that happened in the playroom. She was characterized as anxious and fearful.

When the caregiver attempted to discuss matters with Faith's mother, the divorce and problems with her father were always given as reasons for Faith's behaviour. Several months later, Faith was removed from day care because her mother had been hospitalized for a mental health problem. In retrospect, many of Faith's problem behaviours seemed to make sense. When her mother received special help and the family entered counselling, Faith's behaviour settled down.

This scenario illustrates how children's behaviour may be affected by the circumstances in which they live. It is typical for children to react to changed circumstances with changes in their behaviour (for example, regression or acting out). Early childhood professionals should consider the causes of changes in behaviour from a variety of perspectives.

IMPLICATIONS FOR OTHERS

Adults often seem to think that children have more control over their environment than they actually do. For example, many think that if people in poverty just handled their finances better or would just find a job, all would be well. Often, however, change is not possible or very difficult. Blaming the victim does little to help people, particularly the children we work with (who have even less control). It is always important to examine your attitudes toward families and children.

Role of the Early Childhood Professional

The most beneficial intervention for children at risk is quality day care. Apart from enabling parents to pursue necessary education or employment and providing respite from parenting responsibilities, quality early childhood education has measurable benefits for the children. Perhaps the most well-known preschool study comes from the Perry Preschool Project in Ypsilanti, Michigan, which indicated that children in early childhood enrichment programs consistently had fewer problems throughout their teenage years. For every dollar Ypsilanti spent on early childhood education, the city saved six dollars on the cost of remedial education, jails, and social services. (Callwood, 1997, p. 92)

Early childhood education should not be considered merely an economic issue. What is important in these studies is the positive growth and development of the children involved in quality day care. Although it presents early childhood educators with a monumental task, it also can be seen as a testament to the success of quality day care. As primary-intervention agents with children and families, caregivers must realize that their knowledge, skills, and values are instrumental both in helping to identify children with special needs and in planning to meet those needs.

Children in Stress

It seems unusual to talk about children experiencing stress. Childhood should be a carefree, stress-free time. But children are increasingly experiencing stress in their lives. It may result from trauma such as death or illness, divorce, or poverty. All these issues affect children of all ages, although this has not often been considered for children under the age of 5 years (Shimoni and Baxter, 1996).

Adults often do not explain or provide information to young children because they feel the children will not comprehend or will be adversely affected by stress. However, no matter what adults choose to say or not say, their children will be affected by the circumstances in which they live.

SCENARIO

Tannis began the early childhood education course at a community college in Calgary in the fall. She had relocated from Montreal in August to prepare for school. She had left her two sons — Harris, aged 18 months, and Ho, aged 3 years — in the care of her parents. Ho arrived in Calgary with his grandmother in mid-September and went to day care on the two days that Tannis attended classes all day. Harris arrived with his grandfather at the end of September and stayed with relatives while Tannis attended classes. Each week, Tannis would report a new concern: neither child would sleep, Harris would not come to her, Ho refused to go to day care and would cry for the entire day, Harris was biting, Ho was clingy. With each new concern, Tannis questioned her parenting.

After class one day, we began to consider all of the changes that had occurred for these two young boys over a short period of time. As the list grew, Tannis began to see the changes from their perspective and to realize how they contributed to their changes in behaviour. Although the changes were necessary and understood by her, they likely were not understood or accepted by her young sons. Harris and Ho were letting her know about their difficulties in their own ways.

This scenario portrays children's stresses and reactions. Understanding that stress may be an issue for children and then determining the source of the stress may be instrumental in helping to alleviate it.

Adults are often reluctant to discuss "adult" problems with young children, but all children will understand that something is wrong and try to find out what and why. It is not unusual for children to blame themselves ("If I was good, Daddy wouldn't want to live somewhere else") or to develop their own explanations for what has happened ("Grandma died and went away on vacation"). These explanations may be a result of what children are told or of their having no access to information and thus filling in the details themselves. Providing children with correct, adequate information is crucial. This may need to be done repeatedly in order for them to understand the situation.

Just as we have typically not considered the consequences of such life events on the development of children generally, little consideration has been given to children with special needs. These children are more likely to experience such stresses than are normally developing children; for example, the rates of abuse and divorce among families with special-needs children are consistently high, and high levels of marital strain are common (Deiner, 1993). Thus, these children too will recognize that something is different or wrong and need caring adults to explain things to them.

Implications for the Child's Development

Children may react to stress in a variety of ways. Regressions are common; children may return to thumbsucking and needing a soother or comfort toy. Children often cry more readily and may experience distress upon arriving at the day-care centre. They may engage in more aggressive behaviour or become more withdrawn than usual. Nightmares and difficulties in sleeping are common as well. The child who slept well has difficulties now; the child who made transitions easily gets upset now; the child who was passive and easy-going is more aggressive. When a child's behaviour changes, it is important to observe how it has changed and to talk to the parents and child in order to determine the source of the difficulties or stress.

Role of the Early Childhood Professional

The role of the caregiver may not be to alleviate the sources of stress; this may be impossible to do. Nor may the caregiver be able to treat the stress, either for the child or for the family. One of the roles the caregiver may play is to assist children in coping or building resilience. This may be as simple as listening to them and allowing them to talk about what is bothering them. It may involve validating their feelings. It may not even require an action or solution: having a caring adult listen and seriously consider their concerns is a key factor in the lives of resilient children.

Caregivers may need both to listen to the parents and to help them understand the child's perspective. In the previous scenario with Tannis and her children, Tannis was better able to understand the situation from the perspective of her two sons after discussing it with her class. She stopped thinking that Harris and Ho were "bad" or that she wasn't coping. Once she came to this awareness, she was better able to explain the situation to Ho and Harris and to cope with their behaviours.

Young children's experience of stress may affect their behaviour in the playroom. Caregivers can observe them in an attempt to determine the source of the stress: the playroom? the routine? the children? the environment? It may be useful to discuss their observations and concerns with parents.

SCENARIO

Jacinthe had been a caregiver for several years. She was well liked by the children and worked hard to maintain open communication with their parents. In the spring, she began to notice changes in 4-year-old Sam's behaviour. Usually he was easy-going, played with everyone in the group, and was helpful, but lately he had been getting into more conflicts with peers, was more selective about who he played with, was less cooperative during cleanup, and cried more often when his mother left in the morning. Initially, Jacinthe thought these changes in Sam's behaviour were a result of the long, cold winter. However, the weather changed but Sam's behaviour did not. He continued to engage in the same behaviours and appeared to be withdrawing from the group more and more.

Since there was nothing new or different in the context of the day care, Jacinthe decided to share her observations with his mother. When Sam arrived the next morning with his mother, Jacinthe described what she had observed and asked his mother if she had any explanations. "No," his mother replied. Jacinthe then asked if there was anything different at home. "Well," she replied, "that's none of your damn business."

The particular approach used will depend on the situation, the parents, and the caregiver's rapport with them. Needless to say, children may be experiencing stress simply because their family is experiencing stress.

Summary

This chapter has highlighted the concerns of several groups of children not discussed elsewhere in the book. Although every child with special needs has different needs, the caregiver's approach and strategies remain similar:

1. Check your attitudes regarding children with diverse or special needs. Are you afraid of children with health concerns? Are you uneasy about the possibility of witnessing a seizure or having to give an injection? Do disfigurements or amputated limbs bother you? Do you believe that children would not be considered disadvantaged if their parents spent more time and/or money on their needs? Do you believe that the child's problems are the parents' fault? Do you think that young children with special needs understand what may be happening in their families? Do you believe they should be given an explanation for family stresses?
2. Get to know each child as an individual. The child with a seizure disorder whom you knew last year may be nothing like the child with seizures whom you are dealing with this year. Get to know the child's likes, dislikes, interests, and needs.

SCENARIO

A rehabilitation student began a practicum with children who were severely physically and developmentally delayed. One boy she was paired with had no communication skills, and the student's task was to develop an introductory communication program. After she decided upon the words to teach and the type of communication that was appropriate, she was ready to begin the program. She was, however, stumped in trying to find something that the boy would consider reinforcing. He had severe digestive problems and was tube fed, so eating was not a desirable activity. The student tried a series of toys, noisemakers, music, sounds, and sights in an attempt to get a consistent positive reaction from him.

After days of trying, she was becoming quite frustrated when she noticed that when she slid her chair back and it scraped and made a certain noise, he would look at her and smile. She tried this several times in succession and got a clear smile and laughter from him. She was so surprised at his reaction that she asked for a second opinion. Her practicum supervisor came to observe, and the connection between the chair scraping and his smile was clear.

The student began the program using this noise as a reinforcement and soon was able to find other noises and environmental events that the boy seemed to respond to. Although it took some time and effort, finding that special something that the child related and responded to was significant not only in meeting program goals but also in their relationship.

Again, the significance of getting to know each child's unique interests, needs, and abilities cannot be understated.

3. Make a concerted effort to get to know the parents and develop ways that you can work together so that you can get information about their child and feel comfortable in asking questions. Parents want what is best for their child, although they may have a narrow focus or are so absorbed with the child's condition that they appear not to be considering the whole picture. Parents can be your best resource and ally.
4. Find resources in your community that you can access for support or information about particular situations or conditions. These resources may take the form of conferences, colleagues, or local associations or clinics that have specialized information.
5. Take time to find ways to care for the caregiver. Find support. You may find it difficult to deal with some children and their needs or some parents and their demands. Find someone who can provide direction, advice, or assistance: someone to share the load or share your feelings with.

These ideas and strategies are not only useful for children at risk, but also beneficial for the many children with diverse and special needs in your care.

ACTIVITIES

1. Develop a resource file for the key resources in your community that may be useful for the children and families in your day-care program. Find out about the organization, what it has to offer, and who your contact person would be for future reference. Although contact people or organizations may change over time, this information may provide a starting point for future inquiries.
   Ask the following questions to ensure that the service can be useful:
   - Does it work specifically with children under 5 years of age?
   - Does it work with families of young children?
   - What is the cost of the service?
   - What commitment will families need to make?
   - Is the service run by professionals or parents in similar situations?
   - Can it work with children who have special and diverse needs?

   Knowing these basic facts about agencies and organizations will help to ensure that sufficient and appropriate information is passed on to parents.

2. Choose a particular health or medical concern and search the World Wide Web for information about it. List or bookmark sites that offer useful information for you or for parents.

3. Talk with parents or individuals from diverse cultures and religions. Ask them about their views regarding children with special needs, children with health needs, or children at developmental risk. How might these views affect the parenting and care of the child?

4. Talk with other children about children with different health needs or children at developmental risk. What information do they have about these children? What attitudes do they have?

DISCUSSION QUESTIONS

❶ Discuss children at risk for developmental delays. What are these children typically called in your area? What does this mean to you in your day-care centre or community? What special needs might these children have? What resources may they need?

❷ Discuss the adaptations your day-care centre may need to make to accommodate a child with health and medical needs in terms of space, materials, equipment, toys, and staffing.

❸ Discuss stress in relation to the young child. How is it manifested? What events and situations cause stress for the children you care for? What are some ways of dealing with it?

❹ Discuss how you explain each of the following issues to young children. Consider and practise the actual vocabulary you might use in speaking with children of various ages. Be sure to explain the situation thoroughly in a way that doesn't stigmatize the child or frighten other children:

- Explain a seizure.
- Explain why the child with diabetes needs needles.
- Explain why the child with allergies can't drink milk.
- Explain death.
- Explain what being homeless means.
- Explain what it means to be poor.

❺ Discuss why families with children who have special needs may experience more stress and marital strain than other families. Consider the whole family, including their life cycle, siblings, and extended family, in relation to the child's diverse needs.

Parental Involvement

CHAPTER 9

Introduction

Most young children have several key adults in their lives, including mother, father, caregiver, aunts, uncles, and grandparents. Although all of these adults play important roles in the lives of children, their direct influence on children's development is partly determined by their physical location and by the amount of time they spend together. In almost every case parents spend the most time living with their children and their influence, together with that of brothers and sisters, is the greatest. For a child attending an early childhood program, the caregiver, who may spend up to eight hours each day with the child, is a major non-relative influence on his or her development.

It is traditional within early childhood services for full recognition to be given to the crucial role that parents play in the development of their children. It is to parents that children turn for direction, appreciation, and love. Parents provide continuous learning opportunities for their children. Bronfenbrenner (1979) discusses the need of all children for someone to believe in them and to be totally committed to them. He describes the role of parents as that of being "crazy" about their children. Despite professional acknowledgment of the importance of the parents' role, however, the relationship between early childhood professionals and parents remains a difficult issue. Caregivers speak of working in "partnership" with parents or of "involving" parents in their program. However, difficulty in deciding what these terms mean and in implementing policies to put them into practice have left many early childhood professionals and parents unsure about their roles.

Closeness in the relationship between early childhood professionals and parents is considered important for a number of reasons.

1. It will help the child to make the transition from home to the early childhood program, especially if the communication between adults is open, friendly, and concerned about the child's well-being.

2. It assists in ensuring optimal development for the child, as efforts made to encourage the child's growth and development are consistent in various settings.
3. It helps parents to maintain closeness with their child and to feel competent about their efforts as parents, especially when caregivers share stories of their child's experiences, efforts, and creations.

After reading this chapter, you should have a better understanding of:

- the possible experiences of families that include a young child with special needs;
- the stages that parents may undergo as they learn about and adjust to the implications of their child's special needs;
- how others in society may influence families that include young children with special needs;
- how early childhood professionals may work effectively with families of children with special needs.

Parents of Children with Special Needs

Understanding the Experience

For those of us who have not had the experience of parenting a child with special needs that threaten to seriously impede his or her development, the heading of this section may seem a little absurd. Perhaps the most that we can understand is that parenting a child with a disability often involves a process of adapting to the child, to other members of the family, and to society. It is important to note that the experience of parenting is unique to each family, whether or not the family includes a child with special needs, and there is no single experience of parenting a child with special needs. All parents bring different experiences to the task of parents, have different beliefs about and expectations for their children, and are influenced by a myriad of factors in their environment. Thus, any discussion of the experiences of parenting a child with special needs must recognize the unique quality of each parent–child relationship.

The most accepted description of the process that parents go through in adapting to their child's disability is a stage model. Not all parents of children with special needs experience all of these stages or experience them in the order presented here. Parents may be in one stage for a few days or weeks, or they may experience particular feelings for several years. They may also re-experience these emotions at different developmental stages of their child's life (Shimoni and Baxter, 1996). However, this description will help to increase your understanding of parents as they travel on a continuum of reactions in coming to terms with their child's condition.

SCENARIO

Nora was a 5-year-old girl with significant developmental delays and health concerns. She was included in her local community day-care centre and kindergarten program and had a one-to-one assistant for most of the day. Nora's mother, Hanna, decided to send her to a segregated special school, where she believed Nora's special needs would be more thoroughly attended to. Hanna was convinced it was the right decision and that Nora's best interests were at the heart of the decision.

As the new school year approached, however, Hanna became increasingly anxious and revisited her decision many times, often saying that she wasn't absolutely sure that Nora needed so much extra support. She snapped at the school administrator and the bus driver when arrangements didn't go as she planned. One day she met with Nora's day-care provider and burst into tears. "I never thought going to school was going to be such a big deal, but when I saw all her little friends from kindergarten walk off together while we waited at the side of the road for the special bus, it hit me that she'll never be like them."

Shock

Whether their child is diagnosed at birth or at some later time, parents report feeling numb, helpless, and confused. Many parents say that they are unable to take in the information given to them by the doctor, psychologist, or other professional.

Denial

Some parents may spend a great deal of time and energy in attempting to prove (to themselves) that the diagnosis was incorrect. One mother, after being informed by the pediatrician that her 14-month-old daughter had a profound bilateral hearing loss, spent days "proving" him wrong by bashing together cooking pots and sounding the car horn so that she could report to him how her daughter responded to "environmental" sounds. Some parents search for second opinions or diagnoses that are more favourable than the original one.

Anger and Guilt

Parents may search for a cause for the disability and ask, "Why me?" or "Why should this happen to my child?" They may blame themselves or medical personnel, or they may direct their anger at those closest to them — their spouse, "helping" professionals (including early childhood professionals), or the child.

Depression

Parents may feel sad or despairing about their situation or about their child's future. This may result in them appearing to "give up" or to be less caring.

Detachment

Their depression may lead parents to feel detachment — periods when nothing seems to matter and they feel empty and flat. The joy and meaning of life eludes them.

Reorganization

For many parents, positive adjustment begins with a period of re-energizing and reorganizing their time and energy. It is usually accompanied by feelings of realism and hope.

Adaptation

The parents' acceptance of the situation and their child's condition is characterized by their expression of realistic expectations for the child, advocating on the child's behalf, and working collaboratively with others for the well-being of the child.

Noting the various conditions that parents of young children with disabilities may experience may enhance our understanding of their reactions. Thus, it is not surprising to find some parents who are more difficult to understand. Sometimes they are more critical or demanding, or they make statements that are difficult to understand.

> **SCENARIO**
>
> I once worked with a family that included Julia, an 8-year-old girl who was severely disabled and totally dependent on others for her everyday living. Her parents were extraordinary, dedicating themselves to Julia's well-being. As the father of two young, apparently healthy, and typically developing children, I was shocked when Julia's mother told me that she hoped Julia would die before she did. It was so powerful a statement and ran so contrary to my own hopes and dreams for my children that I could not fully understand how she could say such a thing. She went on to say that she worried every day about what would happen to Julia when she and her husband were no longer there. "I'm sure other people would care," she said, "but they have other cares and they wouldn't care about Julia as we do."

When we consider the myriad of emotions this mother may have experienced, her comments make more sense and demonstrate her deepest feelings and fears for her daughter.

Since parents react and deal with situations differently, it is important not to make every parent of a child with special needs fit into the model presented above. It has been presented here to provide a framework that may increase your understanding and help in your practice with parents. Keep in mind that it is not uncommon for parents to direct strong feelings toward early childhood professionals; often they are the most accessible professionals available.

> **SCENARIO**
>
> Jack was a 2-year-old boy with multiple disabilities involving his physical development, including his health, hearing, and vision. His parents were beginning the long journey of

locating the services and equipment Jack needed. Each time they returned from an appointment with a medical professional, they were visibly frustrated and agitated. They expressed their frustration by increasing their demands on Jack's caregivers. The caregivers soon began to dread Jack's return to the day-care centre after any professional appointments. The day-care director intervened and offered to accompany Jack's parents to their next appointment at the local hospital.

The next week, they headed off to the neuromuscular clinic at the hospital, where Jack was seen by several doctors, therapists, and nurses. The director was amazed to discover that Jack's parents remained quiet throughout the day and answered the doctors' requests with rather meek statements of agreement. This was a far cry from the assertive parents that she and her staff were used to seeing in the day-care centre.

Three other factors influence the development of parenting a young child with special needs.

The first factor is "ignorance." At the time of their child's initial diagnosis, whether at birth or later, most parents know little or nothing about the implications of the condition. Sometimes medical personnel are not able to adequately describe the child developmentally. One parent, for example, remembers her family doctor telling her that her son with developmental delays would grow normally but would always have "the mind of a two-year-old." The description was difficult to comprehend and more than a little frightening. Parents, on learning that their newborn baby has Down Syndrome, for example, may not be familiar with the term or with the developmental implications for their child. It is only later, after thinking, talking, and reading about other children with Down Syndrome, that they begin to understand and to ask questions.

The second factor is "stress." Parenting a young child with special needs brings various stresses in addition to those of parenting a child with typical development. Among the factors that may increase stress are the reactions of others to the child, working with medical and educational professionals, and concern about the child's future — not to mention caring for the child 24 hours each day.

The third factor is "lack of assistance." Parents may not know where to look for appropriate help, especially if they have no relatives or friends nearby to offer physical and emotional support and relief. The normally straightforward task of finding a baby-sitter who can cope competently with the child may be very difficult: it may not be as simple as hiring the 13-year-old neighbourhood baby-sitter from down the street. The early childhood professional may be one of the primary supports to parents of young children with special needs.

OTHER INFLUENCES ON THE FAMILY

Families that include a child with special needs are subject to pressures beyond those typically experienced in a family that does not have a child with special needs. Parents in particular face a variety of physical, social, and emotional stresses that are affected by, and that affect, their ability to develop optimal parenting skills and experience regular family life.

ECOLOGICAL APPROACH

The family that includes a child with special needs may be considered a microsystem, in which the parents, the child, and the siblings influence each other directly and daily. For the child with special needs who attends an early childhood program, the microsystem may also include friends and peers in the program as well as the caregiver with whom he interacts frequently. The settings and relationships that exist within the microsystem affect the dynamics of the system, including the development of the child with special needs. The relationships between members of the microsystem (for instance, the extent to which the parents of the child with special needs know his or her friends and the caregiver in the early childhood program) will have a profound effect on the development of the young child; they will influence transitions from home to program, the consistency of approaches, and the child's sense of belonging. The relationships between members of the microsystem are referred to as the mesosystem.

The inner circle of people who directly and frequently influence each other is, in turn, affected by the exosystem. The exosystem consists of social institutions such as the education system, church, social agencies, members of the extended family, and the parents' work settings. Although these setting have a less direct influence, they still affect the family. For example, the attitudes and opinions of grandparents, even though they may live some distance from the family, will influence the child's development. So will the parents' work settings, which involve many issues: whether the parents' work is secure, involves shift work, includes benefits, and is well paid.

Finally, the macrosystem encompasses the beliefs and influences of society and is reflected in economic and political policies. For instance, in Canada in the 1960s, the prevalent belief was that all people with special needs (including very young children) were better cared for in large institutions, where therapeutic and rehabilitative services could be concentrated. This societal belief changed slowly through the 1970s and 1980s, leading to political and economic support for community-based programs of integration and inclusion.

The ecological model in Figure 9.1 helps to clarify the many influences and sources of support or stress in the family's life.

● ● ● ● ● ●
Role of the Early Childhood Professional

ADVOCACY

Early success in developing services for young children came as a result of effective advocacy by parents. Parents learned quickly that they could be effective when they worked together. Parent associations were formed across Canada, some with national and others with regional and local perspectives. They lobbied governments, social institutions, and private businesses for improved services. For example, families that included children who were classified as "mentally retarded" were often excluded from regular school settings until well into the 1970s. Beginning in the 1950s, parents banded together to start their own programs and schools

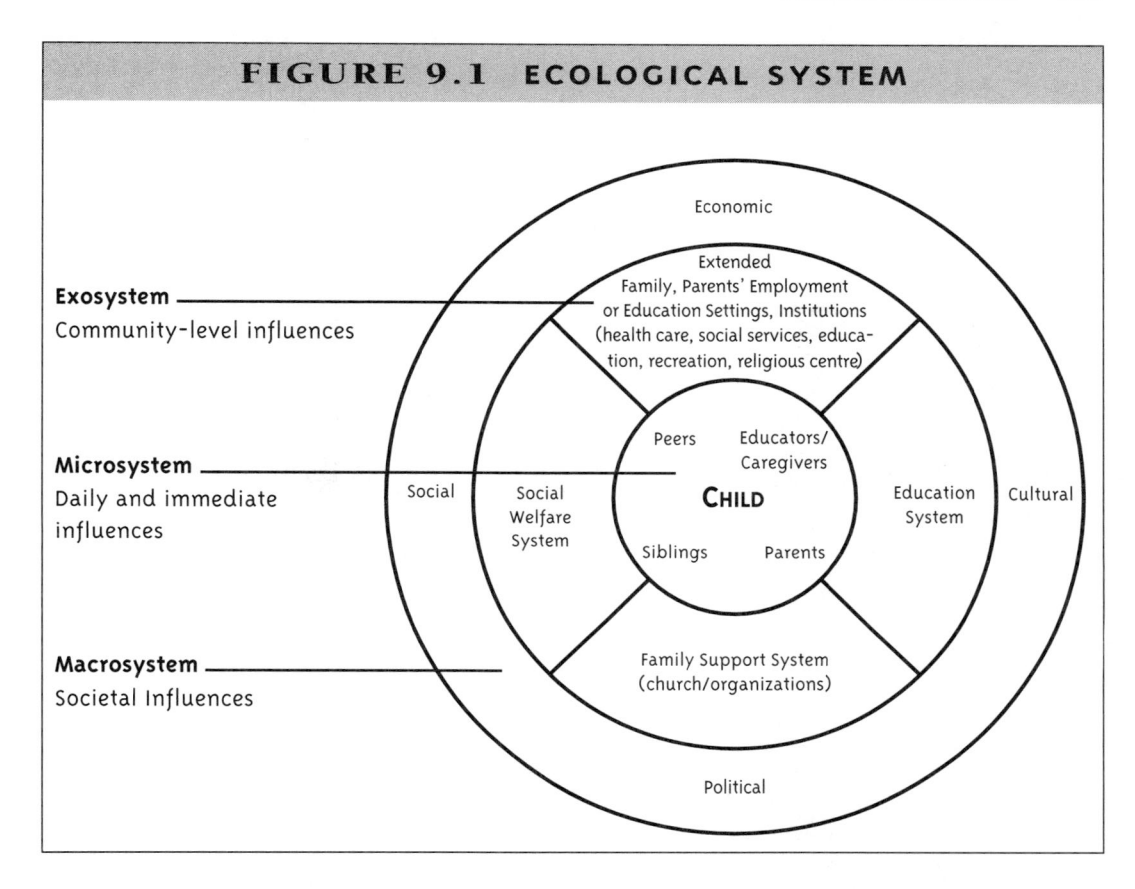

FIGURE 9.1 ECOLOGICAL SYSTEM

Exosystem — Community-level influences

Microsystem — Daily and immediate influences

Macrosystem — Societal Influences

Outer ring (Macrosystem): Economic, Cultural, Political, Social

Middle ring (Exosystem): Extended Family, Parents' Employment or Education Settings, Institutions (health care, social services, education, recreation, religious centre); Education System; Family Support System (church/organizations); Social Welfare System

Inner ring (Microsystem): Peers, Educators/Caregivers, Parents, Siblings — surrounding CHILD

Source: Based on U. Bronfenbrenner. (1979). *The Ecology of Human Development: Experiments by Nature and Design.* Cambridge, MA: Harvard University Press; and D. Peters and S. Kontos. (1987). *Continuity and Discontinuity of Experience in Child Care.* Norwood, NJ: Ablex Publishing.

especially for children with mental retardation. Some of these schools continue across Canada today. They are either operated by local associations of parents or have been taken over by local school boards.

Typically, individual parents, particularly following the initial diagnosis and assessment of their child's condition, are overwhelmed with the intensity of the care needed by the child. They may not be in any position to advocate on behalf of others, on behalf of their child with special needs, or on their own behalf. They may need others to advocate on their behalf for services, support, and information. Early childhood professionals are in an excellent position to provide advocacy support for parents, but advocating on behalf of others cannot be assumed. It is therefore important for early childhood professionals either to wait for parents to request assistance or to get their approval before efforts are made on their behalf. In either case, caregivers must be prepared to advocate for the child with his or her family in a positive, well-informed, and professional manner.

SCENARIO

Louise was the single mother of Owen, a 5-year-old boy with cerebral palsy. Owen had many physical and health-related concerns and required specialized equipment for almost everything, including eating, sleeping, manipulating objects, and communicating. This equipment was very expensive and not covered under her medical benefits package at work. Owen's caregiver at the day-care centre suggested that Louise apply for support to a local foundation that provided funding for people with disabilities.

Louise applied and was required to make a verbal presentation to a panel that would then decide upon the level of support. She was very apprehensive and refused to attend the panel. Owen's caregiver offered to accompany Louise and to assist with the presentation. Together they planned what they would say and how they would answer any questions. With the support of the caregiver, Louise was able to attend, make an effective presentation, and receive funding to help pay for Owen's special equipment.

Parents may express concerns over any number of factors in the early childhood program, from issues of diet, sleep, and toileting to concerns about the child's developmental progress. Caregivers are in a helpful "in-between" position to help parents with these concerns. On the one hand they are able to explain and show parents the various options available to them in the program, and on the other hand they are able to seek help for the parents or child by directing requests to supervisors or program directors.

When the needs of the family involve advocates outside the early childhood program, it is important for the caregiver to know how and where to obtain information that will help. For instance, an early childhood professional may perceive that the parents of a young child with cerebral palsy are quite lonely. They may speak of not having family or friends living nearby who could understand and help them with their situation. An advocate's response may be to inform the parents about local associations or support groups (particularly if there is a local association with a focus on young children with special needs or, more specifically, young children with cerebral palsy) or to ask the parents whether the caregiver could give the association their names for possible future contact. It is important in these situations not to push parents into meeting others with children who are similarly disabled. Whereas some parents may want to do this as soon as possible, others may not wish to meet others for months or even years after their child's diagnosis.

One situation in which parents of a young child with special needs may need support is in formal meetings or case conferences designed to discuss the child's progress and needs. Typically at such meetings the parents, together with all the professionals who work with the child, meet to report on their work to date and to plan future interventions. Parents may feel overwhelmed in meetings at which professionals from various disciplines talk about their child and sometimes use technical language that is difficult for them to follow.

As an early childhood professional, you may be in an excellent position to develop a relationship of trust with the parents and to assist them to be self-advocates in such situations. This may involve spending time with the parents before the meeting, describing for them who else will be present, and outlining the procedures that will be followed. Helping parents to prepare the questions they want answered and the information they want to provide to the various professionals may be a useful service to them.

Showing Respect for the Child and Family

Just as it is important to evaluate your attitudes regarding disabling conditions, it is important to be aware of and understand your attitudes toward the child and her or his family. Do you, for instance, believe that the parents are doing enough, could be doing more, do too much, baby the child, overprotect the child, treat the child differently from other siblings, or have unrealistic expectations of you or other professionals? These and other views need to be considered in light of the stresses, supports, and care needs that the child and family situation demand. An increased understanding of families will assist you in creating an atmosphere of mutual respect.

All parents can contribute important information about their family and the child with special needs. Parents generally not only know their child better than anyone else, but often have a greater understanding of the child's particular condition than do most other people. One of the important ways for you to convey respect for the family is to act upon information you have obtained from the parents regarding their child — his or her likes and dislikes, strengths and needs, and other educational and medical details. Consistently demonstrating respect for the parents requires you to be authentically interested in contributing your knowledge so that the parents are better able to meet the needs of their child. Creating an atmosphere in which information, concerns, and joys are freely and frequently expressed by both the parents and the early childhood professional is an important goal.

You should also be aware of, and consider, the child's siblings. Their roles and concerns will contribute to the dynamics of the family. Siblings may have a variety of needs, such as realizing that other families may include children with special needs and getting to know the friends and caregivers of the sibling with special needs. Including siblings in events, just as we include the siblings of children who are following more typical patterns of development, may help them to feel included in the family.

Similarly, you too can demonstrate respect for the child with special needs. There is always the danger that you as a caregiver will be overwhelmed with the idea that the child has a disability and that the disability will be the focus of your attention, concern, and interaction. It is important to remember that the child with special needs has needs and interests similar to those of other children in the program and that these need to be responded to.

Your attitudes and actions of respect for the child with special needs are important for the parents of that child and provide positive modelling for others in the program. When you play, talk, and clearly enjoy interacting with the child, parents are able to savour the ordinary but delicious pleasure of parental pride and delight — an opportunity they may not often experience because of time restraints and other demands. Parents and siblings, including the child with special needs, need frequent opportunities to interact in playful and fun ways.

Providing Emotional Support

Parents of children with special needs may experience feelings of inadequacy, loneliness, and guilt. The routine sharing of advice and information about child-rearing that occurs naturally among friends and relations becomes irrelevant when parents discover that their child is in some way disabled. Few friends, neighbours, or relatives have faced these situations. Often parents turn to professionals for the support and guidance that is hard to find elsewhere.

SCENARIO

Troy is a child with muscular dystrophy. His mother recounts her need for support: "When Troy was very young I actually looked forward to my doctor's appointments with him, even though they often brought disappointment and pain. In this setting I felt taken care of. My husband, friends, and parents were all eager to help with Troy, but with them I felt desperately in charge and didn't ever feel like I could say "I don't know" or "I need help.""

Although early childhood professionals need to be alert to these feelings, they must at the same time recognize that they are not therapists or medical doctors — they cannot provide all the support that parents may need. One of the most important roles for you as caregiver is that of being a good listener. Encourage parents to express their feelings and attitudes during their period of adjustment. They often need help in feeling comfortable with daily exchanges of information and in expressing their concerns. In addition, it is important for you to act and make comments in support of the efforts of the parent. Sometimes people in professional positions are critical of the efforts of parents, perhaps because they do not live up to expectations of the professional. It is essential for you to look for ways to build the parents' self-confidence. While the child with special needs is the primary focus of such a relationship, remember also that parents are more than parents. They too will have other interests and abilities. Sometimes they may wish to talk about other things that interest or concern them.

Finally, parents of children with special needs often provide emotional support for each other. Look for opportunities for various parents to interact with each other. This may be as simple as introducing them to each other at drop-off or pick-up time, or as formal as referring parents to professional counselling services or parent support associations. You may want to include other family members, such as siblings and grandparents, in these efforts. Some support associations have programs oriented toward other family members in an attempt to ensure that other stresses do not occur.

SCENARIO

Thelma had worked with 4-year-old Zoe for a little over three months. Zoe was described as being developmentally delayed, with a particular problem in the area of speech and language. Together with the speech pathologist, Thelma had focussed all her energies on Zoe's language production and had visited Zoe's home to encourage the family to help with the program. It came as a shock, then, when Zoe's mother stormed angrily into the early childhood program one day and expressed her dissatisfaction with the demands of the language-based program.

During the conversation between Thelma and Zoe's mother, it became apparent that Zoe's mother did not object to the language program. She had other pressures and priorities. In addition to bringing up Zoe, she had to care for 18-month-old twins. She needed help with their toilet-training because all three children were still in diapers. She was so overwhelmed with the day-to-day demands of three preschool-aged children that even a few minutes each day devoted specifically to Zoe's language was too much for her.

Early childhood professionals need to be mindful of the context in which the family operates and to consider it when making requests or demands. What may seem like a simple request to a parent may be too much for the family to cope with. In thinking about what experiences are meaningful for the child it is important to talk with parents. They may disagree with your professional view and find it difficult to maintain enthusiasm and interest in your program. Most parents know their children well and can tell you what interests them and what strengths they will bring.

Providing meaningful experiences for the child with special needs, however, includes more than teaching the child in the areas of identified need. Families that include a child with special needs will be encouraged if they see that the early childhood professional identifies and works with the child's other interests and abilities. This may mean involving the child in play activities; using materials and playing with or alongside other children in appropriate ways; participating in real conversation (not merely teaching-directed commands or rhetorical "small talk") whether the child has sophisticated language abilities or uses mainly gestures; and learning self-help skills, such as dressing, eating, and toileting. These strategies are not only critical to the child's development but demonstrate to parents, in a very real way, that your interest in their child is first and foremost.

Young children are occupied with understanding themselves, the world they live in, and the power or influence they have over their world. Those with special needs are no different. They also want to understand themselves and their world to find out what they like and dislike, what they can and cannot do, and how to get along with others. Meaningful experiences are those that help children to move forward in this process in ways that are developmentally and culturally appropriate.

KNOWLEDGE, ATTITUDES, AND SKILLS

Early childhood professionals hold a unique place in the lives of young children with special needs. Among all professional groups they are the only ones who live, work, and play with and among children in environments designed specifically for children. Psychologists will typically spend time with children (and sometimes the parents) in a "clinical" office setting, at an appointed time to complete activities initiated and controlled by them. When psychologists do visit children at home or in an inclusive early childhood setting, it is usually a brief visit with a particular goal or purpose in mind and does not include "living with" children in any real way. This is also true for medical personnel such as doctors, nurses, and specialists, as well as therapists, including physiotherapists, occupational therapists, and speech therapists.

Although caregivers share the experience of living and playing with children with their parents, however, the experience is different from that of parents in many significant ways: the type of relationship, the reciprocity of belonging that characterizes parent–child realities, and the permanence of a parent–child relationship compared with the temporariness of caregiver–child relationship. Thus, to effectively assist the young children with special needs who are temporarily entrusted to their care, caregivers must have particular skills, knowledge, and attitudes. They already bring a wealth of knowledge regarding the ways in which children typically develop in the early years and of the importance of interactions through play and with the environment. As Chandler (1994) states, "You probably know more than you realize about caring for and teaching children with special needs. If you know about the development of children you know a great deal about children with special needs because they are, first of all, children" (p. 21).

As a caregiver, you should continue to use this knowledge base and to include the child with special needs in your decisions regarding the preparation of the environment and the planning of appropriate group and individual experiences. Additional knowledge that may benefit the relationship between you and the parents includes having a sound understanding of their process of adaptation to the fact of having children with special needs. If parents sometimes react in ways that are difficult to understand or accept (strong expressions of anger or dissatisfaction, for instance), you should learn to accept this, without becoming defensive, and to help them work through these feelings.

Your knowledge base should include an understanding of the dynamics of the family — its work schedules, recreation pursuits, particular beliefs as they relate to raising children, and the extended family and general community supports. This will help you to plan experiences for the child that complement his or her home life.

It is important to provide accurate, and if possible, personal knowledge of other community-based supports. It is helpful for them not only to know of the existence of an agency or association that may help them, but also to know the names of contact people and processes for referral. For example, some parents may desire contact with other parents, while others only want professional contact. Parents need to know if there is a cost for the service, how to access the service, and if there is a waiting list. Providing inadequate or partial information may create additional stress for the family.

SCENARIO

Mary was the single parent of Martin, an active 5-year-old boy with developmental delays. Martin was included in the local day care and, although his needs were being met, his mother really felt that he needed to spend time with adult males because he had no male role models in his life. The caregiver assisted by finding brochures about local programs that paired fatherless children with male volunteers. Mary became excited about the possibilities, but her excitement was short-lived when she discovered they did not accept children with special needs. If the caregiver had checked beforehand, she might have saved Mary this disappointment.

The three fundamentals of good interpersonal communication with children and their parents are listening, understanding, and deciding what action to take. Good listening skills are essential, not merely to hear what parents are saying but to allow them to fully express their feelings and frustrations. Listening is a part of conversation, however, and good listening does not necessarily mean standing in silence while the parents talk. Good listening involves engaging in meaningful conversation with the parents in which it is apparent that you hear what they are saying and respond to them with authentic interest and concern. It requires that you meet and converse with a minimum of other distractions; this may involve setting up times and places to meet other than at drop-off and pick-up times.

In listening, it is important not to contradict or argue with the opinions voiced by the parents but respond with open questions and comments that invite them to fully clarify their thoughts and that will assist you in more fully understanding their views. It is helpful to use techniques such as paraphrasing or active listening, as well as describing what you believe to be the possible implications of the parents' points of view. Finally, try to help parents decide what course of action they should take and what role they should play in it. As a part of this, try to describe what you see as the advantages and disadvantages of particular courses of action.

Collaborating successfully with the family requires you to be committed to the well-being of the child and his or her family, to be authentically interested and involved in ensuring their well-being, and to reflect understanding and empathy for their situation. Authenticity requires that your attitude not be that of the "know-all expert." You must be interested in lending your expertise and in learning more to help the child's development. It is important to be able to admit when you "don't know" rather than pretending to have knowledge and understanding.

Professionalism does not mean hiding behind a professional image or using technical language to promote your own status; parents of young children with special needs do not expect you to know all there is to know, but they do expect honesty. Attitudes of respect, reflected in your efforts to keep parents informed, to ask their opinions, and to follow their suggestions, are also important. Even when the parents' wishes and opinions run contrary to yours, they should be respected. Only on the rare occasion that parents' wishes contravene what you believe to be in the best interests of the child should you point out your reasons for not following those particular requests.

Most importantly, try to view the child and the situation from the parents' point of view. As a caregiver, it is important for you to be empathetic. It is unlikely that the child will experience success or even a sense of belonging in a situation in which there is little or no contact between the parents and the early childhood professional, or where the contact is mostly antagonistic or confrontational. The primary efforts for securing a relationship that is comfortable, is based on trust, and provides for reciprocal information sharing, rests with the early childhood professional. These efforts need to be undertaken sincerely and sensitively for the well-being of the child and family.

• • • • • •
Summary

Respecting children with special needs, their parents, siblings, and other family members may be the first and most important step in establishing a working relationship or partnership with them. Establishing and maintaining the relationship may be, at the same time, the most rewarding and most frustrating experience. Your particular approaches and attitudes will either make this a stressful and frustrating experience or a supportive and nurturing experience for the child, his or her family, and for yourself.

ACTIVITIES

1. List the community organizations that offer services to children with special needs and their families. Are their services "inclusive"? If not, what criteria do they use to include and exclude some children?

2. Ask students and/or early childhood professionals to describe the knowledge, skills, and attitudes that are important for working with young children who have special needs and with their families. If possible, ask parents of young children with special needs to provide descriptions of the qualities that they think are important in early childhood professionals. What do you learn from comparing the lists?

3. Interview ten early childhood professionals and ask them to describe the rewards and difficulties of working in partnership with parents.

DISCUSSION QUESTIONS

1. What would you do if you found yourself in conflict with parents over the care of their child? For example, what would you do if a parent made disparaging remarks about the condition of the child at the end of the day in care, or if a parent demanded that you spend less time playing and more time teaching the child "important" skills?

2. You suspect that a young boy may have developmental delays and that these delays are causing an increasing problem for his full participation with the other children. What will you do? Will you talk with the parents? What will you say? Who else should or could be involved?

3. Write a statement of your philosophy of inclusive care and education that could be shared with parents and other staff to help them understand the goals and strategies that you use.

Collaboration for Success

CHAPTER 10

Introduction

Young children today, including those with special needs, have many educators: the family, the community, and the preschool or child-care environment. Although parents and other family members may play the major roles, other adults who are partners in the educational and caring processes contribute to the enrichment of children's lives during their formative years.

Beyond the family circle, the early childhood environment (child-care centre, family day home, kindergarten, and playschool) is the community's main agency for caring for and educating young children. By working closely with parents, other family members, and community agencies, the early childhood program can help determine how educational and therapeutic resources may be adapted to help young children with special needs and their families. Early childhood programs provide an important link in the resources provided for many children with special needs. By strengthening relationships between early childhood programs, families, and community organizations (municipal departments, regional services of various government ministries, volunteer groups, and privately operated therapeutic services), early childhood programs can emerge from their all-too-frequent isolation and evolve into an inclusive educational centre for children and parents.

Developing these collaborative partnerships, however, may require changes in the attitudes of early childhood professionals, the staff of municipal and other government departments, and community agencies. For professional collaboration to succeed, each person must see herself or himself as an integrated part of a support system for all children. All of the parties must work together without undue concern for their "territorial rights." That is to say, that all involved professionals need to work together in the best interests of the child, not any other individual's best interest.

After reading this chapter, you should have a better understanding of:
- the importance of collaboration between the professional personnel who work with young children who have special needs and their families;
- ways in which early childhood professionals may become important contributors to collaborative efforts to assist children and their families;
- the particular contributions that early childhood professionals may make through collaboration with others;
- the particular knowledge, skills, and attitudes that are important in ensuring the success of collaborative efforts.

SCENARIO

Jake, aged 30 months, was integrated into a community day-care centre with his own full-time aide. He was a content, curious little boy, always wanting to be involved and try new things. However, his presence in the program became problematic because his aide adamantly insisted that she worked for Jake's mother. Jake and his aide kept unpredictable hours, would arrive after the regular program start time, and would leave during the day to run errands or prepare dinner. The programming that included Jake became of secondary importance. As a result, work colleagues repeatedly expressed concerns to the aide and to the mother.

Eventually the director called a meeting. It was a difficult issue to resolve because the mother insisted that the aide worked for her, and the aide seemed content with this position. It was only when the director asked whose interests were best being served in this arrangement that the necessity for some change in approach was acknowledged.

Although the family has primary responsibilities in the development of children, often the family by itself cannot adequately respond to the complex demands of a child with special needs. Similarly, it is unlikely that any single early childhood professional, community service, or government agency can provide the wide range of services these children may need as they grow and develop. Only by working collaboratively can all concerned ensure a range of resources to support the family in raising and educating the young child with special needs. Resources from municipal, provincial, and federal governments, together with volunteer and privately operated community agencies, working with the full participation of early childhood programs, may complement one another in supporting children with special needs and their families.

Following are brief descriptions of some of the specialized services and consultants that serve young children with disabilities and their families.

1. *Physiotherapist:* The muscle control of many children with physical disabilities, for instance those with cerebral palsy, is either too lax or floppy (hypotonic) or too rigid and tight (hypertonic). These problems may be made worse if the child is placed in incorrect positions when sitting, lying, standing, or being handled. The physiotherapist assesses the physical condition of the child and suggests exercises and handling procedures that may remedy some of the difficulties. He or she then recommends appropriate equipment, such as specialized chairs and walking frames. Physiotherapists may work out of a hospital or a community-based agency.
2. *Occupational Therapist*: A primary concern of the occupational therapist is the functional abilities of the child with regard to play, self-care, and interacting with the physical environment. Like the physiotherapist, the occupational therapist assesses skills and recommends appropriate adaptive equipment, such as eating utensils, and toys of varying manipulative complexity.
3. *Speech/Language Pathologist*: The speech/language pathologist works with children who have hearing and language impairments. He or she works to promote children's communication skills with their family and peers at home and in the community.
4. *Health Nurse*: The public health nurse assists in the identification of developmental delays or health problems that a child may exhibit. He or she can assist with preliminary screening for visual or hearing difficulties and help to ensure that the highest health and developmental standards are attained at home and in the early childhood program.

Many other professionals work with young children who have special needs and with their families. It is important for early childhood professionals to be aware of all the services provided for children in their community and to understand the mandates or primary purposes of these services, which children they serve, how referrals are made, and how they relate to the early childhood profession.

Figure 9.1 illustrated the many services and influences that may influence the development of a young child with special needs. Based on the works of Bronfenbrenner (1979) and Peters and Kontos (1987), this model shows the child at the centre of a series of concentric circles. The people in the first circle (the microsystem) are those who have the most direct and frequent contact with the child. They are also most influenced by the child because they share much of the child's daily life. The middle circle (the exosystem) shows many of the community-level influences on the child's development. In this circle are various social institutions, such as those concerning health, social services, and education, from which various specialized professionals, such as psychologists, occupational therapists, and early interventionists, work. The third and outer circle (the macrosystem) includes those social and community contexts within which the child and all the various supports exist. For example, if a child with special needs is raised in a society in which disability is regarded as a weakness, the child and the various services provided to her or him will reflect that attitude.

Although it is not illustrated in the diagram, another significant aspect of this model is the mesosystem, which refers to the extent to which the various people and institutions that have some bearing on the child's development know each other and communicate. The greater the understanding and communication between these people, the greater the advantage for the child's development. At the microsystem level, for example, the child is helped if the early childhood professional and the parents know each other and communicate comfortably together. If the parents know the child's peers in the program and the early childhood professional knows the child's siblings, the advantages to the child are obvious. The challenge for the early childhood professional in this communication system is to extend the mesosystem to the middle circle, so that communication, understanding, and knowledge of the child, the family, and each of the services available flow comfortably among all those involved.

The remainder of this chapter looks at several aspects of services and resources that may assist the development of young children with special needs. Particular focus is placed on:

- a more complete discussion of collaboration as it relates to the services and resources provided for young children with special needs and their families;
- a discussion of the roles of the early childhood professional as a participant in these services;
- the particular knowledge, skills, and attitudes required by early childhood professionals to enable them to work collaboratively; and
- the relationships that may currently exist between the various services.

COLLABORATION

In the context of this book, "collaboration" may be defined as the best practice in the way that various disciplines and agencies work together for the benefit of children with special needs and their families. It includes the concepts of co-operation, co-ordination, and sharing. It implies that professionals who work for different agencies and have different job descriptions will work together for the good of children and their families. It also implies that they will co-ordinate their efforts to reduce the possibility of conflicting advice and to minimize gaps in services. Collaboration among professionals also means working together for the benefit of the child, sharing goals for the child's success and an approach that is congruent across all services and disciplines.

Such transdisciplinary collaboration is difficult to achieve. It requires the commitment of all professionals and agencies involved. They need to be prepared to spend the time necessary to develop a thorough understanding of each other and to recognize the strengths and advantages of each other's approaches. They need to be prepared to change their approach if that is in the best interest of the child. Most importantly, they need to talk and to listen to each discipline and agency in an attitude of mutual respect for the perspectives and skills brought by each person.

In some communities a collaborative team approach may be used to assess, plan, and implement programs for working with young children with special needs. Such a team may consist of several professional personnel, representing a variety of agencies and government programs, who meet regularly to discuss their programs and the children with whom they are working. More typically, however, efforts toward team approaches are seen at meetings called to discuss the plans or progress of a particular child who is receiving services from those invited to the meeting. These meetings, sometimes referred to as case conferences, may be held several times each year to check the progress of a child and to plan for future programs and strategies. The success of these efforts at collaboration depends on many factors, including the skill of the person co-ordinating the services and the commitment of the professionals involved.

There are, however, several barriers to the practical success of collaboration. The first of these obstacles is the professional's lack of access or availability. To work collaboratively requires that time, money, and staff be devoted to the process. For some professions availability may be considered an important facet of their work, but for others it may be difficult. For example, a psychologist who creates her or his own schedule of appointments may include regular meetings with other professional personnel as a part of that schedule, but an early childhood professional working in a child-care centre may have less control of his or her schedule and have more difficulty in meeting with other professionals. Access may be affected by geographic location. In smaller, rural communities, access to particular therapists may require considerable travel or may be available on a visiting basis only. Using modern technology, such as communicating via computer, may alleviate this obstacle to collaboration.

A second obstacle to collaboration is competitiveness, or "turf" struggles between professionals, which may hinder their ability to work together. For example, personnel working in an agency designed specifically to provide services to children with speech and language problems may not readily accept that a child with a language problem is receiving services from an agency with a broader mandate. This competitive aspect of professional relationships may be based on a lack of information about the services and expertise provided by others. Closer communication, more frequent meetings, and visits to each other's practice facilities may all contribute to lessening apprehensions and lead to more collaborative efforts on behalf of children and families.

A third obstacle is professionals' attitudes toward their professional discipline and their ability to implement change. There has traditionally been a paternalistic approach associated with professional assistance: professionals dispensed advice and made all the decisions for the family. If professionals are entrenched in the perspective of their own discipline and the orientation toward working with children that it promotes but have less respect for others who work from different perspectives, it may be difficult to achieve a collaborative team effort. It isn't uncommon for caregivers to feel that they have little or no status compared with the "professionals" they collaborate with. However, caregivers possess a wealth of valuable information about child development.

•••••• Role of the Early Childhood Professional

Early childhood professionals occupy a unique position in the lives of young children with special needs. Outside of the child's immediate family, caregivers are typically the only adults who work alongside and nurture the child for extended periods of time in an environment designed specifically for children and adults to live together for several hours each day. Thus, they share more of the parenting experience than do other professional personnel who may work with the child. Most typically other professionals provide services to the child and have direct contact with him or her only for brief periods and by appointment. It is unlikely for these professionals to be involved in the everyday life of the child — feeding, toileting, napping routines, and play — unless they are specifically associated with an assessment or program.

It is from the position of being in loco parentis that early childhood professionals have an opportunity to gain insights and perspectives on the child's development. This knowledge extends from the intimately personal responses of the child to routines such as sleeping to understanding the child's fears, likes, dislikes, ways of communicating, and modes of play. Caregivers are also in the position to know and understand something of the family — its values, stresses, desires, and hopes. Each day, at drop-off and pick-up times, the opportunity for interaction between the parent and the early childhood professional occurs, and ideas and knowledge that may benefit the child are exchanged.

Professionals who work with the child for therapeutic or health reasons outside the centre will also have contact with the early childhood program, and the caregiver there will have a knowledge of the various services, programs, and particular personnel working with the child. The therapeutic professionals may ask the caregivers to follow through with some program

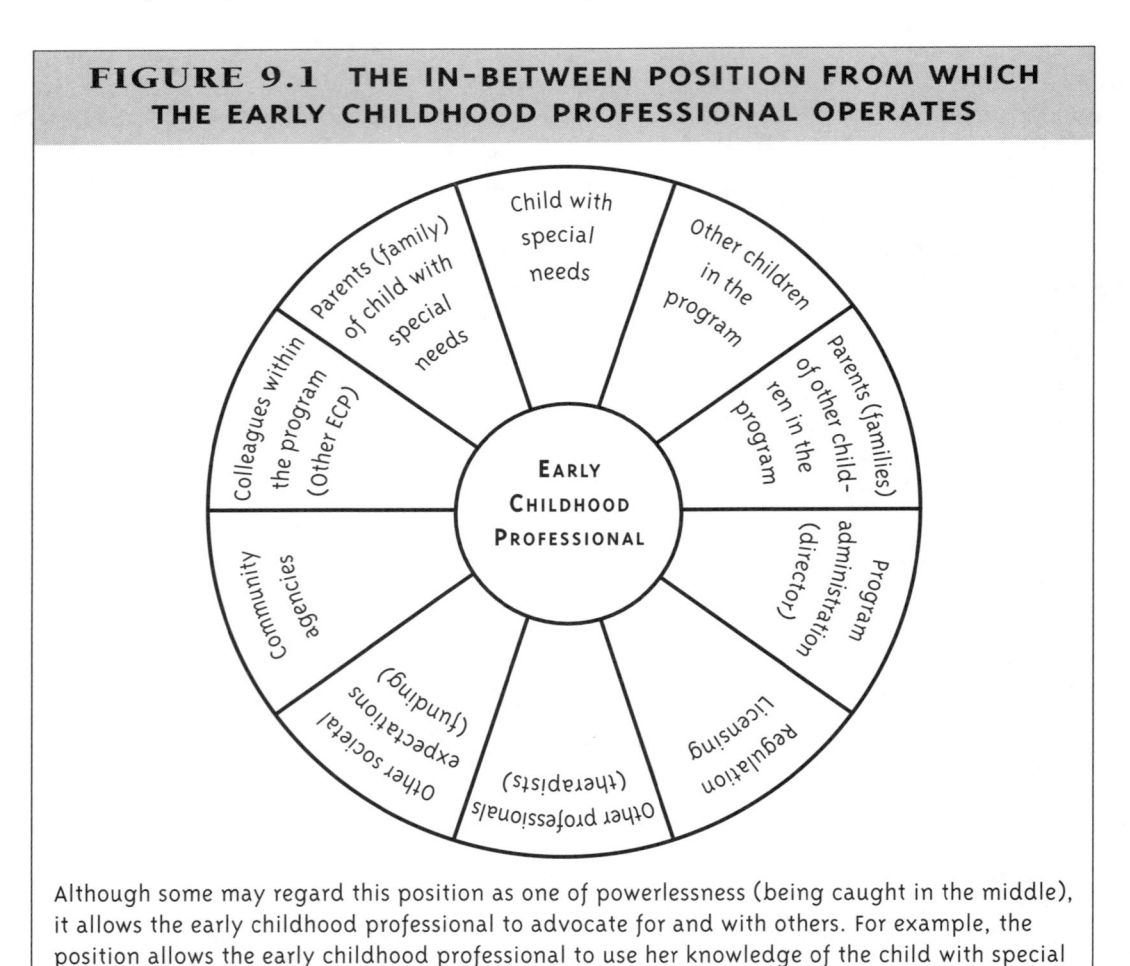

FIGURE 9.1 THE IN-BETWEEN POSITION FROM WHICH THE EARLY CHILDHOOD PROFESSIONAL OPERATES

Segments around the Early Childhood Professional:
- Child with special needs
- Other children in the program
- Parents (families) of other children in the program
- Program administration (director)
- Regulation Licensing
- Other professionals (therapists)
- Other societal expectations (funding)
- Community agencies
- Colleagues within the program (Other ECP)
- Parents (family) of child with special needs

Although some may regard this position as one of powerlessness (being caught in the middle), it allows the early childhood professional to advocate for and with others. For example, the position allows the early childhood professional to use her knowledge of the child with special needs to advocate on his behalf to the administrator, to other parents, and to licensing officials.

recommendations for the child. Indeed, it may be that a primary role of the early childhood professional is to translate therapeutic recommendations into appropriate practice.

The position of the early childhood professional working with children with special needs may, therefore, be described as an "in-between" position. The caregiver is in-between the needs and interests of the child, the wishes and demands of the parents, the expectations of other therapeutic and health professionals, and the policies and practices of the early childhood program as determined by municipal or provincial regulation or by the administration of the program. Viewed from traditional hierarchical structures, with the manager at the top and various levels of supervision down to the front-line early childhood professional, this in-between position may be regarded as one of powerlessness. In this model the early childhood professional is subject to the authority of parents, administrators, and other professionals with specialized knowledge and specific skills. However, if the in-between position is considered in a non-hierarchical model — for instance, as part of a circle of responsibility (more in keeping with our concept of collaboration) — it takes on a central, powerful, and important role.

Being in-between permits the early childhood professional to understand the positions of all others involved in the care and education of the child with special needs and to have a close understanding of the child. It is from this position that caregivers can advocate on behalf of the child, informing therapeutic and health professionals, administrators, and others of the veracity of their assessments, programs, goals, strategies, and ideas. Since caregivers share some of the parenting tasks, they are in a strong position to support the family by representing their views to professional personnel who know the families less well. To take advantage of this position — advocating for the rights and needs of the child and co-ordinating the programs and ideas of various therapeutic professionals — caregivers need certain knowledge, skills, and attitudes.

KNOWLEDGE

The knowledge needed by early childhood professionals as they include children with special needs in their programs begins with a thorough knowledge of child growth and development. It is through the study of, and reflection on, principles of growth and development that caregivers understand the children they work with, have a standard against which to measure the progress of a child, ensure that their expectations are appropriate, and ensure that the experiences they provide for the child are enabling development.

Knowledge of child development includes not only an understanding of what may be considered "normal" standards or milestones of development, but also an understanding of the various theories that explain why development occurs as it does and to present different orientations regarding how development occurs and what factors are important in ensuring positive growth and development. This knowledge of development should not, however, remain at a theoretical or general level. It is important to apply and share that knowledge regarding individual children, so that a caregiver can describe Lois as a child in care, one of whose characteristics is that she is 3 years old, rather than simply talking about 3-year-old children.

Another important area of knowledge for early childhood professionals is personal knowledge of the children in their care. Through living, playing, and working with the child, the caregiver has an opportunity to develop a deeper understanding of the child's abilities, likes, and expressions of emotion. It is in authentic conversations with the young child (whatever the language mode) as well as through sharing in his or her joys, sorrows, frustrations, and hopes, that the caregiver gains a deeper understanding of the child. Such knowledge allows the caregiver to view any special needs in the context of the child's whole life and to bring a sensitivity and understanding that other professionals may not have the opportunity to develop. It also allows the caregiver to represent the needs of the child to the other professionals when advocating on the child's behalf.

As a part of their knowledge of child development, early childhood practitioners need to know the implications of various developmental disabilities. Previous chapters of this book have discussed the developmental implications of each area of disability. It is important, however, not to overgeneralize this knowledge; it is sometimes easy to think that all children with Down Syndrome, for example, are affected in the same way. Caregivers must therefore integrate their knowledge of child development and the developmental implications of a particular disability with their knowledge and understanding of the child.

Other professionals who may be working with the child with special needs have different training and a different orientation to the child. Consequently, they will use terminology about the child that reflects that difference. As a part of knowing about the implications of a disability, it is beneficial for caregivers to be familiar with terms and concepts commonly used by other professionals. This will allow them to participate in conversations and to understand and interpret written reports.

Finally, it is through observing and recording the child's developmental progress that the caregiver can make sense of the knowledge of development and adequately interpret the actions of the child. This is also critical for working collaboratively with professional personnel from other disciplines and services. Observation and recording includes watching and seeing children in a thoughtful way, interpreting those observations, and recording them so that they may be reported to others in a helpful format. The presentation of a well-documented, sensitive, detailed, and accurate record of a child's experiences and development will provide important information to the family and will help ensure that the early childhood professional is a respected member of a collaborative team of professional personnel.

Knowledge of community supports includes knowing what services are available, the focus or purpose of each service, and the process needed for referral. For instance, a physiotherapist working in a hospital setting may work with both patients in the hospital and outpatients. He or she may work with a variety of people, including injury victims, and adults as well as children. The physiotherapist may not be able to schedule appointments outside the hospital, and referrals for physiotherapy services may need to be made by a medical doctor. By comparison, an early interventionist may work out of a community-based agency, provide services directly to young children with special needs at home and in early childhood programs, and may accept referrals from the family or other adults working with the child. The process by which the early childhood professional may either make referrals or simply talk with other professionals in order to get specific advice or information is important in working toward a model of collaboration. It is often difficult to determine which formal processes should be followed in developing such professional relationships; often they develop over time, as trust and respect are established on both personal and professional levels.

Although community services include professional services offering direct educational and medical interventions, the child and his or her family may participate in a variety of other community-based activities. Consider the following questions, for example. What recreation services are available to families with young children, and what efforts are made to ensure the inclusion of children with special needs in these services? Is it possible, for instance, to include a 4-year-old child with cerebral palsy in a swimming experience in the local pool, with his or her siblings and peers? What provisions are made by public transport services to ensure that children confined to wheelchairs have access to public transport? Does easy access exist to all major public buildings, including the early childhood program? Does the public library include taped stories appropriate for children with visual challenges?

A thorough knowledge of these services is important in many ways. First, it provides information that will be useful to the early childhood professional in planning appropriate experiences for young children, including children with special needs. Second, it can be passed on to parents of children with special needs. Third, discovering that some community-based services do not provide for the inclusion of young children with special needs provides an opportunity for the caregiver to advocate on behalf of the child.

The family, including parents, siblings, and other relatives, provides the most powerful context for and influence on the child's development. Developing relationships with parents that are supportive, encouraging, and helpful will enable the caregiver to know and understand the family. Without being intrusive or asking probing and unwelcome personal questions, the caregiver may develop a comprehensive picture of the family — who lives in the home with the child, what are some of the stresses experienced by the family in their work environments, and the hopes, fears, and aspirations of the family for the child with special needs. Such knowledge also helps in the early childhood professional's relationship with other professionals. It enables the caregiver to ensure that recommendations made by a therapist for exercises or practice to occur at home are possible and reasonable for the parent to complete.

There are other important areas of knowledge, including knowledge of self — the caregiver's personal values, abilities, and interests. It may be necessary to re-examine these areas regularly as you gain experience and expertise.

SKILLS

The early childhood professional working in an integrated setting that includes young children with special needs should have a variety of skills to ensure success for the program. Most important are the skills necessary for providing quality care for young children, including the ability to identify each child's interests and needs and to prepare appropriate experiences for each child based on these observations. In addition, however, various skills will assist the early childhood professional to work in collaboration with other professions. Among them are the skills of communication, advocacy, and observation.

Communication is a prerequisite skill for all early childhood professionals. The ability to listen, take turns, engage in meaningful conversation, and to notice and respond sensitively to behaviours in children is an indication of quality in child care. These skills are also necessary to work effectively with other professionals. The ability to question, suggest, and recommend, both verbally and in writing, in professionally acceptable ways requires the ability to listen, interpret, and understand. It is only through a combination of these aspects of communication that caregivers can become effective members of a collaborative team attempting to find solutions to the developmental problems presented by the child. These communication skills include understanding how to address each person on the team, whether in a verbal conversation or in writing a letter or memo; knowing how to express disagreement as well as agreement, in a way that maintains focus on the well-being of the child; and knowing how to ask for advice or help with the child. The ability to provide information, in the form of a written or verbal report giving information that is pertinent, clear and helpful, is another important communication skill.

Although the in-between position of the early childhood professional provides an excellent opportunity for advocacy, the advantage of this position can only be realized if the caregiver develops appropriate and effective advocacy skills. These skills include making sure that the positions taken are in the best interests of the child with special needs, that your advocacy is wanted (usually by the family), and that your methods of advocating are well-informed, assertive, and effective.

ATTITUDES

In addition to the professional attitudes that include maintaining confidentiality, putting one's own needs after those of the child, and searching for improved ways to work with the child, there are attitudes toward working in collaboration with others that are important. First is the notion of acceptance, not only the full acceptance of the child into the program but also your acceptance of the ideas, suggestions, and opinions of others with whom you will collaborate. Acceptance does not mean agreement, but it is an important prerequisite to building a comprehensive picture of the child and of alternative ways of helping her or him. A second important attitude is that of respect. This involves making sure that as a caregiver you act in a way that will cause other professional personnel to respect you and to ensure that you act in a respectful way toward others.

SCENARIO

As the early childhood professional providing care for 2-year-old Henderson, Julie observed that he was beginning to show interest in imitating words. Although the program that she, together with the speech pathologist and other professionals, had designed for Henderson did not include playing verbal imitation games, Julie decided to go ahead anyway. She began to name some familiar objects in the room and to encourage Henderson to repeat them.

After two days of attempting this and finding that Henderson responded well most of the time, Julie telephoned the speech pathologist, gave her a quick summary *of what she was doing and why, and asked for advice. They arranged for the speech pathologist to visit the program, to observe Henderson, and to provide Julie with some more ideas that might help her.*

It is important for the early childhood professionals working in inclusive settings to review their attitudes toward the child, the child's family, and the professionals with whom they work — colleagues within the program as well as therapeutic professionals from other agencies. It is also important for this reflection to include some self-assessment. If your attitude is one of extreme independence ("I know what I'm doing and I don't need others telling me what to do") or one of extreme submission ("I won't do anything with this child until the other professionals tell me what to do"), then you may not be working in a collaborative way for the best interests of the child.

Summary

Traditionally, professionals offered only those resources believed to be appropriate or best for the child. The changing needs of the family were not usually considered relevant or a priority. To be effective, all professionals need to give sound advice, account for and encourage empowerment, respect cultural and religious backgrounds, and respond to specific requests. Early childhood professionals can adhere to these guidelines and ensure that other professionals involved with the family do also.

Professionals must work together to provide the best experience for the child. This collaborative approach is premised on the belief that no one individual is likely to have the knowledge or skill to meet all of the child's emerging needs. The early childhood professional is in an ideal position — in-between — to help ensure that this collaboration among professionals and the family takes place. In order to fully utilize this position of advocacy, however, caregivers need knowledge, skills, and attitudes beyond those normally associated with providing appropriate experiences and quality care for young children.

The early childhood professional is an invaluable member of any collaborative effort to assist a child with special needs who is included in an early childhood program. It is important for these programs to move from their relative isolation in providing inclusive care and education for children to full participation in community efforts to provide comprehensive services that help children and their families.

ACTIVITIES

❶ List the various services available to young children and families in your community; include everything from recreation to therapeutic services. How easily are they accessed? Are all of these services available to families that include young children with special needs?

❷ Invite various "therapists" to talk to you about the services they provide and how they work with early childhood professionals.

❸ Invite parents of children with special needs to talk to you about the support or therapeutic services they use. Ask them to identify both their positive and negative experiences in using these services.

DISCUSSION QUESTIONS

❶ In groups, share observations about ways in which people (especially children) are treated differently in our society on the basis of their ability. In what ways does such treatment affect how people think about themselves?

❷ Discuss the pros and cons of the "in-between" position of the early childhood professional in working with the child, with parents, and with community-based professionals.

❸ What do you consider the major contributions that an early childhood professional can make to interagency collaboration? What are some of the difficulties that need to be addressed?

REFERENCES

Allen, K., and L. Marotz. (1994). *Developmental Profiles: Prebirth through Eight.* Albany, NY: Delmar.

Allen, K.E., and L. Marotz. (1994). *Developmental Profiles.* Albany, NY: Delmar.

Allen, K.E., C. Paasche, A. Cornell, and M. Engel. (1994). *Exceptional Children: Inclusion in Early Childhood Programs.* Scarborough, ON: Nelson Canada.

American Psychiatric Association. (1994). *Diagnostic and Statistical Manual of Mental Disorders* (4th ed.). Washington, DC: American Psychiatric Association.

Bailey, D. (1987). Collaborative goal setting with families: Resolving differences in values and priorities for services. *Topics in Early Childhood Special Education* 7 (2): 59–71.

Bailey, M., and M. Wolery. (1992). *Teaching Infants and Preschoolers with Disabilities.* New York: Macmillan.

Batshaw, M., ed. (1997a). *Children with Disabilities.* 4th ed. Baltimore: Paul H. Brookes.

Batshaw, M.L., and B.K. Shapiro. (1997). Mental retardation. In M. Batshaw.

Berk, L.E. (1996). *Infants and Children: Prenatal through Middle Childhood.* Boston: Allyn and Bacon.

Bloom, B. (1964). *Stability and Change in Human Characteristics.* New York: John Wiley & Sons.

Bloch, M.N. (1992). Critical perspectives on the historical relationship between child development and early childhood education research. In S.A. Kossler and B.B. Swaderee (eds.), *Reconceptualizing the Early Childhood Curriculum: Beginning the Dialogue.* New York: Teachers College Press.

Blum, N.J., and M. Mercugliano. (1997). Attention-deficit/hyperactivity disorder. In M. Batshaw.

Bobath, K., and B. Bobath. (1984). Neuro-developmental treatment. In D. Scrutton, ed., *Management of the Motor Disorders of Children with Cerebral Palsy: Clinics in Developmental Medicine,* no. 90, pp.6–18. Philadelphia: J.B. Lippincott.

Bredekamp, S. (1987). *Developmentally Appropriate Practice in Early Childhood Programs Serving Children from Birth through Age 8.* Washington, DC: National Association for the Education of Young Children.

Bredekamp, S., and T. Rosegrant, eds. (1992). *Reaching Potentials: Appropriate Curriculum and Assessment for Young Children,* vol. 1. Washington, DC: National Association for the Education of Young Children.

Bronfenbrenner, U. (1979). *The Ecology of Human Development.* Cambridge, MA: Harvard University Press.

Brown, L.W. (1997). *Seizure disorders.* In M. Batshaw.

Buzzelli, C.A., and N. File. (1989). The special needs of teachers of special needs children. *Day Care and Early Education* Summer: 9–13.

Callwood, J. (1997). Citizen's shame. *Homemaker's* May: 84–92.

Carr, A. (1997). Play and relationships: Programming for inclusion. *Interaction* (Winter): 1997.

Cashin-Sipos, A., L. Serra, P. DiNunzio, K. McCarl, and M. Quesnel. (1996). *Jelly Beans in a Jar: Inclusive Child Care: A Practitioner's Guide to Integration in Preschool Settings.* North York, ON: Roeher Institute.

Chandler, P.A. (1994). *A Place for Me: Including Children with Special Needs in Early Care and Education Settings.* Washington, DC: National Association for the Education of Young Children.

Cook, R., A. Tessier, and M. Klein. (1996). *Adapting Early Childhood Curricula for Children in Inclusive Settings.* Englewood Cliffs, NJ: Prentice-Hall.

Chud, G. and R. Fahlman. (1995). *Honouring Diversity within Child Care and Early Education.* Vancouver: Early Childhood Multicultural Services.

Covel, S.M. (1997). The importance of play. In L. Dunlap.

Cruz, J. (1987). *Interaction Preferences of Nonhandicapped Children.* ERIC Document Reproduction Service, No. ED 316 328.

Deiner, P.L. (1993). *Resources for Teaching Children with Diverse Abilities: Birth through Eight.* Fort Worth, TX: Harcourt Brace.

Devries, R. (1984). Developmental stages in Piagetian theory and educational practice. *Teacher Education Quarterly* II: 78–94.

Dolinar, K., C. Boser, C. and E. Holm. (1994). *Learning through Play: Curriculum Activities for the Inclusive Classroom.* Albany, NY: Delmar.

Dotsch, J. (1997). Why do I need to address diversity in ECE? *ECDNC Newsletter* 6–9.

Dunlap, L., ed. (1997a). *An Introduction to Early Childhood Special Education.* Boston: Allyn and Bacon.

Dunlap, L.L. (1997b). Infants, toddlers and preschoolers with developmental delays. In L. Dunlap.

Erikson, E. (1950). *Childhood and Society.* New York: Norton.

Featherstone, H. (1981). *A Difference in the Family.* Markham, ON: Penguin Books.

Finnie, N. R. (1981). *Helping the Young Cerebral Palsied Child at Home* (2nd ed.). London: William Heinemann Medical Books.

Frost, J. (1992). Playgrounds for all children. In J. Frost (ed.), *Play and Playscapes.* Albany, NY: Delmar Publishers.

Gartner, A., D. Lipsky, and A. Turnbull. (1991). *Supporting Families with a Child with a Disability: An International Outlook.* Baltimore: Paul H. Brookes.

Gold, M. (1980). *Try Another Way Training Manual.* Champaign, IL: Research Press.

Guralnick, M.J. (1990). Social competence and early intervention. *Journal of Early Intervention* 14(1): 3–14.

Hayslip, W., and L. Vincent. (1995). Opening doors to activities that include all children. *Exchange* 105(9): 44–46.

Hope Irwin, S. (1997). Including all children. *Interaction* (Winter): 1997.

Howard, V.F., B.F. Williams, P.D. Port, and C. Lepper. (1997). *Very Young Children with Special Needs: A Formative Approach for the 21st Century.* Upper Saddle River, NJ: Prentice-Hall.

Hurst, V. (1987). Parents and professionals: Partnerships in early childhood education. In G. Blenkin and A. Kelly, eds., *Early Childhood Education: A Developmental Curriculum.* London: Paul Chapman.

Jambor, M. (1990). Welcoming the child with special needs. *Day Care and Early Education* 17(4): 40–41.

Johnson, J.E., J.F. Christie, and T.D. Yawkey. (1987). *Play and Early Childhood Development.* Glenview, IL: Scott Foresman.

Kamii, C. (1985). Leading primary education towards excellence. *Young Children* 40(6): 3–9.

Kemple, K.M. and L. Hartle. (1997). Getting along: How teachers can support children's peer relationships. *Early Childhood Education Journal* 24(3): 139–146.

Kilbride, K.M., ed. (1997). *Include Me Too! Human Diversity in Early Childhood.* Toronto: Harcourt Brace.

Kuehne, V. (1996). *Working Collaboratively with Parents and Professionals.* Victoria: School of Child and Youth Care, University of Victoria.

Larson, C., and F. LaFasto. (1989). *Teamwork: What Must Go Right. What Can Go Wrong.* Sage Publications.

Lawson, T. (1997). Encouraging friendships among children. *Childhood Education* (Summer): 228–31.

Lerner, J. (1981). *Special Education for the Early Childhood Years.* Toronto: Prentice-Hall.

Liptak, G.S. (1997). Neural tube defects. In M. Batshaw.

Matthews, M.W. (1996). Addressing issues of peer rejection in child-centered classrooms. *Early Childhood Education Journal* 24(2): 93–97.

Mauk, N.E., M. Reber, and M.L. Batshaw. (1997). Autism and other pervasive developmental disorders. In M. Batshaw.

McKey et. al. (1985). Head start evaluation synthesis and utilization project. Quoted in L.J. Schweinhart. Early childhood development programs in the eighties: The national picture. *High/Scope Early Childhood Policy Papers* 1.

Meisels, S. J. (1989). *Developmental Screening in Early Childhood: A Guide* (3rd ed.). Washington, DC: National Association for the Education of Young Children.

Menalascino, F. J. (1987). Mental illness and the mentally retarded: Diagnostic and treatment issues. In J.A. Stark, F.J. Menalascino, M.H. Albarelli, and V.C. Gray, eds., *Mental Retardation and Mental Health: Classification, Diagnosis, Treatment, Services.* New York: Springer.

Michaud, L., A. Duhaime, and M.F. Lazar. (1997). *Traumatic brain injury.* In M. Batshaw.

Neugebauer, B., ed. (1992). *Alike and Different: Exploring Out Humanity with Young Children.* Washington, DC: National Association for the Education of Young Children.

Norton, T. (1997). Special health care for child care settings. Minimize the risks. *Interaction* (Winter): 1997.

Odom, S., and M. McEvoy. (1990). Mainstreaming at the preschool level: Potential barriers and tasks for the field. *Topics in Early Childhood Special Education* 10(2): 48–61.

Odom, S.L., and W.H. Brown. (1993). Social interaction skill intervention for young children with disabilities in integrated settings. In C. Peck, S. Odom, and D. Bricker, eds., *Integrating Young Children with Disabilities into Community Programs.* Baltimore: Paul H. Brookes.

Offord, D. (1991). Growing up poor in Ontario. *Transition* (June): 10–11.

Osofsky, J.D. (1994). Introduction to caring for infants and toddlers in violent environments: Hurt, healing and hope. *Zero to Three* 14(3): 3–7.

Parten, M.B. (1932). Social participation among pre-school children. *Journal of Abnormal and Social Psychology* 24: 243–69.

Pelligrino, L. (1997). *Cerebral palsy.* In M. Batshaw.

Peters, D., and S. Kontos. (1987). Continuity and discontinuity of experience: An intervention experience. In D. Peters and S. Kontos, eds., *Continuity and Discontinuity of Experience in Child Care: Annual Advances in Applied Developmental Psychology.* Norwood, NJ: Ablex.

Phillips, D.A., M. Voran, N. Kisker., C. Howes, and M. Whitebook. (1994). Child care for children in poverty: Opportunity or inequity. *Child Development* 65: 472–92.

Piaget, J. (1962). *Play, Dreams and Imitation in Childhood.* New York: Norton.

Prochner, L. (1994). A brief history of day care in Canada: The early years. *Canadian Children* 19(2): 10–15.

Pucket, M., and J. Black. (1994). *Authentic Assessment of the Young Child*. Toronto: Maxwell Macmillan.

Rioux, M., and M. Bach., eds. (1994). *Disability is Not Measles*. North York, ON: L'institut Roeher Institute.

Roizen, N.J. (1997). *Down Syndrome*. In M. Batshaw.

Russell-Fox, J. (1997). Together is better: Specific tips on how to include children with various types of disabilities. *Young Children* 52(4): 81–85.

Salisbury, C. (1991). Mainstreaming during the early years. *Exceptional Children* (58): 146–55.

Safford, P. and L. Rosen. (1981). Mainstreaming: Application of a philosophical perspective in an integrated kindergarten program. *Topics in Early Childhood Special Education* (1): 1–10.

Saracho, O.N., and B. Spodek. (1987). Play for young handicapped children in an integrated setting. Part I. *Day Care and Early Education* (Winter): 32–35.

Saracho, O.N., and B. Spodek. (1988). Play for young handicapped children in an integrated setting. Part II. *Day Care and Early Education* (Spring): 31–33.

Seligman, M., ed. (1991). *The Family with a Handicapped Child*. Boston: Allyn and Bacon.

Shapiro, E., and B. Biber. (1972). The education of young children: A developmental-interaction approach. *Teachers College Record* (74): 55–79.

Sheldon, K. (1996). "Can I play too?" Adapting common classroom activities for young children with limited motor abilities. *ECED Journal* 24(2): 115–20.

Shimoni, R. (1990). *A Historical Overview of the Development of Early Childhood Services*. ERIC Document ED 334 000.

Shimoni, R., and J. Baxter. (1996). *Working with Families: Perspectives for Early Childhood Professionals*. Don Mills, ON: Addison Wesley.

Shimoni, R., J. Baxter, and J. Kugelmass. (1992). *Every Child Is Special: Group Care for Infants and Toddlers*. Don Mills, ON: Addison Wesley.

Simeonsson, R.J., and N.E. Simeonsson. (1993). Children, families and disability: Psychological dimensions. In J.L. Paul and R.J. Simeonsson, *Children with Special Needs: Family, Culture and Society* (2nd ed.). Orlando: Harcourt Brace.

Smilansky, S. (1968). *The Effects of Sociodramatic Play on Disadvantaged Preschool Children*. New York: Wiley.

Spodek, B. (1985). Early childhood education's past as prologue: Roots of contemporary concern. *Young Children* (July): 3–7.

Stone, S.J. (1996). Integrating play into the curriculum. *Childhood Education* 72(2): 104–07.

Taylor, S., D. Biklen, S. Lehr, and S. Searle. (1987). *Purposeful Integration ... Inherently Equal*. Syracuse, NY: Syracuse University.

Templeman, T., H. Fredericks, and T. Udell. (1989). Integration of children with moderate and severe handicaps into a daycare centre. *Journal of Early Intervention* 13(4): 1–24.

Thomas, A., and S. Chess. (1977). *Temperament and Development*. New York: Bruner/Mazel.

Trachtenberg, S.W., and M.L. Batshaw. (1997). *Caring and coping: The family of a child with disabilities*. In M. Batshaw.

Trawicki-Smith, J. (1997). *Early Childhood Development: A Multicultural Perspective*. Columbus, OH: Merrill.

Trepanier-Street, M.L., and J.A. Romatowski. (1996). Young children's attitudes toward the disabled: A classroom intervention using children's literature. *Early Childhood Education Journal* 24(1): 45–49.

Turecki, S. (1989). *The Difficult Child*. New York: Bantam Books.

Vanier Institute of the Family. (1994). *Profiling Canada's Families*. Ottawa: Vanier Institute of the Family.

Van Manen, M. (1986). *The Tone of Teaching*. Richmond Hill, ON: Scholastic Books.

Van Riper, C. (1978). *Speech Correction: Principles and Methods*, sixth ed. Englewood Cliffs, NJ: Prentice-Hall.

Vygotsky, L.S. (1976). Play and the role in mental development of the child. In J.S. Bruner, A. Jolly, and K. Sylvia, eds., *Play: Its Role in Development and Evolution*. New York: Basic Books.

Wallach, L.B. (1995). Helping children cope with violence. In K.R. Gilbert, ed., *Annual Editions: Marriage and Family 95/96*. Guilford, CT: Dushkin.

Ward, M. (1994). *The Family Dynamic: A Canadian Perspective*. Scarborough, ON: Nelson.

Weikart, D. (1986). What do we know so far? A review of the Head Start Synthesis Project. *Young Children* (January): 44–55.

Winter, S.M., M.J. Bell, and J.D. Dempsey. (1994). Creating play environments for children with special needs. *Childhood Education* 71(1): 28–32.

Winzer, M. (1990). *Children with Exceptionalities: A Canadian Perspective* (2nd ed.). Scarborough, ON: Prentice-Hall.

——— (1997). *Special Education in Early Childhood: An Inclusive Approach*. Scarborough, ON: Prentice-Hall.

Wolery, M., P. Strain, and D. Bailey. (1992). Reaching potentials of children with special needs. In S. Bredekamp and T. Rosegrant (eds.), *Reaching Potentials: Appropriate Curriculum and Assessment for Young Children*, vol. 1. Washington: National Association for the Education of Young Children.

Wolery, M., and J.S. Wilbers, eds. (1993). *Including Children with Special Needs in Early Childhood Programs*. Washington, DC: National Association for the Education of Young Children.

Wolfensberger, W. (1972). *The Principle of Normalization in Human Services*. Toronto: National Institute on Mental Retardation.

Youcha, V., and K.I. Wood. (1995). Answering children's questions about peers with special needs. *Childcare Information Exchange* 105(9): 55–57.

Zeanah, C.H., ed. (1993). *Handbook of Infant Mental Health*. New York: Guilford Press.

INDEX

Able-bodied children. *See* Non-disabled children
Abnormality *vs.* normality, 112–13
Absenteeism, 136
Acceptance, in collaboration, 170
Accessibility
   of community services, 169
   in physical environment, 11, 56
Activity levels, 107 box, 117. *See also* Hyperactivity
Adaptability, 107 box
Adaptation, by parents, 148–50
Adaptive aids, 42, 50, 51, 55–56, 163. *See also* Hearing aids; Orthotic devices; Prosthetic devices; Static devices; Wheelchairs
   for CP children, 47
   for hearing impaired children, 85, 89
   for hydrocephalic children, 48–49
   for visual impairments, 70
Advocacy, by early childhood professionals, 153–55, 169, 170
Aggression, 123, 124, 138, 141
Alcohol abuse, 137
Allen, K.E., vi, 7, 30, 45, 64, 67, 68, 128
Allergies, 128–29, 136
   hearing impairments and, 80
Amblyopia, 65
American Psychiatric Association, 27
Anger
   management, 119
   in parents, 149
Antibiotics, 78
Anxiety, in children, 113
Aphasia, 95
Art, use in hearing impairments, 83
Articulation, in speech, 92–93, 94
Asthma, 129, 136
Astigmatism, 65
Ataxia, 47
Athetoid cerebral palsy, 46–47
Attention deficit disorder, 114–15

Attention deficit hyperactive disorder, 114–15
Attention seeking behaviour, 116, 120–21
Attention span, 107 box, 114, 115, 123
Attentiveness, hearing impairments and, 80
Attitudes
   of adults, 15
   toward behavioural difficulties, 119
   toward children in poverty, 139
   collaboration and, 161, 170–71
   toward communication difficulties, 98–99
   toward developmental delays, 36
   development of, 6
   regarding diversity, 18–19
   of early childhood professionals, 36, 170–71
   toward family, 155
   toward health problems, 133–45
   toward hearing impairments, 83–85
   of non-disabled children, 16–17, 88
   toward physical impairments, 55–56
   positive, 16
   toward special-needs children, 16
   toward visual impairments, 70
Audiometers, 79
Auditory training, 86
Authenticity, 159, 168
Autism, 94, 103, 113–14

Babbling, 103
Babies. *See* Infants
Baby-sitters, 151
Bailey, D., ix
Batshaw, M.L., 27, 28, 30, 113, 114, 133
Baxter, J., 4, 23, 138, 140, 148
Behavioural approaches, 5, 7–8
   to special-needs children, 19–20
Behavioural challenges, 105–24
   assessment, 111–12
   causes, 110–11
   classification, 112–13
   diagnosis, 111–12
   environments for, 119–22

etiology, 110–11
poverty and, 138
role of early childhood professional in, 118–24
Behaviour management, 119
Behaviours
of children in poverty, 139
communication and, 97, 98–99, 102–103
in developmental delays, 33–34
within environment, 33–34
externalizing, 113
hearing impairments and, 87
internalizing, 113
judgements regarding, 111–12
peer relationships and, 14
social, 31–32, 114
stimuli of, 119
stress and, 142
unco-operative, 116
in visual impairments, 69
Bell, M.J., 12
Berk, L.E., 106
Biber, 7, 8
Biklen, D., 6
Biology, as cause of behavioural problems, 110
Birth defects, 137–138
Biting, 113
Bladder dysfunction, 48
Blindness, 63, 64, 65. *See also* Visual impairments
Bloch, M.N., 2
Blood testing, 130
Bloom, B., 3
Blum, N.J., 114
Bobath, B., 46
Bobath, K., 46
Body awareness, 41, 124
Bowel dysfunction, 48
Bowlegs, 49–50
Braille, 64
Brain
fluid in, 48
injuries, 49
Breath, shortness of, 133

Breathing, 129
Bredekamp, S., 20
Brigance scale, 21
Bronchial tubes, 129
Bronfenbrenner, U., 147, 153, 163
Brown, L.W., 132
Brown, W.H., 15
Buzzelli, C.A., 13, 16

Callwood, J., 139
Canadian National Institute for the Blind (CNIB), 71
Caregivers. *See* Early childhood professionals
Carr, A., 13, 16
Case conferences, 154, 164–65
Cataracts, 64
Central nervous system, impairment, 95
Cerebral palsy, 4, 46–47
speech and, 95
Chandler, P.A., vi, 6, 12, 15, 51, 158
Chess, S., 106
Child abuse, 138
Child care, history, 2–8
Child development
behavioural concerns and, 116–17
communication difficulties and, 96–97, 101–102
hearing impairments and, 80–83
knowledge of, 167
language skills, 15
nursery schools and, 2–3
physical impairments and, 50–55
play and, 8–9
visual impairments and, 67–70
Choices, making, 39, 40, 121
Chud, G., 19
Club feet, 50
Cognitive delays, 28
behavioural difficulties and, 117
Cognitive development
behavioural difficulties and, 123–24
communication difficulties and, 103–104
developmental delays and, 31, 32, 40–41
hearing impairments and, 83, 88–89
physical impairments and, 52, 60–61
visual impairments and, 74

Colds, hearing impairments and, 80, 81
Collaboration
　with family, 159
　with other professionals, 85, 99, 161–71
　transdisciplinary, 164–65
Comas, 131, 136
Communication. *See also* Conversation;
　　Language; Peers; Speech
　by early childhood professionals, 169–70
　of hearing impaired children, 77
　with hearing impaired children, 86
　non–verbal, 93
　with parents, 135–36, 147–48
Communication aids, 56
Communication difficulties, 91–104, 113
　assessment, 95–96
　behavioural difficulties and, 116
　causes, 93–95
　diagnosis, 95–96
　environments for, 99–101
　role of early childhood professional in, 97–99
Communication skills
　developmental delays and, 42–43
　hearing impairments and, 93
Community support, 158, 168
　organizations, 161
　Project Head Start, 3
　for special-needs children, 162
　visual impairments and, 71
Compensation
　for impairments, 89
　within impairments, 67–68, 72–73
Conductive hearing loss, 78, 81
Conflict resolution, 15
Constructivist approach, to early childhood education, 7–8
Conversation. *See also* Communication; Real talk
　communication difficulties and, 95, 103
　with parents, 159
　skills, 94
　with special-needs children, 100, 157, 168
Convulsions, febrile, 132
Cook, R.A., 13
Cornea, 65

Cornell, A., vi, 45, 67, 68, 128
Coughing, 129
Covel, S.M., 32
Cruz, J., 16
Crying, 113, 124, 141
Cultural diversity
　behaviour and, 113, 119
　in early childhood education, 17–19
Cystic fibrosis, 129
Day care, 2
Daydreaming
　hearing impairments and, 80
　seizures *vs.*, 132
Day nurseries, 2
Deaf culture, 83
Deafness, 79. *See also* Hearing impairments
Decibels, 79
Deficit model, in behavioural approaches, 19–20
Deiner, P.L., vi, 113, 128, 133, 137, 141
Dempsey, J.D., 12
Denial, in parents, 149
Denver Developmental Screening Device, 20–21
Depression
　in children, 138
　in parents, 149
Destruction of property, 116
Detachment, in parents, 149
Developmental curriculum approaches, 20–21
Developmental delays, 27–43, 137–38
　assessment, 30
　behavioural difficulties and, 116
　causes, 29
　classification, 28
　cognitive development and, 40–41
　communication skills and, 42–43
　diagnosis, 30
　environments for, 37, 38
　knowledge of, 168
　language and, 42–43
　physical development and, 41–42
　physical impairments and, 53–54
　role of early childhood professional in, 35–43, 139–40
　sensory development and, 41

Index • **181**

social, 39
Deviancy, of behaviour, 113
Devries, R., 8
Diabetes, 129–31
Diet
   for cerebral palsy children, 47
   of hydrocephalic children, 49
   management, 47, 129, 130
Disabilities. *See* Developmental delays
Discipline, 110
Diseases, hearing impairments and, 79
Disfluency, 93, 98
Disruptiveness, 114, 116, 117, 122
Distractibility, 107 box, 114, 116, 117, 123, 124
Diversity
   cultural, 113, 119
   in early childhood education, 17–19
   of needs, 42–43
Divorce, 138
Dizziness, 131
Dotsch, J., 18
Down syndrome, 29
Dressing, 157
Drowsiness, 131
Drug abuse, 137
Duhaime, A., 49
Dunlap, L.L., 13, 30, 113, 137
Dyskinetic cerebral palsy, 47

Early childhood education
   behavioural approaches, 5–6
   constructivist approach, 7–8
   interactionist approaches, 7
Early childhood professionals, 157–60
   as advocates, 152–55, 169, 170
   attitudes of, 36, 55–56, 70, 170–71
   children in stress and, 141–42
   collaboration with other professionals, 85
   family and, 169
   knowledge of, 167–69
   parents and, 35–36, 153–56, 158, 164, 166
   relationship with other professionals, 166–67
   relationship with parents, 164, 166
   role, 165–71
   role in behavioural challenges, 118–24
   role in communication difficulties, 97–99
   role in developmental risks, 139–40
   role in health impairments, 135–37
   role in hearing impairments, 83–89
   role in physical impairments, 55–61
   role in visual impairments, 70–75
   skills of, 169–70
Early childhood programs, 161
Early intervention, 4
Ears, infections, 78, 80, 81
Echolalia, 94
Ecological approach, to special-needs children, 152, 153 fig., 163–64
Emergencies, 136
Emotional challenges, 105–24
   poverty and, 138
Emotional development
   behavioural difficulties and, 122
   communication difficulties and, 94–95, 103
   delays in, 39–40
   hearing impairments and, 88
   physical impairments and, 52–53, 60
   visual impairments and, 72
Emotions
   awareness of, 122
   of children at risk, 133–35
   dealing with, 119, 120
   expression of, 123
   of parents, 156–57
Empathy, 159–60
Engel, M., vi, 45, 67, 68, 128
Enrichment programs, 139
Environmentally delayed children, 137–38
Environments
   accessibility in, 11, 56
   behavioural problems and, 110, 119–22
   behaviour within, 33–34
   for communication difficulties, 100–101
   control over, 32
   for developmentally delayed children, 37, 38
   for hearing impaired children, 85

inclusion in, 11–13
for independence in children, 101
language-rich, 94, 99
for physically impaired children, 56, 57
play-focussed, 100
for special-needs children, 158
for visually impaired children, 69, 70–72
Epilepsy, 132
Epipens, 128–29
Erikson, E., 9
Eustachian tube, 78
Exosystem, social institutions as, 152, 163
Experience-based approach, to early childhood education, 22–23
Experiences
disadvantages in, 94
meaningful, 157
for physically impaired children, 60
for special-needs children, 158
Expression, of feelings and thoughts, 15
Expressive language problems, 96, 104
Eye glasses, 65, 73, 75
Eye patches, 73, 75
Eyes, 64–65. *See also* Visual impairments

Faintness, 133
Falling, physical impairments and, 51, 58
Family. *See also* Parents; Siblings
context of, 157
dynamics, 158
as microsystem, 152, 163, 164
relationship with early childhood professional, 169
respect for, 159
Fathers. *See also* Parents
absent, 138
Febrile convulsions, 132
Feelings. *See* Emotions
Feet, 49–50
Fetal alcohol syndrome, 115–16
Fever, 132
File, N., 13, 16
Finger spelling, 86
Finnie, N.R., 47
Fit, goodness of, 106–108
Fragile X syndrome, 114

Frequency modulator auditory trainers, 82, 85
Friendships, 13–16
Frost, J., 39, 56, 68, 69
Frustration levels, 114
Fuhlman, 19

German measles, hearing impairments and, 79
Glaucoma, 64–65
Gold, M., 6
Goodness of fit, 106–108
Grand mal seizures, 132
Guilt, in parents, 149
Guralnick, M.J., 13

Hartle, L., 13, 14, 15
Hayslip, W., 73
Head injuries, 49
Head Start, Project, 3
Healing, diabetes and, 131
Health clinics, 136
Health impairments, 128–35
poverty and, 138
role of the early childhood professional in, 135–37
Health nurses, 163
Hearing aids, 82, 85
Hearing impairments, 41, 77–90
assessment, 79–80
causes, 78–79
communication skills and, 93
diagnosis, 79–80
environments for, 85
role of early childhood professional in, 83–89
visual impairments and, 73
Heart problems, 133
Help, for parents, 151, 154
Hemophilia, 133
Hierarchy, of support systems, 167
Hip problems, 50
Hitting, 113, 119
Homelessness, 138
Hope Irwin, S., 6
Howard, V.F., 46, 47, 48, 67, 129
Howes, C., 138

Hunger, diabetes and, 131
Hydrocephalus, 48
Hyperactivity, 114, 115. *See also* Activity levels
Hyperopia, 65
Hypertonicity, 46, 163
Hypotonicity, 29, 46, 163

Images, physical impairments and, 60
Imitation, 113
   communication skills and, 97
   learning through, 88
Impulse control, 114, 115, 122
In-between position, of early childhood professionals, 154, 167, 170
Inclusion. *See also under* Environments
   of children with developmental delays, 28
   of hearing impaired children, 83, 87–88
   in physical environment, 11
   of special-needs children, 6–7, 169
Independence, in children, 101, 105
Infants
   communication, 98–99
   visual impairments, 69
   vocalization, 103
Infections
   hearing impairments and, 79, 80
   respiratory, 133
Inhalers, 129
Injury to self, 116
Insulin, 129–30
Integrated curriculum approach, 22–23
Integration, of special-needs children, 6
Intelligence, 88
Interactionist approaches, to early childhood education, 7
Intervention
   in behavioural difficulties, 119
   in developmental delays, 30
   early, 4, 168
   in hearing impairments, 80, 83
Isolation, 113, 138

Jones, 8

Kamii, C., 8
Kemple, K.M., 13, 14, 15
Kindergartens, 3
Kisker, N., 138
Klein, M., 13
Kontos, S., 153, 163
Koontz scale, 21
Kugelmass, J., 23

Language, 81, 82–83. *See also* Conversation; Speech
   developmental delays and, 32, 42–43
   in environment, 94
   oral, 91
   pathologists, 163
   spoken. *See* Speech
   verbal, 88–89
Language development, 15
   behavioural difficulties and, 105, 116, 117, 123
   communication difficulties and, 103–104
   hearing impairments and, 77, 79–83
   physical impairments and, 51–52, 60
   visual impairments and, 68
Lawson, T., 13
Lazar, M.F., 49
Leaders, among children, communication difficulties and, 99
Learning
   behavioural difficulties and, 116
   developmental delays and, 31
Legs, 48, 49–50
Lehr, S., 6
Lepper, C., 46, 47, 48, 67, 129
Libraries, public, 169
Limbs, absence of, 49
Linguistic diversity, in early childhood education, 17–19
Lip reading, 83
Lips, bluish colour, 133
Liptak, G.S., 48
Listening skills, 141, 156, 159

Macrosystem, society as, 152, 163
Make-believe play, 87–88
Marotz, L., 64
Matthews, M.W., 13, 14
Mauk, N.E., 113, 114
Measles, 80

German, 79
Medical professionals, 22, 158, 163
Medication, 136
   for asthma, 129
   for diabetes, 130
   for epilepsy, 132
Meetings, 154, 164–65
Memory
   developmental delays and, 31
   language and, 104
Mental retardation, 114
   definition, 27–28
Mercugliano, M., 114
Mesosystem, special-needs support as, 163–64
Metabolism, 29
Michaud, L., 49
Microsystem, family as, 152, 163, 164
Mobility. *See also* Physical impairments
   of children, 45
   of physically impaired children, 48–49
Monitoring
   of communication development, 99
   of health conditions, 135
Mood, quality of, 107 box
Mothers. *See also* Parents
   working, 2
Motor-skill development
   behavioural difficulties and, 124
   developmental delays and, 32–33, 42
   of Down syndrome children, 29
   hearing impairments and, 83
   physical impairments and, 52, 53, 58–59
   visual impairments and, 67, 73–74
Mumps, 80
Muscles
   contractions, 132
   control, 163
   eye, 65
   speech development and, 51–52
   tone, 29, 46
Muscular dystrophy, 47
Myelomeningocele, 48
Myopia, 65

Neglect, of children, 2

Nightmares, 138, 141
Noise
   background, 85, 123
   hearing impairments and, 78, 79
Non-disabled children. *See also* Peers
   attitudes, 16–17, 88, 134
   behavioural difficulties and, 117–18
   developmental delays and, 33–34
   pairing with special-needs children, 39
   physical impairments and, 51
Non-disabled people, responses to special-needs children, 33–34
Non-verbal communication, 93
Normality vs. abnormality, 112–13
Normalization, 27
Norton, T., 128
Nursery schools, 2–3
Nurses, health, 163
Nystagmus, 65

Object permanence, 9
Observation
   by children, 36
   of children with health needs, 136
   of communication development, 99, 101
   learning by, 39
   of problem behaviours, 121–22
   of special-needs children, 168
Observations, about behaviour, 111–12
Occupational therapists, 58, 163
Odom, S.L., 15
Offord, D., 138
Oral language, 91
Orthopedic impairments. *See* Physical impairments
Orthotic devices, 47
Osofsky, J.D., 138
Overprotection, of children with health needs, 134–35

Paasche, A., vi, 45, 67, 68, 128
Pairing, of children, 39
Paraphrasing, 100, 159
Parent-child relationship, 13–14, 119–20
Parenting
   as cause of behavioural problems, 110
   respite from, 139

Parents
  adaptation to special-needs children, 148–50, 158
  of children with health needs, 135–37
  communication difficulties and, 99
  conversation with, 159
  early childhood professionals and, 35–36, 147, 153–56, 158, 164, 166
  emotions of, 156–57
  hearing impairments and, 85
  information from, 35–36
  interaction with other parents, 156
  involvement, 3–5, 147–60
  professionals vs., 4–5
  reaction to special-needs children, 153–54
  self-advocacy by, 155
  single, 138
  of special-needs children, 148–52
  support for, 156–57
  teenage, 137
  temperamental traits and, 106–108
Parten, M.B., 9
Peer acceptance, communication difficulties and, 103
Peer relations, 13–16, 53, 54, 73. *See also* Communication; Play
Peers, 164. *See also* Non-disabled children
  interactions with, 84–85, 103, 115
  modelling by, 16
Pelligrino, L., 46, 47
Perry Preschool Project, 139
Persistence, 107 box
Personalities, 112
Pervasive developmental disorders, 113–14
Peters, D., 153, 163
Petit mal seizures, 132
Phillips, D.A., 138
Phonemes, 91
Physical development
  behavioural difficulties and, 124
  developmental delays and, 41–42
  visual impairments and, 67, 73–74
Physical impairments, 45–61
  causes, 46
  child development and, 50–55

  classification, 45–46
  correction of, 49–50
  developmental delays and, 53–54
  environments for, 56, 57
  images of, 60
  role of early childhood professional in, 55–61
Physical therapists, 58
Physiotherapists, 163, 168
Piaget, Jean, 7, 8, 9
Play, 8–11, 58–59, 157. *See also* Peer relations
  behavioural difficulties and, 122–23
  behaviours, 113
  communication difficulties and, 95, 101–102
  co-operative, 86–87
  in developmental delays, 38–39
  free, 14, 68, 122–23
  hearing impairments and, 79–80, 86–87
  in interactionist approaches, 7
  isolated, 86, 97, 101
  make-believe, 87–88
  onlooker, 97
  parallel, 86
  physical impairments and, 53
  pretend, 113
  skills, 10–11, 23
  solitary, 68, 99
  stereotypic, 113–14
  visual impairments and, 68, 73
Playrooms, 38. *See also* Environments
  diversity and, 19
  physical impairments and, 57
  visual impairments and, 70, 71–72
Pneumonia, 129
Port, P.D., 46, 47, 48, 67, 129
Positioning
  of cerebral palsy children, 47
  physical impairments and, 51
Poverty
  children in, 3, 137–38
  day care and, 2
Prescott, 8
Prevention
  of head injuries, 49

of health difficulties, 136
Prochner, L., 2
Professionalism, 159
Professionals. *See also* Early childhood professionals; Medical
professionals
attitudes of, 165
collaboration with. *See* Collaboration
competitiveness between, 165
parents vs., 4–5
relationships among, 37, 168
relationship with early childhood professionals, 166–67
teams of, 164–65
Project Head Start, 3–4
Prosthetic devices, 49, 50. *See also* Adaptive aids
Psychologists, 158
Public libraries, 169

Public transport services, access to, 169
Punishment, 120

Questions, of children, 16

Reaction, intensity of, 107 box
Reading, 82
visual impairments and, 64
Real talk, 97, 157
Reber, M., 113, 114
Receptive language problems, 95–96, 104
Recreation services, access to, 169
Regressions, 141
Rejection, by peers, 14
Relocation, of children, 138
Reorganization, of parents' reactions, 150
Resilience, in children, 141
Respect
in collaborative relationships, 170
for family, 159
Respiratory infections, 133
Responsiveness, threshold of, 107 box
Rett syndrome, 114
Rhythmicity, 107 box
Risk, children at, 127–44
Ritualized behaviours, 113
Roizen, N.J., 29

Role models
early childhood professionals as, 16, 36, 54–55, 155
peers as, 6, 16
Romatowski, J.A., 16
Rosen, L., v
Rubella, hearing impairments and, 79
Rules, setting, 121

Safford, P., v
Salisbury, C., 7
Saracho, O.N., 30, 31, 67, 68, 73
Searle, S., 6
Seizures, 114, 132, 136
Self-advocacy, by parents, 155
Self-assessment, by early childhood professionals, 171
Self-concept, physical impairments and, 57–58, 60
Self-esteem
behavioural difficulties and, 116, 122
of children in poverty, 138
communication difficulties and, 98
developmental delays and, 32, 39
of hearing impaired children, 88
toileting and, 48
Self-help skills, 157
Self-talk, 94
Sensorineural hearing loss, 79, 82
Sensory deprivation, communication difficulties and, 93
Sensory development, 124
developmental delays and, 41
hearing impairments and, 89
physical impairments and, 60–61
visual impairments and, 72–73
Sensory disabilities, visual impairments and, 67–68
Shaking
diabetes and, 131
injuries from, 49
Shapiro, B.K., 27, 28, 30
Shapiro, E., 7, 8
Shimoni, R., 2, 3, 4, 23, 138, 140, 148
Shock, in parents' reactions, 149
Shunts, in hydrocephalic children, 48

Shyness, 113
Siblings, of special-needs children, 155, 164
Sight impairment. *See* Visual impairments
Sign language, 77, 83, 84, 86
Skills development, 21–23. *See also under* Play
    adaptive aids in, 10, 56–57
Skinner, B.F., 5
Sleeping difficulties, 141
Smilansky, S., 9
Social contact. *See also* Peer relations
    visual impairments and, 69
Social development, 13–14
    behavioural difficulties and, 123
    communication difficulties and, 94–95, 102–103
    delays in, 39
    hearing impairments and, 83, 87–88
    physical impairments and, 52–53, 59–60
    visual impairments and, 75
Social institutions. *See also* Community support
    as exosystem, 152, 163
Social interactions, 37–38, 113. *See also under* Peers
    communication difficulties and, 101
    developmental delays and, 31
    hearing impairments and, 79–80, 83
    visual impairments and, 68
Social interations, 116
Socially disadvantaged children, 137–38
Social workers, day care and, 2
Society. *See also* Community support
    as macrosystem, 152, 163
Sounds, of speech, hearing impairments and, 78, 79
Spastic cerebral palsy, 46–47
Spasticity, 114
Special needs, information sources, 35–36
Special-needs children
    parental adaptation to, 148
    personal knowledge of, 167–68
    respect for, 155
    services for, 162
Speech, 91–92
    communication difficulties and, 103
    disabilities, 92–93
    disorders, 96
    of Down syndrome children, 29
    pathologists, 163
    physical impairments and, 51–52, 60
    sign language vs., 84
    sounds of, and hearing impairments, 78, 79
    therapists, 99
    visual impairments and, 68
Speech development, hearing impairments and, 80
Speech reading, 86
Spina bifida, 48–49
Spinal cord injuries, 49
Spodek, B., 2, 30, 31, 67, 68, 73
Spoken language. *See* Speech
Static devices, 47
Stereotyped behaviours, 113, 114
Stereotyping, 53–54
Stone, S.J., 22
Strabismus, 65
Strain, P., ix
Stress
    children in, 140–42
    in parents, 151, 152
Stuttering, 93, 98
Success, in children, 14–15, 123
Sugar, diabetes and, 130, 131
Support. *See also* Community support
    for children with developmental delays, 28
    community-based, 158
    groups, 154, 156
    integrated systems, 161
    for parents, 156–57
Tasks, developmental, 23
Taylor, S., 6
Teacher-directed learning, 22
Teams, of professionals, 164–65
Teasing, 15
Technological aids. *See* Adaptive aids
Temperament, 106–109
Terminology, familiarity with, 168
Tessier, A., 13
Theatre, use in hearing impairments, 83
Thinking, language and, 104
Thirst, diabetes and, 131

Thomas, A., 106
Thumbsucking, 141
Tiredness, diabetes and, 131
Toileting, 48, 57, 157
Tonic clonic seizures, 132
Toys, 11, 37. *See also* Play
   behavioural difficulties and, 123
   physical impairments and, 57
Traits, temperamental, 106–109
Transfers, of physically impaired children, 50, 58
Transitions, 115, 121, 141, 147
Trauma, 140
Trawicki-Smith, J., 13
Trembling, 131
Trepanier-Sreet, M.L., 16
Turecki, S., 106
Turn taking, 88, 95, 99, 100

Unresponsiveness, 113
Urination, diabetes and, 131
Urine testing, 130

Values, positive, 16
Vanier Institute of the Family, 138
Van Manen, M., 98
Van Riper, C., 91–92
Verbal communication. *See* Communication; Language; Speech
Vicious cyle, in parent-child interactions, 119–20
Vincent, L., 73
Violence, 138
Vision, diabetes and, 131
Visual displays, for hearing impaired children, 85
Visual impairments, 63–75
   assessment, 65–67
   attitudes toward, 70
   causes, 65
   child development and, 67–70
   classification, 64–65
   diagnosis, 65–67
   environments for, 69, 70–72
   legal definitions, 64
   resources regarding, 71
   role of early childhood professional in, 70–75
Vocabulary, 15
   developmental delays and, 42
   physical impairments and, 54
   visual impairments and, 74
Voice problems, 93
Voran, M., 138
Vulpe scale, 21
Vygotsky, L.S., 13

Waiting times, 121
Wallach, L.B., 138
Ward, M., 138
Warning signs, of health difficulties, 136
Watson, A., 5
Weakness, 131
Weight
   gain, 129
   loss, 131
Wheelchairs, 49, 51, 57, 169
Wheezing, 129
Whitebook, M., 138
Williams, B.F., 46, 47, 48, 67, 129
Winter, S.M., 12
Winzer, M., vi, 7, 29, 30, 63, 66, 68, 111, 116, 117
Withdrawal, 107 box, 113, 124, 138, 141
Wolery, M., ix
Wolfensberger, W., 6, 27
Women. *See also* Mothers; Parents
   responsibility for child rearing, 2
Wood, K.I., 15, 18

Youcha, V., 15, 18

READER REPLY CARD

We are interested in your reaction to *Children First: Working with Young Children in Inclusive Group Care Settings in Canada*, by Joanne Baxter and Malcolm Read. You can help us to improve this book in future editions by completing this questionnaire.

1. What was your reason for using this book?

    ☐ university course ☐ college course ☐ continuing education course
    ☐ professional ☐ personal ☐ other _____
       development   interest   _____

2. If you are a student, please identify your school and the course in which you used this book.

3. Which chapters or parts of this book did you use? Which did you omit?

4. What did you like best about this book? What did you like least?

5. Please identify any topics you think should be added to future editions.

6. Please add any comments or suggestions.

7. May we contact you for further information?

    Name: _____
    Address: _____
    Phone: _____

(fold here and tape shut)

MAIL / POSTE
Canada Post Corporation / Société canadienne des postes
Postage paid / Port payé
If mailed in Canada / si posté au Canada
Business Reply / Réponse d'affaires
0116870399   01

0116870399-M8Z4X6-BR01

Larry Gillevet
Director of Product Development
HARCOURT BRACE & COMPANY, CANADA
55 HORNER AVENUE
TORONTO, ONTARIO
M8Z 9Z9